"Having devoted my life to creatin
uplifts, I know how powerful a tool n
I am so enthusiastic about *The Chanter's Guide*. This simple
yet insightful manual teaches the reader how to tap into the
healing power of music. Through sacred music, we can usher
in a new era of peace and understanding on this planet. I
believe that the wisdom contained in *The Chanter's Guide*
can help inspire this important transformation."

—*GuruGanesha Singh, Sacred Chant Artist
and Founder of Spirit Voyage Music*

"Dr. Shamas' book is a fresh and clear presentation of ancient
tools that have the power to inspire all of us to come together
and participate in the global transformation that is so needed
today. It is a call of awakening for many to remember their
role as healers through the vehicle of chanting, both as a
personal practice and in community."

—*David Newman, Chant Artist
(www.davidnewmanmusic.com)*

"*The Chanter's Guide* is a beautiful story of healing and transformation. I appreciate the thoughtfulness and style of writing. It is
a must read for anyone expanding their consciousness."

—*Alice Anderson, Unity Minister and Musician*

"This is a wonderful, clear and accessible offering into the
delicious, heart-opening practice of chant. I highly recommend
Dr. Shamas' book to anyone interested in immersing themselves
in the powerful vibrations of sacred chant."

—*Gina Salá, Sound Healer, Voice Coach, Chant Leader
(www.ginasala.com)*

The Chanter's Guide:

Sacred Chanting
as a Shamanic Practice

Victor Shamas, Ph.D.

Foreword by Dr. Pablo Singh

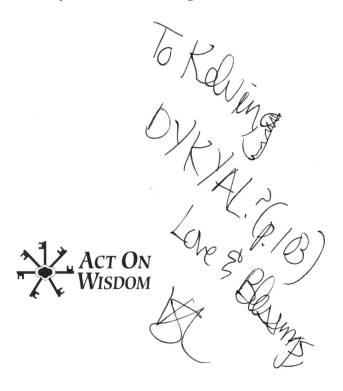

ACT ON
WISDOM

THE CHANTER'S GUIDE
Sacred Chanting as a Shamanic Practice by Victor Shamas, Ph.D.

Act on Wisdom
Post Office Box 12484
Tucson, AZ 85732-2484
www.ActonWisdom.com

Cover Illustration by Mary Bodine
Book and Cover Design by Marnie Sharp

First Edition 2007
Printed in the United States of America

Publisher's Cataloging-in-Publication
(Provided by Quality Books, Inc.)

Shamas, Victor.
  The chanter's guide : sacred chanting as a shamanic
practice / Victor Shamas ; foreword by Pablo Singh.
   p. cm.
  1. Shamanism. 2. Incantations, Shamanist.
3. Healing--Religious aspects. I. Title.
BL2370.S5S53 2007   201'.44
QBI07-600063   2007900902
ISBN 978-0-9793628-0-4

For my teachers, elders,
and guides, without
whom this book would
not be possible.

Contents

Foreword

Shamans have many healing tools at their disposal. Some use herbs and medicinal plants. Others use dancing, drumming, or visual art. The shamans in my lineage have all been Chanters. We rely on the powerful chants and incantations that have been passed down from our ancestors.

I first learned about the healing power of chants when I was five years old. That is when I began my apprenticeship with my uncle Leonardo, who was a Master shaman. I accompanied him to healing ceremonies but my role was simply to observe, and more importantly, to listen.

For seven years, we traveled from village to village through the mountains of Oaxaca, either on horseback or on foot. Rarely did my uncle speak directly to me, and it was even more unusual for him to listen to anything I had to say. And yet, I learned everything I know about being a Chanter from him. At my uncle's feet, I learned how to use sacred chanting as a shamanic tool.

Since my apprenticeship with Uncle Leonardo, I have had many other teachers. It was they who insisted that I come to the United States to live and teach. My teachers told me that I would share the wisdom of the Chanters with many spiritual seekers, but that one in particular would help convey this wisdom to millions of others.

When the author of this book, whom I know affectionately as Omar, began his apprenticeship with me in the summer of 2004, I knew immediately that he was the one who would write about the teachings of my lineage. All the pieces were in place for Omar already. From the first time he came to me, I could see the intensity of his passion for chanting and for spiritual life. By then, Omar had already been leading a chanting circle called Global Chant for nearly a decade. He was also an established lecturer at the University of Arizona, where he had been teaching Psychology for many years, and he was a successful and very skilled writer.

The only question I had was: How long would it take Omar to put all the pieces together? My answer came just a few weeks later. Omar came to me one day and asked me to put him on what he called "the fast track." He wanted me to push him as hard as I could in his spiritual training, and that is exactly what I did.

I never saw a spiritual student work harder than Omar to grasp the teachings of the Chanters or to put those teachings into practice. At the same time that he was immersing himself in this training, he was also documenting his experiences. Omar knew that it was important to have a record of the extraordinary events that were taking place in his life.

Whenever he read his writings to me and to my other apprentices, Omar would delight us all with the beauty and honesty of his narrative and with the depth of his understanding. His light-heartedness and sweet nature came through in these writings, as did his willingness to look at himself critically and to expose his greatest weaknesses.

As wonderful as these qualities are, the most impressive thing about the writings that were to become *The Chanter's Guide: Sacred Chanting as a Shamanic Practice*, is the powerful wisdom that they manage to capture. I have no doubt that this beautiful book is divinely inspired. Omar himself will admit that the spiritual concepts he describes in the book did not come from him. He simply transformed himself into a pipeline through which the great teachers in our lineage could deliver some of their most powerful messages.

The Chanter's Guide contains profound spiritual wisdom that is especially pertinent to this time in history. Much of the information in the book was hidden for centuries. This information is not simply about chanting, or even about shamanism. It is a way to find true peace in turbulent times, to heal oneself and then to spread that healing to others. And it is also as simple a guide to enlightenment as I have ever read.

Omar has given me credit, throughout this book, for making spirituality look easy. But he is the one who has captured that simplicity on paper. Besides being a wonderful story about this man's spiritual development, *The Chanter's Guide* is also a straight-forward roadmap that can take you as far on your own spiritual path as you are willing to go. I can assure you that it will start working its magic from the moment you start turning the pages. It will open you to a new way of living, with no conditions and no limits.

The publication of *The Chanter's Guide* represents a mile-stone for me. It is the culmination of the teaching mission that took me to the United States in the first place. I am happy to have been a good servant during my stay there, but I am equally happy to return to my homeland, where I can follow in the foot-steps of my mentor, Uncle Leonardo. If I am blessed, I will live out my days as he did, serving the healing needs of simple people living in the mountains of Oaxaca.

Everything I have to say to you about your spiritual life can be found in the pages of *The Chanter's Guide*. If you seek me out, you will need to look no further than this book. I am here in spirit, as are the teachers who came before me. Every word you will read is imbued with our essence and our wisdom. Whatever you do not find directly in the book, you will need to search for within your own heart.

When Chanters come together to perform rituals, we gather in a circle. The circle is an important symbol of our relationship to one another as Chanters. No point along the circumference of the circle is more significant than any other. We are all teachers, and we are all healers. I ask that you not put any one teacher above the rest. All of the points of the circle are equally valuable to you. And remember that you too are in that circle now.

You do not need me, or Omar, or anyone else for that matter, to tell you what you need to know about the pursuit of your spiritual life. The circle is contained inside of you, as are all the teachers and guides you will ever need. You will see. Just read the book.

—Dr. Pablo Singh (Written in Oaxaca, Mexico, December 21, 2006; Delivered by courier January 15, 2007)

Acknowledgments

One of the chants that my fellow Chanters and I use as part of our healing ceremonies starts with the words: "Open up the circle of healing and love." This chant serves two purposes: First, it is an invocation of all the forces and beings that make up our circle of healing and love. It is also an opportunity to extend the circle outward to encompass the individuals that we touch through our own healing intentions and actions.

Every moment that I have spent writing *The Chanter's Guide*, I have been aware of the circle of healing and love that already exists in my own life, nourishing me spiritually and supporting my endeavors. This circle begins with my family: my parents, Sara and David; my brother, Daniel; his wife, Susan; and my two beautiful nieces, Jenna and Sarina. Although my grandparents are no longer living, they continue to serve as sources of inspiration and guidance for me.

The circle also includes my teachers, for whom I have the greatest esteem and respect. Besides the Masters whose wisdom I have sought to share in this book, I want to acknowledge all of the teachers who have mentored me. I have had the privilege to learn from so many wonderful individuals at every institution I have attended: Seattle Hebrew Academy, Roosevelt High School, the University of Washington, The Evergreen State College, the University of California at Santa Cruz, and the University of Arizona. It is my particular honor to have had the chance to study under the following individuals: Victor Walling, Ariel Lind, Jerry Elarth, Dr. Norman Rose, Dr. Fred Tabbutt,

Dr. Byron Youtz, Dr. Frank Andrews, Dr. Joseph Bunnett, Dr. Eugene Cota-Robles, Dr. Adela Allen, Dr. John Kihlstrom, Dr. Kenneth Forster, Dr. A. J. Figueredo, Dr. Lee Sechrest, and Dr. Gavi Salomon.

Since 1996, I have hosted a weekly chanting circle called Global Chant, which is undoubtedly a big part of my circle of healing and love. With gratitude, I acknowledge the hundreds of individuals who have taken part in Global Chant over the past 11 years. They have taught me so much of what I know about the spiritual power of chanting. I would especially like to thank the following people: Jhan Kold, James Counts, Caroline Ragano, Erin Madden, Mark Gouhin, Mary Bodine, Wanda Poindexter, Alice Anderson, Shannon Olesen, Jonathan Reese, Heidi Wilson, Sabine Gillespie, Peter McLaughlin, Marnie Sharp, Jean Mulvaney, Mary Eiland, Jack Spring and Connie Stoessel, Amy Gleeson, Mary "Ranjani" Blake, Marilyn Kaler, Luno Martinez, Pamela Cooper, David Christy, Abigail and Will Bergeron, Teresa Banks, Michael Sigler, Dash Oquitadas, Tony Paniagua, Anna Simon, Miriam Bloomfield, Philip Franchine, Jackie Hesford, Patricia Noble, and Jeanne Burrows-Johnson.

I also offer thanks to all of my students and colleagues at the University of Arizona, and especially to Dr. Alfred Kaszniak, who has been a wonderfully supportive mentor, supervisor, and friend. For the past several years, the classroom has been my laboratory, offering an ideal setting for me to apply and test many of the spiritual principles described in this book. I have had the privilege to work with thousands of young men and women who are earnest in their pursuit of a life filled with purpose and meaning.

I am blessed to have many other dear friends in my circle, including Kenn Goldman and Deb Mechigian; Sal Balakrishnan and Mary Jo Benjamin; Peter Epperson and his family; Lisa, Logan and Piper Crabtree; the Perotti-Orcutt family; Tom Ofe; Lewis Humphreys; Wendy Kohatsu; the Counts family; Yolanda Aguirre; David Bean; the Edman family; Rick and Josie Savelli; Randi Beck; Fernando Galvez; Gina Salá; Jesse and Amber

Wiesenfeld; Peter Axelrod; the Brauer family; Liz Hedger; Cliff and Danielle Berrien; the Rodriguez family; Guy Josserand; Janet Page; David Newman; Steve Rooke; the Policar family; Steve Roach and Linda Kohanov; Susan McGovern; Dale Luke; the Rodriguez family; Jagjit Hayre; Mary DeCamp; William Weir; the Gosch family; Dr. Edythe London; Mariana Cacciatore; Keith Mau, Mary Rulewicz and their family; Gail Pruitt; the Hamrick family; Ginger Trumpbour; Dr. Isidro Bosch; John and Rich Phillips; the Nepomechie family; Iris Rink; Meryl Beck; and Richard Utt.

Many members of my circle have contributed directly to this book, reading early drafts of the chapters, offering editorial feedback, and writing reviews. I am grateful to Merrie Wolfie for the image that appears on the book cover, which is inspired by the work of Huichol artist Lorena Benitez Rivera. Many thanks, as well, to the folks at Act on Wisdom who handled this project with such care.

Finally, I would like to honor my darling Estrella, who inspires me every day with her sweetness, compassion, wisdom, and gentle, loving heart. I am blessed beyond measure to have such a radiant, joyous presence in my life.

I am also blessed that my circle continues to grow each day—so rapidly, in fact, that there may be a number of loved ones that I have failed to acknowledge here. In no way does this oversight reflect how I feel about them. In fact, I am reminded of the words of one of my favorite chants, which expresses my feelings about all of the wonderful people without whom my circle of healing and love would not be complete: "You are in my heart, living in my heart, always in my heart."

Introduction

There are sounds in the universe that can make miracles happen. The most surprising thing about these sounds is that they are produced by the human voice. Each sound carries the power to heal cancer, end hunger, or create world peace. The outcome depends only on the awareness and the intention of the person from whom the sound emanates.

One way to tap into this extraordinary power is through the practice of sacred chanting. The first Chanters in human history were the ancient shamans who used their voices as a tool for healing and spiritual transformation. Through their chants and incantations, these individuals could access a limitless source of creative power and harness that power for the good of their communities.

For centuries, the wisdom possessed by the Chanters was all but lost. Although most of the world's spiritual traditions incorporate some form of chanting into their rituals and prayers, only a few living masters know how to use the practice of chanting as a shamanic art. In 2004, I began a two-year apprenticeship with one such master. This is the story of my apprenticeship, but it is also a detailed manual containing the wisdom shared with me by this extraordinary spiritual teacher.

Chanting has been the most effective tool I have ever encountered for finding happiness, fulfillment, and unconditional love. For me, it has been the missing piece in a lifelong spiritual quest. Through chanting, I have been able to discover a sense of peace that had always eluded me. Doors have opened that I never even knew existed, leading me to new insights, unexpected adventures, and spiritual transformation. As I share my story with you, I anticipate that similar doors will open in your life.

My story begins on a pilgrimage to Oaxaca, Mexico. I am one of four Americans being guided on a journey by our beloved friend, mentor and spiritual tour guide, Dr. Pablo Singh. Dr. Singh is a medical doctor and shaman who was raised in Oaxaca and trained as a healer and visionary since the age of five. As his surname would indicate, someone on his father's side is Sikh and immigrated to Mexico from India; the rest of the family has been in Oaxaca for generations.

Dr. Singh's sweet face and roly-poly physique belie the depth of this man's wisdom. All of us who accompany him on this journey know him to be a master, not just of the traditional practices of the local Mixtec and Zapotec people but of something even more profound. The glimmer of mischief and delight in Dr. Singh's eyes gives a slight hint of the staggering power that lies within.

On this particular day, which happens to be Halloween, the four Americans walk behind Dr Singh as he escorts us through the ruins at Monte Alban. We are his apprentices, even though we are all in our late 40s or older. Carmina, who has been with Dr. Singh the longest, is a gentle, good-natured ex-hippie girl who hides her considerable light under the disarming Southern drawl and down-home charm gained from a youth spent in Arkansas and Alabama.

Her older sister, Harper, can be the model of serenity. Harper's disguise is the soft round body and quiet demeanor of a Kansas housewife—a role she played to perfection in her home life for two decades. Her gentle lilting voice and Mona Lisa smile have a soothing effect on those who meet her. In the relatively short time that I have known her, she has become perhaps my closest friend and confidant.

Harper's ex-husband, Ricardo, is an interesting paradox. Part holy man and part good-old-boy, he can bully you one minute and nurture you with genuine tenderness the next. Fiercely independent, Ricardo is determined to go his own way, even if it means running into an occasional brick wall. In some ways, though, he is the reason I am here. Ricardo was the first member of this ragtag Band to reach out to me.

I am known to the group as Omar. As you may have guessed, our names have been given to us by Dr. Singh. Each name is a blend of wisdom and whimsy. Sometimes, it takes months or years to unravel the significance of the name you have been assigned. I know that my name derives from Hebrew and Arabic. It has several meanings, including: "one who speaks the word of God," "long-lived," "flourishing" and "ultimate devotee." But I believe that the reason Dr. Singh has chosen this name is that it contains the two Sanskrit words, MA and OM. These words, which represent Divine Love and Divine Light respectively, have become very significant in my life. I chant them every day.

My story is that I have always been a dilettante in the true sense of the word. In Latin, this word means "seeker of delight." My quest has led me here to Monte Alban, but the route has not been exactly what I would call a straight line. In 1980, I fell in love with a girl named Julia. When she entered the Peace Corps a year later, I followed her to Ecuador, even though I was enrolled in graduate school at the time. During my six months in Ecuador, I traveled to the Galapagos Islands, where I first discovered my passion for coral reefs.

This obsession led me to Fiji five years later, where I met some folks with unusual mental powers. That is when I became fascinated with questions related to human consciousness. Because of this fascination, I moved to Tucson, Arizona and enrolled at the University of Arizona, where I studied with one of the country's leading consciousness researchers. While working on my Ph.D. in psychology, I became intrigued with topics like meditation, hypnosis, and biofeedback. I even started a weekly meditation group. My love of sacred music transformed the meditation group into a chanting circle, which is basically the kind of sing-a-long you might experience if you were sitting around a campfire with a group of monks.

I had been drawn to sacred music since the age of three, when I first heard the voice of the legendary gospel singer, Mahalia Jackson. Every weekday at noon, she would come on the television for five minutes to sing gospel. I was so compelled by Mahalia and her inspirational songs that I would cry if I missed her program.

By the time I was 12, I was playing hymns on the guitar and singing in my school choir. As an adult, I gravitated to everything from Jewish liturgical music to Hindu ragas. But I always had a special place in my heart for chants. A chant is a prayer, mantra, or incantation that is either sung or uttered in a rhythmic fashion. Usually, chants have a simple refrain that gets repeated. The mere repetition of the words or sounds comprising the chant can have a profound spiritual effect.

I discovered this while living in a college dorm. One of my dorm roommates gathered a group of friends together and taught us a Sufi chant. As we stood in a circle and chanted the words, "Love, love, love, love, people we are made for love," I was filled with a sense of lightness and joy. Part of the reason I started the chanting circle years later was to share that feeling with others. It was through this circle, which I named "Global Chant," that I first met Ricardo and then was introduced to the rest of Dr. Singh's Band.

A few weeks after my first meeting with Dr. Singh, he and Carmina took off on a journey to Oaxaca by themselves. After returning to Tucson, he began to discuss plans to return to Oaxaca with the entire group. A year later, we all arrive in Oaxaca—the master and his four apprentices. The four of us are innocents, exploring this strange and wonderful landscape with wide eyes and absolutely no expectations. Only Dr. Singh knows what is in store for us.

After passing through the turnstiles at the entrance to Monte Alban, we stop to look at a large site map showing the layout of the ruins. Dr. Singh shows us the location of the temples. He points to them and says, "These were the ancient equivalent of the Kennedy Space Center."

Taken aback by his words, I ask. "Are you saying that the people who lived here were capable of space travel?"

Dr. Singh gives me a mischievous smile. "That is just part of the story," he says. "We were also able to travel through time and into other dimensions. The most impressive thing, though, is that we did it all without the use of rockets or spacecraft."

As we continue walking, I am wondering about his choice of words. Why did he say that *we* were able to do these things? Could he be referring to his family lineage?

A few moments later, we arrive at the main plaza of Monte Alban. Surrounded by ruins in every direction, I feel an overwhelming sense of awe but also something else—a hint of familiarity. Looking into the faces of my three fellow apprentices, I can tell that they are feeling the same thing.

Dr. Singh instructs us to sit on the grass at the base of one of the temples. He says, "All of you were among the first people to settle in Monte Alban. See if you can remember who you were."

Now, my head is spinning. I begin to get glimpses of an ancient time and suddenly I am remembering details of a past life. The four of us—Carmina, Harper, Ricardo and I—had been part of a powerful civilization that used sacred music not just as a spiritual practice but as a basic tool of everyday life. Through the simple act of chanting, this civilization gained the inspiration it needed to create a highly sophisticated system of government, health, and education.

Our people built Monte Alban as well as many of the other temples scattered throughout Central America. To the tribes that surrounded our communities, we became known as Chanters because of the central role that chanting played not just in our rituals but in every aspect of our lives. Regardless of where we went or what we were doing, we chanted. Even toddlers who were just learning to speak or elders who were too feeble to say more than a few words could be heard singing the sacred chants of our people.

Where and how the Chanter societies originated remains a mystery, but there is little doubt that these societies were among the most advanced of their time. Chanters knew how to tap into the extraordinary power generated by the spiritual practice of chanting. We used this power to engage in a form of astral projection called flying. Through the process of flying, we could project our awareness not only through space and time but also into other dimensions of reality. We often visited these dimensions and the people who inhabited them. Among these inhabitants were a number of great spiritual Masters, many of whom shared their wisdom with us.

At the feet of these Masters, we learned how far chanting could take us. Through this simple practice, we were able to transform ourselves into healers and our societies into true spiritual communities. We were also able to propel ourselves into other dimensions and make contact with the most advanced civilizations in the universe. In our visits to these civilizations, we gained access to their science, medicine, art, and technology, which we were more than happy to share with our neighbors. We co-existed peacefully with other tribes, who were often advanced enough to comprehend and apply the system of knowledge we were sharing but not to develop it for themselves.

Sitting among the temples here, I am reminded of the book *Contact* by Carl Sagan. An advanced civilization shares a technology that permits an individual to travel across entire galaxies in a matter of seconds. The core of this technology is a series of tunnels through which the traveler can exit the dimensions of time and space at will. Now, for the first time, I understand that this system of tunnels lies within the human spirit and that chanting can be the vehicle for moving through these tunnels.

After a decade of chanting, I was somewhat aware of the power contained in even the simplest of chants. I had seen the transformative effect of chanting on those who would come to Global Chant. Some of these friends healed physical and mental illness through chanting. Others opened doors into their spiritual lives. For me, chanting brought a continuous flow of blessings, including new friendships, a sense of purpose, and the opportunity to meet and work with Dr. Singh.

Yet, until this day at Monte Alban, I had no idea how powerful chanting really could be. On the one hand, it was the foundation of spiritual life for Chanter societies. Through chanting, these societies discovered a direct path to healing and enlightenment. On the other hand, the use of chants had practical ramifications for everyday life. The practice of chanting provided a technology that connected Chanter societies to an information superhighway much vaster and more profound than any Internet: It linked them to the knowledge and wisdom of the entire universe.

Over time, Chanter societies arose in various parts of the world, including Egypt, India, Tibet, and Central America. These communities were populated by skilled teachers whose mission was to share the vast wealth of knowledge possessed by more advanced civilizations. From the beginning, our settlements attracted members of neighboring tribes who recognized the value of what we had to offer. We welcomed them into our communities and trained them as we would our own people.

Not all of our neighbors were open to our way of life. Many could not understand our intentions and felt threatened by our power. They allowed themselves to be controlled by leaders who knew how to play on their fears and suspicions and whose intention was domination. At first, they waged a secret war on us, infiltrating our settlements with saboteurs and spies. Once they had amassed strong enough armies, they ordered full-fledged invasions.

Being a peaceful civilization, we Chanters did not defend ourselves against these attacks. Many of us were killed; those who survived either went into hiding or were enslaved by conquering tribes. Before our cities could be captured, however, we succeeded in hiding our vast knowledge within the temples we had built. We knew that the leaders who had waged war against us were only capable of misusing this knowledge, finding ways to benefit from it at the expense of their own people.

And so, the wisdom of the Chanters went underground in the most literal sense possible. Our temples were buried and sealed.

In Central America, churches were built right on top of these temples, preventing all access to them. Even if the temples were unsealed, however, the knowledge they hold would not necessarily become accessible. The secrets that were stored inside the temples would have to be unlocked, and the only keys to unlock them were also hidden. These keys were buried in the safest place possible—within the hearts and minds of the Chanters who had established the first settlements at Monte Alban and elsewhere.

The keys to the temples were not made of iron or steel. They were elements of our spiritual practice, which allowed us to free ourselves from the limits imposed by our bodies and minds so that we could project our awareness into multiple dimensions of reality. Through this spiritual practice, we could access the wisdom of beings in other dimensions. When the last of the Chanters died, we took our spiritual practice with us. Through many incarnations, our souls remained unconscious of the extraordinary power at our disposal. The Masters who had taught us the spiritual power of chanting had also prophesized that the time would eventually come in which we would need to rediscover this power for the good of the planet. At the right time, the temples would be unsealed and reopened.

The builders of the temples designed them to be vehicles for multidimensional travel. Inside the temples, sacred chants would open portals into other dimensions. A properly-trained Chanter could chant his or her way out of the dimensions of space and time and into more than 40 other realms of existence. To be able to do this, every Chanter had to undergo a rigorous training regimen, which included an initiation into an entirely new way of life. We had to learn to live in accordance with a spiritual path that used the practice of chanting to free the spirit and heal the body and mind.

To fly into other dimensions, a Chanter had to be able to travel light. Not only can you not take your physical body into these dimensions; you also have to leave your ego behind. That means stripping away all of your emotional attachments, including the sum of all your hopes and fears. As Chanters, we had to live in a perpetual state of serenity—any perturbation at all could keep us grounded. We also had to practice humility.

Each of us understood that the powers we were accessing through the practice of chanting could only be used in the service of others. All Chanters had to abide by a code of selflessness. We were the servants of our communities, acting as healers, counselors, and high priests. Through our chants, we could tap into deep reservoirs of wisdom that could be used to alleviate suffering and provide illumination.

The spiritual path that Chanters followed was much easier to understand than it was to practice. For this reason, we learned from spiritual Masters who taught primarily by example. The Masters were role models who personified the ideals to which the Chanters aspired. Some of these Masters have taken human form and are alive today, along with thousands of us who are reincarnations of the original Chanters. There are also millions of others who are at a point in their development when they are ready to follow this path for the first time. It is an extraordinary time to be alive!

This book is an introduction to the spiritual life of a Chanter. It will give you access to the profound power contained in the practice of chanting. This practice represents a unique path that focuses on action rather than beliefs. To live the life of a Chanter means to act in ways that serve not only your own spiritual needs but those of others. When you approach the practice of chanting with an attitude of selflessness, you will become an extraordinary resource to your community. Not only will you be able to fly, but you will also gain access to universal wisdom that can serve the spiritual and healing needs of the people in your life.

If you once were a Chanter, then this book will simply trigger memories of a not-so-distant past. And if you are discovering this path for the first time, then the teachings you are about to encounter will open doors to an entirely new and extraordinary way of existing. The life of a Chanter is simple, fulfilling, balanced, and free of worries. It is also filled with loving relationships and genuine happiness.

You may be wondering if something as simple as chanting can really have such a profound impact on a person's life. From direct experience, I can tell you that it definitely can. And yet chanting itself is not enough. Although sacred chants are among the most powerful transformative tools I have ever come across, they only work as part of an integrated way of life. For Chanters, the practice of chanting is the centerpiece of our spiritual path, but it is certainly not the only piece. What matters most to us is the way we experience the present moment and how we conduct ourselves in our daily lives. We Chanters are artists and our lives are the canvas. By applying the simple spiritual principles described in this book, each of us is capable of creating a masterpiece.

While sitting among the temples at Monte Alban, I knew not only that I would be writing this book but exactly how it would be structured and what information it would hold. All I am sharing with you is the set of teachings I received from Dr. Singh during the two years of my apprenticeship with him. He calls these teachings kindergarten, not with the intention of denigrating them in any way but to indicate that they are the fundamentals that every Chanter must know.

Although Dr. Singh views the content of this book as basic, he also recognizes its potency. This is why he has asked me to include a disclaimer. He once told me, "If you were writing a book on how to build an atomic bomb, you would start with a disclaimer, wouldn't you? Because the technology you would be describing has the potential of pulverizing the reader and turning his or her world into dust, you would want to state explicitly the dangers that are likely to be encountered."

This book is a detailed manual for the spiritual bomb-builder. The practices that I will be sharing with you have the power to annihilate you and everything you have ever known. And so I offer this disclaimer: Read the book only when the timing is right for you. If you are not ready to let go of your attachments to your identity, your reality, and your most cherished possessions, then set this book down. Otherwise, the forces that have guided me in writing it will start working on you, and they will not stop until all your ego attachments have been stripped away and you are ready to devote yourself to your true purpose.

The time has come for the wisdom of the Chanters to reign once again on this planet, and if you are reading this book, chances are that your purpose—your spiritual mission—involves playing a role in the changes that are coming. There are too many of us alive today who are ready to follow our spiritual path for these changes not to take place. It would be impossible to hold us down any longer.

The current world leaders are the descendents of those who once vanquished the Chanters and whose power was based on domination rather than wisdom. At this point, they can no longer hide the failure of their leadership. Their decisions are choking the planet and leading to the destruction of humanity.

Several months before our trip to Oaxaca, Dr. Singh first told me of the prophesy that the Masters had revealed to him. According to this prophesy, millions of people will learn or rediscover the powers associated with chanting, and in doing so, they will unlock the wisdom hidden in the ancient temples. The re-emergence of this wisdom will bring about a revolutionary shift in global politics that will cause the governments of the world to be reorganized into seven major nations. These nations will live peacefully and co-exist with the Earth's other animal and plant species.

Within the next century, war will become obsolete. So will the uneven distribution of wealth that now permits most of the Earth's resources to be controlled by a small percentage of the population. Although the fall of the current political and economic system will not be painless, it will be surprisingly peaceful. The reason bloodshed will be avoided is that spiritual teachings such as the ones contained in this book will prevail.

There is a good chance you will live to see the changes I am describing. But you can be more than just a passive witness. By adopting the simple practices outlined in this book, you will set in motion the chain of events that fulfill the prophesy. You are capable of becoming a powerful player in this whole process, but first you have to overcome your doubts—especially your self-doubt. In the next chapter, I will give you specific guidelines for doing just that.

For me, any doubts I ever had about the nature of my spiritual mission dissipated at Monte Alban. I spent the day immersed in memories of my past and revelations of my future. That day, I rediscovered my true identity as a Chanter—an identity that is more vital and important now than it has ever been. When the five of us returned from the temples to the home where we were staying, our music-loving hosts asked us to share a few songs with them. That night, we sang one of Dr. Singh's favorite songs: "Imagine" by John Lennon.

As we sang the lyrics, they gained new significance for me. I realized that Lennon's ideal of a world without countries, religion, or possessions was not that different from my own. More importantly, the ideal seemed not only attainable but inevitable. In keeping with the vision expressed in this beautiful song, I ask the following of you:

Imagine unlocking the wisdom of the universe through the practice of chanting. Imagine traveling to other dimensions. Imagine making contact with the most advanced civilizations in the universe and sharing their knowledge. Imagine feeding people with sunlight and building vehicles that run on water. Imagine healing without medicines or surgery. Imagine extending the lifespan to hundreds of years. Imagine a world where peace and balance prevail and where enlightenment is the rule rather than the exception.

I can imagine all of these things because I know they are the future. We are much closer to living this dream than we realize. Let me show you how close.

CHAPTER 1

Ready to Jump

One of the first chants I ever learned was based on the Hebrew prayer, *Ana El na refa nala*, which means "Please, God, heal us." When I learned the meaning of this chant, I began to discover the link between chanting and healing. Many of us seek healing through the act of chanting. We look to create a sense of wholeness and balance in our hearts, in our bodies, in our relationships, and in every other aspect of our lives. In many cases, we also seek to extend this healing to our circle of friends, our family, our community, our nation, the ecosystem, and the planet as a whole.

Every chant is imbued with the power to heal, even if its words are not as direct as "Please, God, heal us." What matters most is the intention with which we chant. Those of us who are living spiritual lives as Chanters are driven by the desire to tap into the healing power locked away in each chant and to direct that power to those in need. Through our intention, the act of chanting becomes a shamanic process: We undergo a spiritual transformation through our chanting that allows us to serve and benefit others.

The spiritual path of a Chanter is wonderful and fulfilling, but it is far from easy. The hardest part is getting started. When you set out on this path, you are going to find yourself at the edge of a cliff, looking down. All of your fears, doubts, and concerns will rise to the surface and you will face an important realization: If you want to follow this path, first you are going to have to jump.

The cliff on which you are standing represents the security and familiarity of the life you have led up to now. You are about to begin an entirely new life—one that is dedicated to serving the spiritual needs of others. On this path, the only certainties are that healing and enlightenment are the priorities and that chanting is a powerful means to those ends. Everything else that takes shape is spontaneous, unpredictable, and ever-changing.

To jump off the cliff means to face your fears and to let go of everything. Just past the edge of the cliff begins a journey into the unknown.

The Love Letter

I remember the exact moment I jumped. It was in September 2004, six weeks after I first met Dr. Singh's apprentice, Ricardo. For nine years, I had been hosting my weekly chanting circle, Global Chant, on Wednesday nights at a local chapel. One summer evening, a striking man in a bright orange robe appeared at the chapel. When he introduced himself, he said his name was Ricardo. The name definitely didn't go with this man's pale skin and freckled complexion.

I could hardly take my eyes off him. Ricardo cut a Christ-like figure with his long silver-specked red hair, full beard, and serene face. All the members of the chanting circle gravitated to him instantly—especially the women. At the end of the session, Ricardo introduced himself to every person in the room and gave each one a hug. There was something different about Ricardo's embrace. When he hugged me, it felt like an acknowledgement of some part of me that had never been fully acknowledged before.

I casually asked Ricardo the same question I ask every new person. "How did you hear about the group?"

"My teacher sent me," he replied.

This answer surprised me. "And who's your teacher?" I asked intently.

"His name is Dr. Pablo Singh. He's a shaman from Mexico."

Instead of quenching my curiosity, Ricardo's response added fuel to the fire. Questions flew through my mind: *Who is this shaman? How did he know about my chanting circle? Why did he send Ricardo here? What interest does he have in this group? AND WHEN COULD I MEET HIM?*

Without even knowing anything other than Dr. Singh's name and that he was a shaman, I felt drawn to him. I wondered why I was so eager to meet this man. I had met plenty of people over the years who had claimed to be shamans. But I could sense something different about Dr. Singh. In fact, a few weeks later I would discover that he was much more than just a shaman. I had known people who had used the title of shaman to elevate themselves. Dr. Singh used it because he had no other term to describe what he did. Most of the people he met would not understand what it means to be a Chanter and would not recognize a Master if they saw one.

Two weeks later, I met Dr. Singh for the first time. I was invited to an event called the Sound Circle, which was held in a small wooden building that Dr. Singh had built next to his house and that he had named the Tabernacle. From the outside, the Tabernacle looked like a tool shed. It had obviously been built from scrap materials. And yet when I stepped into the little room, it had the unmistakable feel of a sanctuary. Inside the Tabernacle, I met Harper for the first time, as well as Ricardo's mother, whom Dr. Singh had named "Tía Luz." They both welcomed me as if I were a long-lost relative.

Within minutes, the Tabernacle was packed with people—spiritual seekers, those in need of healing, and others who were just drawn to the place without knowing exactly why. Dr. Singh was the last to arrive. He walked in smiling and radiating such sweetness that I felt a sense of warmth just looking at him. He greeted each one of us in the room by placing his hands together as if in prayer, bowing slightly, and then giving us a powerful embrace. When he approached me, he said, "Master, it is so good to see you again."

Hearing those words, I nearly burst into tears. Indeed, there was something so familiar about him that I knew instantly we had been together before. At that moment, my heart was filled with intense love, and I felt a desire to be as connected as possible to this man.

He addressed the group briefly, welcoming each of us and speaking to us about the importance of serenity, detachment, and unconditional love. His voice was so soft and soothing that I became engrossed in the mere sound of it—the low resonant tones and the elegant Spanish accent. In fact, the hypnotic quality of his voice had such a powerful effect on me that I started feeling as if I were high on a drug.

The purpose of the Sound Circle was to use chanting, drumming, musical instruments, hand-clapping, and any other appropriate sounds to generate healing energy. That night, Dr. Singh told us that we would be doing a form of chanting called toning in which we would be making sounds without words. He asked us to dedicate our toning to someone or something in need of healing. Each of us made our dedication aloud in front of the group. Some members of the group dedicated their chanting to friends or family members, and others to Mother Earth. I directed my intention to the people of Sudan, who had been suffering the severe effects of tribal warfare for over a decade.

Once we had set our intention, the toning began. Dr. Singh had encouraged us to just allow our voices to make whatever sounds felt right. Starting with Tía Luz, who was the senior member of the circle, each of us began toning until the room was filled with sound. At first, all I could hear was cacophony. Random squeaks, growls, hums, moans, and other strange noises emanated from the people in the room.

Within a few minutes, though, a subtle change happened. The voices began coming together, almost effortlessly, and the initial noise was eventually transformed into a series of beautiful harmonies. At one point, I felt like I was part of a heavenly choir—a host of angels singing the praises of the Divine. The toning started having a strange effect on me, making me feel as if I were levitating. Although my body never moved, I felt myself floating above the circle, looking down at the gathering. The rest of the ceremony became a blur to me. When it ended, I stumbled out of the Tabernacle like a drunken sailor.

Although I did not understand fully what had happened to me that night, I knew I had made an important connection. So, I kept coming to the Tabernacle every week. One evening, Dr. Singh asked me to stay and talk with him after the Sound Circle. Once everyone else had left, he and I sat on the floor of the Tabernacle, leaning against a wall.

In a gentle voice, he asked, "How has your summer been?"

Any other summer, that might have seemed like a perfectly casual question. But for me, this was my summer of discontent. Starting in June, I had descended into a period of spiritual crisis the likes of which I had never known before. On the surface, my life looked as if it were rolling along smoothly. I was living in my dream house, doing work that I enjoyed, and earning more money than I ever had. And yet something was missing.

Here I was in my mid-40s and I had not yet discovered—let alone realized—the true purpose of my life. Somehow I had steered off course, veering away from my spiritual path. After years of pursuing enlightenment, I had the sense of getting no closer to it than when I had started. All of my efforts, my meditation practice, my chanting, and my study of spirituality, had not transformed me in the ways I had expected to be transformed. Rather than finding peace, I had become increasingly restless. I had succeeded in finding all kinds of distractions for myself: parties, casual dating, movies, concerts, and sporting events. It was a self-centered existence. Although the chanting group and my teaching work were benefiting a few people, I knew I could be doing much more to be of service in the world.

The void in my life just kept growing. By late June, when I traveled to California for a meditation retreat, I was so filled with despair that instead of meditating, I pleaded with the universe: *Please let me find my purpose.* I repeated this prayer silently for three straight days. Two weeks after the retreat, I lost a lucrative consulting job with a publisher of educational materials. That same week, I met Ricardo at Global Chant.

In response to Dr. Singh's question, I said, "It has been a hard summer." When he heard my reply, his body jerked back slightly, as if recoiling.

"This is a time of big changes for you," he explained, "but those changes are hard only if you choose to make them hard. Remember the words of the song: 'Summertime and the living is easy.' This is the season when people go outside and celebrate together with picnics and barbecues. Are you sure you want to describe it as a hard summer?"

I understood what he was saying: This was a time of transition for me, and although the transition was dramatic, it didn't have to be traumatic. In truth, the changes I was experiencing were all positive. First, I had the good sense to recognize that my life was not aligned with my ideals. This is not an easy realization to make. When you are immersed in your day-to-day life, you can miss the subtle changes that are happening to you. It is not as if you just lose sight of your hopes and dreams overnight. The erosion of your ideals happens a little at a time. Each day, you move slightly more off-center.

Once I saw what was happening, I prayed for a change with all my heart. That too was a blessing. My despair made me focus more intently than I ever had before. Because of my intention, my prayers were answered almost immediately. There is a great deal of truth to the saying: "Be careful what you pray for." Sometimes, the most shocking thing that can happen is that our prayers get answered. That was certainly the case for me.

I liked my consulting job well enough but I also knew that it had become a burden for me. At first, I had found the work enjoyable, but after four years, my interest was waning. By the end, I was in it more for the financial rewards and the status it provided me. In terms of my spiritual progress, I knew that the job was a dead end. I had wondered at times if I would have the courage to leave it. When the time came, that door just closed on its own.

Then I met Dr. Singh. Somehow, he was a significant player in this transition I was undergoing. I had not yet discovered his role in my life, but that was about to change.

"What do you want out of life?" he asked.

I did not hesitate. "I want to be enlightened," I replied, "and to help others experience enlightenment."

This was a particularly easy question for me because I had spent the past two months thinking of virtually nothing else. For me, enlightenment was just a word, but I had a sense of the condition to which it referred. I had experienced a few moments in my life of what might be called illumination, inspiration, or epiphany. Each time I had had one of these experiences, I had felt as if I were coming home to a part of myself that was at the very core of who I am. At those moments, I knew perfect clarity, connectedness, and peace. When the feelings dissipated, as they always had, I felt as if I had fallen from grace or had been thrown out of paradise and forced to return to a dark hovel.

Dr. Singh said, "You can have your wish, but there is one condition: You have to want it 24/7."

"But I do." Once again, there was no hesitation in my response. This was my chance to really have my prayers answered, perhaps more so than I had ever imagined possible. I was not going to let the opportunity pass me by.

"I am happy to hear that," Dr Singh replied. "If you want to pursue this path, then I will be honored to serve as your teacher. But I want you to take some time to think it over before you give me your answer. When you feel you are ready to jump, let me know."

In some ways, I was ready to jump at that moment. I had some idea of what the jump would entail because I had given it a great deal of thought already. In fact, a few weeks before meeting Dr. Singh, I had written the following words in my journal:

"I want to be healthy, happy, and balanced. I want to give myself the best chance at enlightenment in this lifetime. I want to know God in all people and all things. I want my humility to be genuine, as well as my compassion, unselfishness, love, kindness, decency, and integrity. Let me heal, not hurt, with my touch. Let me be touched by spiritual people at the deepest level of my being. Let me do right by myself and by my God so that I can die in peace one day, knowing that I made the most of my opportunity to shine, to feel, and to be of service to those in need."

In retrospect, I also understand why Dr. Singh asked me to think it over. The decision to jump into this path—into this new way of existing—is the most significant decision you can make. And once you jump, there is no going back. In one of my favorite movies, *The Matrix*, the protagonist, Neo, is asked to make a similar choice. The character of Morpheus sits facing him, holding two pills in his hands: one red and the other blue.

He tells Neo, "This is your last chance. After this, there is no turning back. You take the blue pill, the story ends, you wake up in your bed and believe whatever you want to believe. You take the red pill, you stay in Wonderland, and I show you how deep the rabbit hole goes."

Dr. Singh had a rabbit hole of his own, but at the time I had no idea how deep it would take me. I didn't know what it meant to be a Chanter. It never occurred to me that one day Dr. Singh would show me how to create miracles through the practice of chanting or that he would take me to new worlds and new dimensions of reality. All I knew was my own heart. I wanted to connect to something profound within myself, and I felt this desire so strongly that I ached for it. My heart also told me that Dr. Singh had come into my life at just the right time to open doors for me and to facilitate this connection. Even though I had only just met him, I was beginning to feel a profound and intense love for this man. I could see that he was not just talking about the spiritual path but actually walking it.

At the end of our conversation, Dr. Singh invited me to the Conservatory. This was a small parcel of land in a Mexican border town called Sonora, about 100 miles outside of Tucson. A few years earlier, the Band had acquired the land and had built a few simple structures on it. Every weekend, they would make the drive south along an empty stretch of highway populated only by wildlife and Border Patrol agents. After being greeted at the tiny border crossing station by hung-over Mexican crossing guards and a few stray dogs, they would go another 100 yards or so down a bumpy dirt road to the Conservatory.

When I first arrived there on a Saturday morning, I felt surprisingly at home—especially considering that I was on foreign soil in the middle of nowhere, surrounded by the neighbor's squawking chickens and unfriendly goats. Immediately upon our arrival, the eight of us who had caravanned from Tucson gathered in a room called the Song Chamber to perform the ritual of Opening the Four Corners.

There was something magical about this room. On one of the walls was a mural of a jaguar walking through the mist. The room had a white cement floor with a circular pattern etched in it. In the center of the room were a few crystals, the candles that provided the only light in the room, a Navajo ceramic bowl containing feathers, and a set of Tibetan prayer flags spread in a circle. On the sides of the room were cushions that looked as if they had been salvaged from old sofas.

Certainly, there was nothing luxurious about the Song Chamber, and yet it was as powerful a place as any I had ever experienced. The moment I entered it, I was transported into another world. During the invocation prayers that Dr. Singh asked Ricardo and Harper to recite, a whirling energy began to move through the room, building force like a dust devil. I began to sense an unfamiliar vibration in my body, as if I were a guitar string being played. As I sat there trying to become accustomed to this sensation, I felt the vibration increase in frequency. This happened a little bit at a time, but I knew the guitar string was being tuned—gradually tightened so that it could reach ever higher notes. The experience was not at all unpleasant, but at the same time I felt like I was being put through a vigorous workout. I could hardly keep my eyes open.

We chanted a Sikh prayer, *Ra Ma Da Sa, Sa Say So Hung*, which translates to "Sun, Moon, Earth, Infinity. I am that Infinity I belong to and contain." As we chanted, I began drifting in and out of consciousness. As soon as the chanting was over, I felt so overwhelmed by the intensity of the energy in the room that I had no choice but to lie down on the cushions and rest. Within seconds, I fell asleep. It was not a typical sleep, either, but a silent and peaceful state with no dreams or thoughts of any kind. And it lasted no more than a few minutes.

Afterwards, I got up and went into the kitchen, where Harper was busy making lunch. When Dr. Singh had asked me if I would be willing to help her with food preparation, I was more than happy to comply. I had always enjoyed cooking and it was relatively easy for me. Plus, kitchen duty meant staying indoors, where we had heat in the winter, shade in the summer, and a boom box playing music year-round. Most importantly, I wanted to work with Harper because I was drawn to her warmth and openness. That morning, I had a lengthy conversation with her that would be the first of many.

I began by remarking about Dr. Singh's happy disposition. "Is he always this way?"

Harper paused to reflect for a moment. "I guess so," she replied. "I can't ever remember seeing him get upset."

"And how long have you known him?" I asked.

"About five years."

This was amazing to me. Harper had spent nearly every weekend with him for the past five years and had never seen him lose his cool, even for a moment. At that point in the conversation, Harper's sister, Carmina, walked into the kitchen.

I turned to her and asked, "How long have you known Dr. Singh, Carmina?"

"Let me see," she said. "I think it's going on twelve years now."

"Have you ever seen him lose his temper?"

"Oh no," she replied cheerfully. "I've been with him in situations that would drive most people nuts, but he never gets angry or frustrated. And nothing seems to make him sad."

I wondered how this could be. Surely, Dr. Singh must get bad news like the rest of us—rejection, plans gone awry, the loss of loved ones. To not feel even a hint of disappointment or resentment in these circumstances seemed almost superhuman.

A few minute later, Dr. Singh came into the kitchen and asked me to go help him move a table in the Amphitheater, an enclosed porch that served as the Conservatory dining room. After we were done with the task, I asked him, "How do you manage to avoid anger or sadness?"

He invited me to sit down on a couple of cushions that were in the room. "Oh, that's easy. You just choose to be happy."

"That's it?" I said, with a hint of surprise.

"Yes, it's really that simple, My Friend. No matter what is happening around you, the choice is yours: You can either be in heaven or you can be in hell. Either way is fine. Hell is not such a bad place." Then he smiled.

When I looked over at him, I began to laugh. I was delighted to realize what a wonderful role model I had, sitting right in front of me. Dr. Singh was teaching my by example, and he made it all look so easy. I was reminded of the time I had taken sailing lessons back in Olympia. The instructor, Tom, took the class to Budd Inlet one cold gray Saturday morning to practice on a small fleet of 16-foot racing boats. Because most of us had never sailed before, Tom decided to assign us to boats in teams of two. One student on each boat would control the rudder and main sail while the other would handle the jib.

The morning was a disaster. We floundered more than we sailed. Even though our boats were on an open stretch of water, we somehow managed to crash them into each other. I remember having a hard time just keeping track of the wind direction, which kept shifting. The idea of trying to steer the boat and control the sails at the same time seemed impossible.

Finally, we took a lunch break. Tom had us tie the boats together, and while we ate our lunch, he took one of the boats out and sailed it by himself. We watched in awe as he controlled the boat effortlessly, steering it in a perfect figure-eight pattern around the inlet. Tom moved in his boat with impeccable grace, as if he were Fred Astaire gliding across the dance floor. There was not even a single moment of wasted effort.

When we got back on the boats after lunch, everything was different. Watching Tom sail with such ease, we began to understand that this was something we could do, too. In the afternoon, the boats sailed under our control, and for the first time, I felt the real joy of sailing.

Now, instead of sailing, I was learning to be happy. I felt so fortunate just to be in the presence of someone like Dr. Singh, who had found genuine happiness and peace. For him to be here, showing me how to find these qualities in myself, made me feel even more blessed. But I had not yet realized the extent of my good fortune.

Then he asked me the following question: "Do you know why I sent Ricardo to your chanting group?"

I shrugged. "No, but I've wondered about that."

"I heard your heart calling out for us," he explained.

I was speechless. In one brief sentence, Dr. Singh had told me volumes about his relationship to me. Now, I knew beyond a doubt that he had come into my life in response to my prayers. But I also realized that Dr. Singh had heard my prayers himself—that he had the power to feel what was in my heart. He knew about my despair; that is why he had asked me about my summer when we had spoken at the Tabernacle.

But I also felt something else, which filled me with a sense of awe and overwhelming gratitude. For the first time, I understood that I had not found Dr. Singh; he had found me. I could feel the depth of his love for me and the strength of his commitment. Knowing the pain that was in my heart, he had sent Ricardo to look for me. Dr. Singh understood that I would be drawn to the very mention of his name, that I would be compelled to meet him, and that I would get a sense of our connection just by looking at him.

Suddenly, I remembered something that he had told me the first time I came to the Tabernacle. As I was saying good-bye to him at the end of the drumming, he leaned over and said softly, "We are coming together at just the right time. You and I almost met a few years ago but you weren't ready yet."

Recalling this, I told myself: I may not have been ready before, but I am now. Dr. Singh had waited patiently for me to come around and now I was here at last. When I came home from Sonora that afternoon, I wrote him the following letter to let him know that I was ready to jump:

My Dear Friend,

I have no words to describe how fortunate and honored I feel for the opportunities you are offering me. I am astonished and overjoyed at the extraordinary set of circumstances that has brought us together.

I thank you with all of my heart. The fact that you came looking for me touches me as much as anything that has ever happened to me. I feel so very blessed to have a teacher like you—gentle, humble, powerful and wise. I can't say that I was waiting for you; it was more of a hope and a dream. Now that you have come into my life, there is no way I am letting this opportunity slip through my fingers. Yes, yes, yes! That's my answer to your question.

I feel like I'm falling in love with the whole world. My heart is so full that I want to sing songs of love and joy all the time. You helped me find the piece that was missing in my spiritual life, and for that I am eternally grateful. I send many blessings and much love to you, my friend.

Genuinely yours,
Omar

Beyond Dr. Singh

The act of jumping onto my spiritual path was never about Dr. Singh; it was about me. For most of my adult life, I had been searching for my true calling, my purpose in life, and a way to find lasting happiness—not just for myself but for those I would eventually serve. Dr. Singh happened to be the one who opened the door and pointed me in the right direction. That is what a good teacher does.

A good teacher also knows when to get out of your way. That is why Dr. Singh has chosen to remain in the shadows. If you go searching for Dr. Singh, you do not need to look any further than the pages of this book. His wisdom permeates everything you are reading here. There are no secrets when it comes to pursuing your spiritual path, whether you choose to become a Chanter or to go in an entirely different direction.

For me, chanting is the path that works best. I knew that long before I met Dr. Singh. Sacred music has been a driving force in my life since I was a little boy. And my search for happiness has never ceased for even a moment. In terms of my spiritual path, all of the pieces were already in place when Dr. Singh came into my life. He just showed me how the pieces fit together, and he did so in a way that made it all look easy.

I was pursuing a spiritual path before my decision to jump, but I could not see what the path looked like or where it was leading me. As a result, I had a tendency to get sidetracked. It was as if I were trying to follow an overgrown trail through a dense, dark forest. The terrain in which I was walking was lush and beautiful, but it was also hard to navigate. In a sense, Dr. Singh provided me with a ladder and a map. The ladder let me climb high enough so that I could see the lay of the land, and the map pointed out some of the landmarks I would find along the way. With these tools in hand, I have had a much easier time finding the trail, although I still manage to take a few missteps here and there.

The difference is that now I know what the path looks like. When I wake up every morning, I have a sense of how my day connects to my overall purpose in life. The big picture has finally come into focus for me. Much of what I do is aligned with my spiritual path, and whatever is not seems like wasted effort. I have a better sense of where to invest my time and energy. My life has a level of integration and coherence that it lacked before. For the first time, I know what it takes to live in a manner consistent with both my ideals and my passion.

When I made the decision to jump, I opened myself up to the wisdom of a number of spiritual teachers. Dr. Singh just happened to be one of them. There is no denying that Dr. Singh played an important role in my decision to jump fully into my spiritual path, but my decision was based on something very personal: the pressing need to find my spiritual purpose in this life. No matter how inspiring I have found Dr. Singh's teachings to be, I know that they are simply a means to an end. I know in my heart that my pursuit of healing and enlightenment is the most important priority in my life, and that I am going to take that pursuit in whatever direction it needs to go.

For two years, this pursuit brought me in close contact with Dr. Singh, for which I am grateful. But he knew that our association was only meant to last a short time. The role of a spiritual teacher is to give you wings and to show you how to fly. At some point, you have to be ready to take flight, and that is something you have to do on your own. You cannot rely on anyone else to do it for you.

Dr. Singh was with me long enough to give me the insights I needed in order to write this book. Once the book began to take form, he returned to his native Oaxaca and disappeared from my life. I have heard that he is living in the mountains of rural Oaxaca, but his exact whereabouts are unknown to me or to any of his former students.

Very early in our acquaintance, Dr. Singh told me, "I prefer to remain invisible. Otherwise, I draw too much attention to myself. The only thing that matters is the wisdom contained in the teachings. I am just an instrument."

When Dr. Singh told us of his decision to go underground, I was not particularly surprised by his announcement. I knew that anyone reading this book would be tempted to go out and find him. But Dr. Singh has always been more interested in having you find yourself. Everything you need to know in order to get started on your spiritual path—especially if you are pursuing the path of a Chanter—is contained in this book. But the pursuit of any path is not simply a matter of knowing what to do. At some point, you need to take action, which is a bold and courageous step. It is up to you to decide when you are ready to do so.

A Deeper Level of Commitment

When I wrote my letter to Dr. Singh, it was easy to jump. I was in love—with Dr. Singh, with life, and with my newfound direction. But that initial passion was short-lived. Dr. Singh knew it would subside, which is why he started calling me *llamarada de petate* a few weeks after he received my letter. In Mexico, a *petate* (prounounced "peh-TAH-teh") is a bedroll made of woven straw. The *llamarada* (prounounced "yah-mah-RAH-thah") is the flame produced when one of these straw bedrolls catches fire. For Mexicans, a *llamarada de petate* is a passionate fling—an intense flame that burns out quickly.

Throughout my adult life, I had experienced my share of such flings, not just in my relationships but also in my career and my spiritual life. It had never been hard for me to fall in love—with people, places, or ideas. The challenge had always been to maintain my intensity over time. Just as suddenly as I would fall in love, I would also fall out of love.

After my first visit to Sonora, I entered a honeymoon phase in which I felt like I was gliding above the clouds. Two months later, the honeymoon ended and I came crashing back to Earth. There was no apparent reason for this change; I just lost my momentum. I still wanted the same things that had drawn me to Dr. Singh, and I knew he was someone who could teach me what I needed to learn. Yet the initial flame had died out. That is when Dr. Singh began referring to me as *llamarada de petate*.

When I discovered what the term meant, I was deeply hurt by it. But the more I reflected on it, the more I realized that the term was accurate. I had rarely sustained my passion for anything

longer than a few months. Here I was, a few weeks into my training with Dr. Singh, and I was already running out of steam. My
spiritual path was in jeopardy and I had no idea what to do.

Finally, I went to Dr. Singh and let him know about my struggle. I said, "I don't want to be a *llamarada de petate* anymore. I
know that my flame has burned out quickly in the past, but I
want this particular fire to last."

Dr. Singh smiled at me and said, "Alright. You are no longer
llamarada de petate. Now, find a way to keep the fire burning."

Within a few days of that conversation, I discovered what Dr.
Singh had really meant when he first asked me if I was ready to
jump. He wanted to know if I could make a lasting commitment
to my spiritual path—a commitment that would withstand
moments of inner turmoil and confusion. The decision to jump
is not something you make just a single time. You have to renew
the decision every day.

Initially, I made my decision based on passion. But once the
passion had subsided, I needed to make the same decision based
on courage. In other words, I knew this path was the right one
for me, and so I had to keep going, even though it meant facing
my fears. At that moment, my biggest fear was a life devoid of
passion. I was afraid that the thrill had gone out of this path and
that it would never return. But I also understood that I had to
push through this fear. Otherwise, my commitment would have
been meaningless.

Some men—and a few women—get accused of being commitment phobic, but I believe that nobody is afraid of commitment
per se. What we fear is making a sacrifice in pursuit of a dream
that is unattainable. Most single people would sacrifice their
freedom, for instance, in exchange for marital bliss. But we just
have to look at our married friends to see that such bliss is
elusive, at best, and that it might even be a bit of a pipe dream.

The one commitment that makes sense—at least in my
mind—is to what Dr. Singh calls the Big Beautiful Spirit. This is
the infinite source of consciousness and energy that permeates
all things, including ourselves. Jumping is an act of faith. I am

not talking about faith in the existence of a Big Beautiful Spirit. Knowing that the Big Beautiful Spirit exists is a matter of direct experience—not faith. You have either experienced it for yourself, or you have not.

The faith to which I am referring is in the path you are pursuing. If you are seeking enlightenment, then you want to know that the direction you are taking is the one that is going to connect you in the deepest and most lasting way possible to the Big Beautiful Spirit. For me, this is what matters most. Everything else is just icing: our chanting, our ability to fly into other dimensions, our link to the ancient temples, and our role as healers. Nothing else matters if we do not have this connection.

For the first several weeks of my acquaintance with Dr. Singh, I was in a state of continuous bliss. In this state, I had a sense of connectedness to all things. My heart was open and filled with more love than I had ever experienced. Although I wanted to stay in that state, I also knew that I was not ready for it. I was in the process of being tuned like a guitar string so that I could vibrate at higher frequencies. But if a guitar string is over-tightened, it snaps. I knew that I was in no danger of snapping because I was in the hands of Dr. Singh. He had a good idea of my limits—of how much I could take. When it got to be too intense for me, the blissful feeling just dissipated on its own.

After that feeling went away, it was replaced by a sense of loss. I had become so attached to the sensation of bliss that I could hardly live without it. That is when Harper told me something that I hated to hear at the time but that I would later come to appreciate. She said, "Right now, you think that enlightenment is a state of perpetual ecstasy, but maybe it's not quite that sensational. What if enlightenment is more a condition of serenity than of bliss? Then to be enlightened, all you would have to do is to let go and find peace within yourself."

In her own gentle way, Harper was letting me know that I was allowing myself to become distracted from what really mattered most, which was my pursuit of enlightenment. It seems ironic that something as beautiful as what I had been experiencing could end up interfering with this pursuit. And yet, an addiction to bliss is still just an addiction.

From the moment I had met Dr. Singh, he had emphasized detachment. Now, I was beginning to understand why. Although I have never been enlightened and make no such claims, I have one strong belief about enlightenment: It happens through a process of subtraction—not addition. If the Big Beautiful Spirit permeates all things, then it is already inside each one of us. So, why would we be unable to connect with it? As far as I can tell, the only reason for this inability is that there must be something in our way.

The interference comes from everything to which we feel an attachment: our possessions, our self-concept, our memories, our loved ones, our thoughts and feelings, our goals and aspirations. Imagine letting go of all that. I once heard a Tibetan lama say, "Oh, that's easy. It's called death. The trick is to do it while you are still alive. That's called enlightenment."

But why would anybody want to let go of everything they have? At the beginning of this chapter, I compared the process of getting started on this path to the act of jumping off a cliff. What I did not tell you is that the cliff is not solid ground. In fact, it is crumbling beneath your feet. No matter how attached you are to something, you are destined to lose it eventually. In the meantime, the attachment itself is keeping you from making the most precious connection of all, which is with the Big Beautiful Spirit.

Our destiny as human beings is to merge with the Divine, to identify with our infinite nature, to melt into the flow of love. For those of us who are Chanters, our destiny is also to be selfless servants, to act as instruments of divine love, to tap into the spiritual power at our disposal so that we can benefit others. To fulfill this destiny does not mean that we have to go and give away everything we own. It does mean, though, that if all our possessions were taken from us tomorrow, we would be unaffected because our happiness and well-being would not be dependent on them.

The Obstacles

When you jump, you are choosing to meet your destiny head-on. You enter the path of enlightenment and begin your life as a Chanter. This choice is clearly not for everyone. In my first year with Dr. Singh, I saw many wonderful people try to jump unsuccessfully. Each one of them genuinely wanted to follow a spiritual path but got tripped up by an attachment of some kind. I want to share a few of their stories with you, not to disparage them in any way but to let you know the kinds of obstacles that others have faced. I honor the efforts of these friends and feel a great deal of love and compassion for each of them. I also know in my heart that they have all taken important steps in their spiritual lives and that each of them will find what they seek when the time is right.

White Horse. This was the spiritual name Dr. Singh had given to a dear friend of mine who had taken part in Global Chant for many years. Dr. Singh invited her to attend the Sound Circle a week after my first visit to the Tabernacle. The first time I went to Sonora, White Horse rode with me.

White Horse had a hard time fitting in with most groups. She had a tendency to intimidate people with her size—at 5'8" and 350 lb—and her gruff demeanor. But I also knew her to have a very tender side, with a childlike sense of playfulness and joy. When she met Dr. Singh and the rest of the Band, she took to them immediately. She was thrilled to have found a spiritual teacher and a community that accepted her.

And yet, White Horse rarely did anything that Dr. Singh asked of her. She resisted even the smallest things, such as the request that people wash their hands when entering the kitchen in Sonora. This policy was adopted to protect visitors from hepatitis, which was a serious health concern in that part of Mexico. But White Horse reacted to it as if it were an affront to her civil liberties.

Because of her weight and her limited mobility, she was accustomed to receiving special treatment. The rest of us who came to Sonora on the weekends would devote some of our time to accommodating White Horse and tending to her needs. Dr.

Singh felt that we were indulging her too much and began to set limits on what we could do for her. He wanted to encourage White Horse to be more independent and less demanding. These limits made her feel resentful and after a few weeks, she threw a profanity-laced tantrum in the Amphitheater. As a result of this incident, Dr. Singh asked White Horse to conduct ceremonies in Tucson on the weekends, partly so that she would stop coming to Sonora.

One weekend, when Dr. Singh asked White Horse to do a chanting ceremony by herself at a Tucson shrine, she invited several people she knew to accompany her. White Horse wanted her friends to see how well she could conduct a spiritual ceremony. Some of the people who attended the ceremony were so impressed by it that they asked her to lead a weekly chanting circle.

Dr. Singh supported this idea; he wanted White Horse to gain a lesson in humility. The group began meeting every week at the same time as the Sound Circle in the Tabernacle. But White Horse ran her chanting circle like a dictator, imposing her will on the group at every turn. After a few weeks, the members of her circle rebelled and voted her out as leader. She reacted to the "overthrow" by quitting the group altogether.

For White Horse, the major stumbling block was her desire for attention and special treatment. The idea of selfless service did not appeal to her. She preferred to be served by others, to the point that it kept her from taking advantage of the learning opportunity that Dr. Singh had offered her.

Dr. Llamarada. After Dr. Singh stopped calling me *llamarada de petate*, he decided to pass along the name to a retired osteopath who had come to him for spiritual help. To simplify the name, Dr. Singh referred to him as Dr. Llamarada.

Like many of us, Dr. Llamarada had studied different forms of spirituality and had read all kinds of books on the subject. But in spite of all his efforts, he was restless and unhappy. He became so miserable that his wife started encouraging him to spend the weekends with us in Sonora. This was an act of desperation on her part. She did not expect that Dr. Singh would be able to pull her husband out of his funk, but it was pretty much her last resort.

When I would watch Dr. Llamarada's behavior around us, it was as if I were looking in the mirror. The first time he came to Sonora, he became enamored of us instantly. He was especially drawn to Dr. Singh and to Harper, just as I had been. And right away, he began to have the kinds of intensely blissful feelings that I had experienced when I first started coming to Sonora.

Soon, he became a mainstay of the group, spending at least part of every weekend with us. He was feeling so grateful to Dr. Singh that he insisted on giving him one of his cars. His wife was so elated at the change in Dr. Llamarada's demeanor that she would send a loaf of her homemade bread with him every weekend. Although the bread was delicious, it was made with white flour. Dr. Singh had set a policy that we would only serve nutritious food in Sonora, including whole grains. He did this to set an example for the local townspeople who would eat with us on occasion.

Meanwhile, Dr. Llamarada was becoming seriously infatuated with Harper. She gave him the same attention she showed everyone else who came to Sonora. There were no mixed signals in her approach to him. Nonetheless, his infatuation grew to the point that his wife picked up on it. Suddenly, she was becoming much less enthusiastic about having her husband spend the weekends with us.

One day, when Dr. Singh met with Dr. Llamarada and his wife, he asked her politely if she would be willing to use whole wheat flour in her bread. She took offense at the request and stormed out of the room, accompanied by her husband. A few days later, Dr. Llamarada called Harper and told her that he would not be coming to Sonora anymore and that he was deeply hurt by the way that Dr. Singh had insulted his wife. It was ironic how quickly Dr. Llamarada's passion had turned into resentment. The name that Dr. Singh had given him fit perfectly.

The reason Dr. Llamarada left the group is that he had a strong attachment to his marriage, even though his wife did not share or support his spiritual interests. Dr. Llamarada took great pride in his loyalty to his wife. He was also proud of the fact that she was significantly younger than he was. Although he was not particularly happy in his marriage, he was unwilling to put the relationship in jeopardy. It was his infatuation with Harper that made his wife uncomfortable—not Dr. Singh's request. The bread incident was an excuse for her to pull him out of the group.

Montana. I had known Montana and her husband, Rob, for a few months before I met Dr. Singh. They were the kind of people you cannot help but like: kind, ethical, modest, and caring. When Montana announced that she was pregnant, I was thrilled for her. But she started having complications midway through the pregnancy and sadly, her baby did not survive.

Montana was devastated by the death of her little boy. Even before his death, she had been susceptible to depression and anxiety. Plus, she was physically frail and had a number of chronic medical problems, including fatigue and pain in her joints. The loss just seemed to compound all of her symptoms. Seeing her so miserable, I decided to put her in touch with Dr. Singh.

As soon as she met him, Montana started feeling better. She began coming to the Tabernacle for the weekly Sound Circle. A few weeks later, she and Rob came to Sonora for the first time. Spending time with us seemed to do them both good. Montana was noticeably happier and more energetic around us. At times, she would run around and play with the local children in Sonora—something that I had never imagined her being able to do. Rob thrived in our company, as well. He seemed to enjoy being around us and helping out with little handyman jobs around the Conservatory.

Montana and Rob befriended one of the local children—a 10-year-old girl named Betsy who would hang around the Conservatory on the weekends because she had nowhere else to go. Betsy's mother had recently remarried, and the new husband wanted nothing to do with either of the children from the mother's first marriage. Betsy became unwelcome in her own home. Knowing this, Dr. Singh had encouraged Montana and Rob to spend time with her. As they became closer to Betsy, they considered adopting her. Both of them seemed thrilled by the idea—especially Rob, who wanted to start a family. They even began discussing the possibility with Betsy's mother.

As Rob began to make arrangements to adopt Betsy, Montana's health began to worsen. All of the mental and physical symptoms she had experienced before meeting Dr. Singh began to reappear. After a while, Montana and Rob stopped coming to either the Tabernacle or to Sonora, presumably because of Montana's failing health. But there was another reason they distanced themselves from the group: The closer Montana and Rob came to adopting Betsy, the more Montana felt threatened by the prospect of having Betsy live with them. As long as she and Rob lived by themselves, she had his undivided attention. Rob was Montana's caretaker; he looked after her and doted on her as much as he could. This behavior was part of the reason that the improvement in Montana's health did not last. Whether or not she realized it, she depended on the attention she received by being ill.

Montana and Rob were attached to the dynamic of their relationship. Rob needed to play the role of caretaker and Montana needed to have someone take care of her. In their marriage, they had created a little bubble that engulfed the two of them and isolated them to some degree from the rest of the world. Neither one seemed interested in either stepping out of that bubble or letting someone else into it.

What It Takes to Jump

All of these friends took important steps on their spiritual path, but none of them were ready to jump. When faced with the decision, they all chose to follow a course that was familiar to them. I see nothing wrong with that. In fact, even the tiniest step is significant when it comes to finding your purpose in life. And if you are not ready to take that first step, then dipping your toes in the water can be an important start. At least you know what to expect when you do decide to jump.

In reality, the life of a Chanter is not for everyone. But even for those of us who recognize this as our path, there is the matter of timing. Neither you nor I can be rushed to do something for which we are physically, mentally, or spiritually unprepared. In order for you to jump, the right combination of factors has to be in place.

For one, you have to recognize the significance of the decision you are making. When you reach the turning point, you will be faced with options that are equally attractive to you. In fact, the differences among your choices may appear inconsequential because the repercussions of making the wrong choice may not seem all that great. In his well-known poem, "The Road Not Taken," Robert Frost captures the subtlety of this decision:

Two roads diverged in a yellow wood,
And sorry I could not travel both
And be one traveller, long I stood
And looked down one as far as I could
To where it bent in the undergrowth;

Then took the other, as just as fair,
And having perhaps the better claim,
Because it was grassy and wanted wear;
Though as for that the passing there
Had worn them really about the same,

And both that morning, equally lay
In leaves no step had trodden black.
Oh, I kept the first for another day!
Yet knowing how way leads on to way
I doubted if I should ever come back.

I shall be telling this with a sigh
Somewhere ages and ages hence:
Two roads diverged in a wood, and I--
I took the one less travelled by,
And that has made all the difference.

The difference between the two roads is anything but obvious. One road is "just as fair" as the other. Although Frost claims to have chosen "the one less travelled," we know the claim to be false. The poem tells us that previous travelers along the two roads have "worn them really about the same." Given that both roads are equally attractive and equally well-worn, we are left to wonder how the traveler is able to choose one over the other. Is the decision arbitrary? Or does it even matter which path we choose?

I believe that the choice matters a great deal. Only one direction leads to the full realization of what we really are. For those of us who are Chanters, this path connects us to other stars, other dimensions, the wisdom of the Masters, the rich traditions of our past and the shining promise of our shared destiny as healers, counselors, and high priests.

Our choice has ramifications that extend far beyond our own lives. When we jump, we become spiritual servants to a world in desperate need. As Chanters, we are taking upon ourselves the monumental task that Joseph Campbell describes as "the unlocking and release again of the flow of life into the body of the world." We live in a time when more people are disconnected from the spiritual core of their identity than ever before. In *The Hero with a Thousand Faces*, Campbell writes "The usual person is more than content, he is even proud, to remain within the indicated bounds, and popular belief gives him every reason to fear so much as the first step into the unexplored."

To be a Chanter means to be willing not just to step into the unexplored but to jump in head-first, venturing into even the most mysterious dimensions of the spiritual realm. We do this because the unknown represents the source of creation, the fountain from which miracles and blessings flow into existence. As Chanters, we are also dreamers, envisioning possibilities that have not yet been realized—at least not in the dimensions that most of us are accustomed to inhabiting. The visionaries who reshape the world begin with nothing more than a dream, and this dream always comes from somewhere deep, mysterious, and limitless within the human heart.

When you first decide to jump, you will be armed only with your passion and your courage. As you have already seen, passion was my greatest ally at the beginning. I wanted much more for myself than the life I had been living up to that point. I wanted to experience enlightenment in a lasting way. For me, this was a burning desire. Sometimes, I wonder if anyone else shares that intensity. Do you know what it is like to have that fire burning in you? Have you ever felt a desperate need to find the divine spark within yourself, to know who you are to the fullest extent possible, to be connected to all things at all times?

Here is a prayer I say every morning: "Fill my heart so that I can know you in every moment and in everything." My prayer comes out a passion for the Big Beautiful Spirit. If you are really going to jump, you need to have that kind of passion. Otherwise, you will not be compelled to move forward in the face of hardship. Why should you? Without the feeling that nothing matters more—that life is not worth living without it—you will never know enlightenment. The sacrifices you have to make are just too great to justify unless you know in your heart, beyond a shadow of a doubt, that this is your highest priority.

I have had people ask me, "How do I know if I'm ready to jump?" When I hear this question, I am reminded of another scene from *The Matrix*, in which Neo meets the Oracle, who asks him, "Do you think you are The One?"

He replies, "Honestly, I don't know."

The Oracle points to a sign above her kitchen door that reads *Temet Nosce* and says, "Do you know what that means? It's Latin. It means, 'Know thyself.' I'm gonna let you in on a little secret. Being The One is just like being in love. No one can tell you you're in love. You just know it, through and through, balls to bones."

Jumping into this path is comparable to falling in love. You feel it so strongly in your heart that you just know it is right for you. There is no need for analysis, no need to weigh pros and cons. That is not how love works.

When I greet Dr. Singh, I get a lot of enjoyment just from

asking him the generic question, "How are you?" I know his answer will be anything but generic. He often responds, "I'm in love." And when I hear him say it, I know he means it. Dr. Singh is in love with life. He resides permanently in a psychological space that most of us have only visited. Knowing that someone like him exists is both comforting and inspiring to me. He is one of the role models—and there are many of them alive today— who teach by example, showing us what it might be like to experience happiness and peace all of the time.

With the help of these role models, we can learn to live fully in the moment. But this is not an easy thing to learn. In fact, it may be the greatest challenge of your life. Right away, you will discover, as I did, that passion alone is not enough. My passion could only take me so far because I could not sustain the intensity for more than a few weeks. Unlike Dr. Singh, I could only be in love for so long. After a while, the feelings subsided and then my inner struggle began in earnest.

Albert Einstein described this struggle perfectly when he said, "Great spirits have always encountered violent opposition from mediocre minds." Ironically, the great spirit and the mediocre mind reside in the same body. The difference between the two is striking: Your spirit is limitless; it has never been born and will never die. It is also part of the Big Beautiful Spirit that permeates all things. Your mind, on the other hand, is limited in every respect. It is confined to your body from conception to death. Moreover, its primary function is to impose and enforce those limits—by defining reality and by making sense of it through the faculties of judgment and perception.

Your spirit, which is at peace, requires nothing, whereas your mind, which is restless, requires complete control and safety. The mind can never fulfill either of these needs. No matter how brilliant it may be, your mind is small and weak compared to your spirit. Because your mind knows that its destiny is to die, it is plagued by fear and doubt. From its standpoint, your spiritual life is the ultimate threat because it means that you are pursuing a path that will align you inevitably with your spirit, which is the real source of your power and happiness. And so your mind struggles. It will challenge, question, doubt, and analyze every aspect of your spiritual path.

Most of all, your mind will create fear. You may become preoccupied with worry or suspicion, and you will find plenty of reasons to be afraid: lack of security, trust issues, and loss of control. But all of these worries are really a smokescreen. In *A Return to Love*, author Marianne Williamson identifies the real reason why your mind is afraid of your spiritual path. She writes, "Our deepest fear is that we are powerful beyond measure. It is our light, not our darkness, that most frightens us."

The Courage of Ricardo

The only way to counteract fear is through courage. When you choose to pursue your spiritual path in spite of your fear, then you really jump. One of the most courageous people I have met on this journey is the man who introduced me to Dr. Singh: my friend Ricardo. When I met Ricardo, I felt like I was in the presence of a true holy man. His tenderness and quiet strength were irresistible. I knew from the start that I wanted this man as my friend.

But then the first time I visited the Conservatory in Sonora, I encountered a very different side of him. From the moment I arrived there, Ricardo acted as if I were competing with him somehow. He challenged me, found reasons to ridicule and humiliate me, and did everything he could to assert his position as the alpha male.

At first, I felt that I had been tricked. In a sense, Ricardo had misrepresented himself, pulling the classic maneuver that marketers know as the bait-and-switch. This is the type of dishonest advertising ploy that promises the buyer one thing and then delivers something of inferior quality.

When I watched Ricardo with some of the people who would visit the Refuge, I would catch glimpses of the holy man I had met. He was especially loving and gentle with the children who always seemed to surround him. Once I realized that the version of Ricardo I had seen initially really did exist—at least some of the time—I decided to only acknowledge and respond to that side of him. To me, the seemingly mean-spirited antics were just the last-ditch effort of his mind to hold onto the status quo.

The more I got to know Ricardo, the more I discovered how hard this path has been for him. From the time Ricardo started training as a Chanter, he has had one setback after another. To be fair, these setbacks have to do with his resistance to change. Ricardo had been accustomed to being in control. For much of his life, he has been telling others what to do—in both his home life and his professional career.

The Ricardo I saw every weekend in Sonora had a desperate need for control and refused to admit his mistakes. He challenged virtually everything that was asked of him. I would avoid asking for his help because I knew that his first answer would always be "No." Then if he did offer his help, it would be accompanied by a lecture or scolding.

But I felt compassion for Ricardo because I understood that this behavior was grounded in fear. At times, Ricardo seemed overwhelmed by the demands of his spiritual path. It required a level of self-reflection that was painful for him. Rather than looking critically at himself, he preferred to direct his criticism towards others.

What makes Ricardo so courageous is that he has never given up, no matter how hard things have gotten for him. He keeps plugging away in spite of his fear. I know that he will be at the Tabernacle for the Sound Circle every Thursday night and in Sonora every weekend. I also know that he has been tempted to quit on at least one occasion. But he keeps coming because he knows the importance of what we are doing. Those of us who are learning to fly with Dr. Singh have been given the opportunity not just of one lifetime but of several. Our spirits have been waiting a very long time to be set free and to serve the needs of this world.

When we visited the ancient temples in Oaxaca, Ricardo rediscovered his identity as a Chanter. After that experience, his demeanor changed and he became more consistently the holy man that I had met a year earlier. In the time I have known Ricardo, he has made huge strides in his spiritual development. I believe that his courage has been rewarded in ways he never could have imagined possible. By persisting on his path and overcoming his fear, Ricardo discovered amazing things about himself and about the powers that support him on this journey.

Goethe wrote, "Act boldly and mighty forces will come to your aid." Ricardo is the embodiment of this profound statement. He has shown the courage to act boldly and to jump into his spiritual path, in spite of all the obstacles. Now he is discovering the magnitude of the forces that are at his disposal as a result of his decision to jump.

CHAPTER 2

Wake-up Call

When I made my decision to jump, I had the luxury of knowing that I was not operating blindly. No matter what kind of predicament I would face, I knew that I could rely on the guidance of my friend and teacher, Dr. Pablo Singh. What I did not realize is how much guidance I had at my disposal. Dr. Singh was not the only one looking out for me. He was part of a team comprised of the most inspiring mentors imaginable.

Even more surprising is that the wisdom of these Masters is not something that only a few can access. It is available to anyone who is committed to the pursuit of a spiritual path. There is one catch, though: You have to know how to receive this wisdom. In other words, you need to be able to listen to the inner voices that speak to you. The first thing a Chanter learns is how to be a good listener—but not in any traditional sense.

A month after I met Dr. Singh, he told me to expect conversations with him in the middle of the night. "Every morning, a little bird wakes me just after three in the morning," he explained. "That's when I get up and meditate. If I have information to pass along to you, I will give you a wake-up call a few minutes later."

I was certainly not used to receiving phone calls in the middle of the night. But Dr. Singh had no intention of using a telephone. His wake-up calls were of a different kind. These conversations were telepathic. We would communicate with one another using only our sense of intuition.

Two days later, I got my first wake-up call from Dr. Singh. At exactly 3:12 am, I awoke from a deep sleep to the sound of his voice, as if he were sitting on the edge of my bed talking to me. I immediately got up, as he had instructed me to do, and sat at my normal meditation spot. There, I could hear Dr. Singh talking to me at length about a variety of topics, including the need for me to start communicating with the Masters.

The conversation ended up being a wake-up call for me in more than one sense. It marked the beginning of an important new phase of my spiritual life in which I began receiving guidance directly from the Masters. Since that memorable conversation with Dr. Singh, I have been listening more and more to what the Masters have to say. The words you are reading are an example of the detailed information I have received from them.

And who exactly are these Masters? Although they sound like a group of golf pros, they are actually the enlightened beings who have chosen to serve as our spiritual teachers and guides. You are already familiar with a few of the Masters because they have taken human form at some point in history. Many of them, however, have not. There are Masters who have never existed in the dimensions you and I inhabit, or who have lived in galaxies other than our own.

Dr. Singh once confided to me that the decisions he makes in his spiritual life are relatively easy. "I just have to listen to what the Masters tell me," he said. Of course, this is not as easy as it sounds. To receive the guidance of the Masters, first you have to be open to it. This means acknowledging the wisdom you receive from them and being willing to surrender to it. Besides an attitude of openness, you also need a heightened sense of intuition. You must be able to discern their guidance from all the noise that may fill your mind.

There will be a great deal of noise—especially at the beginning. When you begin to tune into the guidance the Masters have to offer, your mind will find a number of creative ways to resist and challenge it. This was certainly the case for me. I doubted the accuracy of the information I was receiving and wondered if I was sacrificing too much autonomy to someone other than myself. But I soon discovered that the guidance I got from the Masters always seemed to lead me in the right direction. An even more surprising discovery was that this guidance was not coming from someone else at all. Ultimately, it was coming from inside of me.

In the Hindu tradition, a spiritual Master is referred to as *guru*. Although this term is widely misunderstood in the West— we tend to associate it with strange little bearded men in white robes—it really means "the embodiment of the inner teacher." This is a profound idea: The Masters who guide us actually reside within us. We would not be able to communicate with them if they did not.

Buddhists have a saying: "If you meet the Buddha on the road, kill him." The point of this saying is that the Buddha is a manifestation of our own enlightened mind. If the Buddha only exists outside of our selves, then it is not really the Buddha. Beware of any spiritual teacher who tells you, "I am an enlightened Master and you are not." This individual cannot be a true Master. When Dr. Singh addresses me, he calls me "Master." This is his way of acknowledging the inner teachers who guide me.

All of my adult life, I have been searching for Masters who would be willing to share their spiritual wisdom with me. I knew there had to be role models who personified the ideals to which I aspired and who were willing to teach me. Little did I know that the Masters I sought were already inside of me, offering their teachings freely. I just had to arrive at the same conclusion that Dorothy reaches at the end of *The Wizard of Oz*, when she says, "If I ever go looking for my heart's desire again, I won't look any further than my own back yard."

Meeting the Masters

My search for spiritual wisdom began long before I met Dr. Singh and took me to some strange and wonderful places. The first time I became aware of the influence of the Masters in my life was while traveling through the South Pacific. I was 27 and didn't know where I wanted to live or what I wanted to do with my life. All I knew was that I had a powerful fascination with coral reefs. So, I decided to use my savings to buy an open-ended airline ticket that would allow me to tour the South Pacific for a year. My only plan was to keep traveling until I either had some reason to turn back or until the ticket expired. In six months of traveling, I had gotten as far as Fiji but had made little progress in finding clarity about my life's direction.

Feeling restless, I wandered to a remote part of one of the islands, where I struck up a friendship with a local farmer named Sanjeet who was of East Indian descent. One day, Sanjeet told me the amazing story of a cousin of his—a wife and mother named Rukmini who lived in the village next to his. A few years earlier, Rukmini had seen an old beggar wandering through the streets of her village. She invited him into her home and fed him. In return, the man offered her his blessing.

Several days later, Rukmini began noticing layers of an unusual dust that was collecting on all the surfaces of her home—the floors, the furniture, and especially the picture frames. This dust was actually a type of ash called *vibhuti* that is considered sacred in Hindu tradition. Within weeks, her house was covered in *vibhuti.* Even more astonishing, the woman herself started to experience spontaneous trances, during which the same ash would emerge from the palms of her hands.

Sanjeet went on to explain that people from all over the island had heard about this miracle and began making pilgrimages to his cousin's home by the busload. Many of these people believed that the beggar had actually been a holy man in disguise who had blessed Rukmini with the ability to channel his power. They came to her home to receive her blessings, to worship in her presence and to take home some of the *vibhuti,* which they believed to have healing properties. Two nights a week, Sanjeet volunteered as an attendant at ceremonies in which hundreds of people would gather in Rukmini's backyard. These devotees sat cross-legged on the ground, chanting, meditating, and waiting to be ushered into the house, where Rukmini greeted them individually.

When Sanjeet described the ceremony to me, I knew I had to see it for myself. I asked him to take me along the next time he went to one of the ceremonies, and he agreed, saying that he could use my help ushering. Two days later, we set out for Rukmini's village. By the time we arrived at her house, three busloads of people were already waiting to be seated. Sanjeet and I worked for nearly an hour, and we somehow managed to accommodate more than 500 people into a backyard that was less than half the size of a tennis court.

Even though people were packed tightly together, this was a surprisingly quiet and peaceful crowd. The congregation began to sing a series of Hindu chants, and as the tempo of the music increased, I could feel a buildup of energy in the gathering until the singing reached a crescendo. At that moment, Sanjeet signaled me to come into the house, where Rukmini was sitting. I had not been able to see her from my vantage point in the backyard, but now that I was less than 10 feet away from her, I could hardly believe my eyes.

Rukmini was wearing a white sari with several floral garlands around her neck. Her eyes were closed and her facial expression was one of complete serenity. While her right hand rested on her thigh, her left hand was extended in front of her, with the palm side facing up. This hand was filled with vibhuti, which appeared to be flowing continuously from her palm. The pile covered her hand and was about two inches high, with the excess pouring out from between her fingers. On the floor in front of her sat another pile of ash that was at least 15 inches high and three feet in diameter.

When Sanjeet had first told me about Rukmini's ability to manifest matter from her hands, I tried to be polite but my mind was filled with doubts. *Was this just a hoax?* I wondered. *Could this woman be performing an elaborate magic trick? How was she benefiting from her powers? Was she making money off the people who came to see her?* As I stood in front of Rukmini, though, my doubts gave way to a feeling of complete openness. At that moment, I was neither a skeptic nor a believer; I was just willing to consider the possibility that she was actually producing sacred ash from her hand.

I wondered how a physicist would interpret what I was seeing at that moment. Was there any law of nature being violated? Or was it just my expectations that were being challenged? As I watched *vibhuti* pour out of Rukmini's hand, I realized that my assumptions about the world had been too narrow, that I had been too willing to rule out certain possibilities simply because they did not conform to my way of thinking. I remember something I had once read, the words of a well-known physicist named David Bohm:

"Whatever we know of the world, there is always more. We find things that we didn't know about, and we find things that contradict what we already know. This is a sign of a reality that is beyond our knowledge, our will, our intention, and our desire, as well as being beyond what we have created."

Here I was, face to face with such a reality, and it was reshaping my perspective on the world.

At the end of the ceremony, after Rukmini had greeted all of the people in attendance, Sanjeet told me that it was now our turn to be greeted by her. When I approached Rukmini, she looked into my eyes intently for several seconds. Then she scooped up a handful of *vibhuti* that had been lying on the floor, poured the ash into my hand, and spoke a few words to me in a language I did not understand. When I asked Sanjeet to translate for me, he replied, "She is saying, 'You will be offered a gift that will change your life forever. Keep an open heart and an open mind so that you can receive it.'"

A week later, while I was staying in a small youth hostel on the other side of the island, I decided to go for a moonlight swim. As I floated on the gentle ocean waves, looking up at the constellations of the Southern sky, I wondered about Rukmini's prediction: *What kind of gift did she envision for me?* As soon as I asked myself this question, a strange sensation came over me. I had a sense of foreshadowing, as if something important were about to happen.

After my swim, I went back to my dormitory and tried to sleep. The room felt stuffy and confining, and it seemed like hours before I could get comfortable on the rickety bunk. Finally, I managed to fall asleep, only to be awakened a short while later by a powerful male voice.

"You are greater than you ever imagined," it said in the darkness.

I raced over to the wall and turned on the light. At that moment, the largest spider I had ever seen ran across the room, under the door, and out into the hallway. I actually followed it, wondering if somehow this spider was the one who had spoken to me. There was certainly nobody else around. After a few minutes, it crawled into a neighboring room and I had no choice but to abandon my chase.

By the time I got back into bed, I was beginning to wonder if it had just been a dream. The words had been so vivid, though, that they felt real. Unlike any other dream I had ever had, there were no visual images. I lay in bed and just repeated the words to myself. With each repetition, I grew more excited as the significance of the statement began to dawn on me.

You are greater than you ever imagined. There was something so beautiful and profound about this statement. It let me know that I was connected to something limitless and all-encompassing. As I repeated the words to myself, I could feel that a door was opening for me. I began to realize how much I had been underestimating myself—and my world. My encounter with Rukmini had given me a glimpse of the enormous creative power that a single individual could have under the right circumstances. Now, I had a surge of energy go through my body as I felt the source of this power pulsing inside of me. It was embedded in the human spirit, just waiting to be tapped. Suddenly, I felt an overwhelming desire to unleash that power, both in myself and in others.

My travels were over. It was time to turn back and head home. I had been ready to end my trip for several weeks, and yet something had compelled me to keep going. Here I was, six thousand miles from home, and finally I understood why I had come this far. I had been on a pilgrimage of sorts—a quest for the central vision of my life that would focus my energy and direct my actions. Now I had what I wanted, in the form of a simple seven-word statement: *You are greater than you ever imagined.* Eventually, I turned this statement into a chant—the first of many chants that I would compose.

In recalling that critical turning point in my life, I now realize some things that I had no way of knowing at the time. The old beggar who had given his blessings to Rukmini was one of the Masters—a powerful spiritual teacher known as the Sai Baba. Among the many powers that Masters like the Sai Baba possess is the power of direct transmission. Through a process that the Hindus call *darshan*, this Master was able to confer his energy and wisdom to Rukmini. In turn, she became a channel through which he could give blessings to those who would come in contact with her, including me.

By coming to Rukmini with an attitude of openness, I showed the Sai Baba that I was ready to start receiving the teachings of the Masters. When Rukmini spoke to me, it was his words that she uttered. The Sai Baba made sure to remind me to "keep an open mind and an open heart." Only by maintaining a state of complete receptivity—free of all judgment, analysis, and doubt—would I hear the messages of my inner teachers. In this receptive state, all I had to do was listen.

Over the next few years, I would become a much better listener. I cultivated my intuition in a number of ways. First, I began tuning into my dreams and writing them down in my journals. I also used intuitive techniques to get answers to yes-or-no questions. One such technique relies on linking certain muscle movements to a "yes" or a "no" answer. For instance, I would use finger movements. A twitch of my left index finger would signal "yes" and of my right index finger would signal "no."

I also started paying more attention to seemingly random occurrences. Dr. Singh once confirmed something that I had suspected nearly 20 years earlier, which is that nothing is random or arbitrary. The more sensitive your intuition becomes, the more you are able to pick up on the significance of even the smallest things, such as the laughter of children playing or the subtle movements of branches in a breeze.

The more I refined and learned to trust my sense of intuition, the more encounters I would have with the Masters. Eventually, I came to know and interact with several of them. Each one communicated with me on an intuitive level, sometimes in extraordinary and dramatic ways. They also connected with me through music and chanting. Here are just a few examples:

Ammachi. One day, I was visiting a friend who had just returned from a meditation retreat with Ammachi, who is known as the "hugging saint." The reason for this moniker is that Ammachi gives *darshan* in the form of an embrace. She transmits her love and blessings to people while holding them in her arms and chanting a mantra in their ear. I have known individuals who have traveled thousands of miles to receive one of her hugs. It is estimated that she has given *darshan* to over 30 million people, one hug at a time.

When my friend described her experience with Ammachi, I was somewhat intrigued but felt no compulsion to meet her or to receive *darshan* from her. That night, however, Ammachi came to me in a dream. She looked into my eyes and said, "Come to Santa Fe, my son." The dream was so vivid that it stunned me. Even though I had never seen a picture of her, my dream showed me a perfect image of her face. And I had no idea if or when Ammachi was scheduled to be in Santa Fe, but I soon found out that she would be arriving there two weeks later.

Accepting her invitation, I packed up my car and drove to Santa Fe. Ammachi was holding a public program in the banquet room of one of the city's historic hotels. When I walked into the room, I found a spectacle the likes of which I had never seen before. At least two thousand people were packed into the room, most of them wearing white. On the stage sat Ammachi, surrounded by several orange-clad swamis. The swamis played musical instruments and accompanied Ammachi as she sang sweet, melodic chants.

From the moment I saw Ammachi, I could hardly take my eyes off her. There was something so beautiful and perfect about this little Indian woman in the white sari. She just radiated a sense of perfect peace, bliss, and unconditional love. When I arrived, Ammachi was leading the congregation in a call-and-response style of Hindu chanting called *bhajan*. She would sing a verse and then the rest of the gathering would repeat it. The first *bhajan* I ever heard her chant was called *Amba Mayi*. I would later discover the English translation of the words: "O Thou who art the Universe itself, Thou art Courage, Truth, and Divine Love."

I stood mesmerized in a corner of the room for several minutes. As I watched Ammachi chant, I was struck by her intensity. She threw herself into the act of chanting completely, in a way that I had never seen anybody do. I was so moved by the strength of her will and the purity of her intention that my heart just filled with love for her. Suddenly, I started crying. This reaction surprised me. I had not shed many tears in my adult life, and I certainly did not expect to be crying at the sight of a strange woman chanting.

But Ammachi was no stranger to me. I recognized her right away as a Master. A few weeks before meeting her, I came across this quotation from the Buddha: "Of all the Buddhas who have ever attained enlightenment, not a single one accomplished this without relying upon a Master, and of all the thousand Buddhas that will appear in this eon, none of them will attain enlightenment without relying on a Master."

When I got in line to receive *darshan* from Ammachi, I kept staring at her, knowing for the first time in my life that I was face-to-face with a true Master. I spent hours in that line without any restlessness or discomfort. It was such a delight to be in the presence of someone like her that I was in no rush to go anywhere.

Finally, I got to the front of the line. Ammachi put her hands on my shoulders and gave me a look of pure love. Then she drew me into her gently, turned my head slightly and chanted the Sanskrit word for love, which is MA, into my ear several times. After that, she leaned my head on her shoulder and rubbed my back.

I could not tell you how long that hug lasted. It felt as if I stayed in her arms for hours, and yet I know that the whole thing did not take more than a few seconds. When Ammachi released me from her embrace, she smiled at me lovingly, handed me some rose petals and a Hershey's kiss, and then moved on to the next person in line.

I stumbled to the nearest chair and sat there trembling, overcome by the waves of energy that were moving through my body. As I basked in the unconditional love that was enveloping me and flowing through me, I sensed a noticeable change in myself. My heart was open in a way that it had never been before. I felt several different emotions at the same time: awe, gratitude, joy, wonder, and love. It was one of the most beautiful sensations I had ever experienced.

That is when I decided to send Ammachi a psychic message. I transmitted these words to her through my thoughts: *Thank you for this beautiful gift, my beloved Ammachi. I ask that my heart stay as open as it is at this moment for the rest of my life. I also ask that I be a good servant, helping others to open their hearts in the way that you have opened mine.*

What happened next came as a shock to me. I heard Ammachi's voice speaking through me. She said, *Tonight you can have anything you ask for, my son.* These words came with such clarity that I had no doubt as to their authenticity. Ammachi had heard my request and had responded to it. This was the first intuitive conversation I had ever had with a Master, in which I not only received guidance but also had a chance to express myself and to say what was in my heart.

Jesus. Having grown up outside the Christian faith, I had rarely set foot in a church, let alone attended a church service. Two years after meeting Ammachi, I was listening to a recording of Mahalia Jackson singing "I'm on My Way to Canaan Land." I had heard this recording many times before; it was one of my favorite gospel songs. For some reason, though, this time was different. I was hearing the despair and longing in the song as I never had before.

One verse in particular moved me to tears. It said, "I had to pray so hard but I'm on my way." My heart was filled with compassion for the spiritual seeker—the individual who kneels quietly in an empty room and prays for guidance in the midst of despair. I know what an act of courage it is to look for the light in moments of utter darkness. As I focused on this feeling, an image of a Roman Catholic church came to me. It was so vivid that I felt that I had been transported to this place. Suddenly, I had an overwhelming desire—for the first time in my life—to attend Mass. The desire came over me with such intensity that I just knew I had to do it.

I decided that I would visit a Catholic church close to my home. When I walked into the church, my first reaction was a sense of familiarity. This church looked very much like the one I had envisioned while listening to the gospel song. I was thrilled by the idea that my imagination could take me to a real place that I had not visited before—at least not in a traditional, three-dimensional sense.

My second reaction was one of embarrassment. I felt out of place, as if I were trespassing somehow or infiltrating the meeting of a secret society. Slinking into one of the pews at the back of the sanctuary, I tried to be as inconspicuous as possible. Once the service began, though, everything started to change. I became more relaxed, and I could sense a powerful force in the room. By that point in my life, I had attended enough retreats with Ammachi to recognize the feeling: I was sensing the presence of a Master.

The sweet loving energy that filled the church was unmistakable. I knew that Jesus was there, circulating through the room like a gentle breeze. Once I became aware of his presence, I delighted in it. As the congregation members began to sing, the feeling just intensified. All I remember about the hymn they were singing was that it contained the words, "Glory to God in the highest." In terms of its sweetness, this hymn reminded me of the Hindu chants that I had heard Ammachi sing. As I listened to it, I began to experience the sensation of Jesus enveloping me in his love. Literally, I could feel his embrace, which was as warm and comforting as anything I had ever known. I allowed myself to just sink into it as I would a warm bath.

Suddenly, the congregation began to stand—one row at a time—and to form a line down the center aisle of the Church. I had only heard about the sacrament of Communion, but I knew enough about it to realize that I was not supposed to receive it, and so I stayed out of the line. As I sat and watched the ritual, I heard a voice saying, *Go receive my Communion.* It was gentle yet insistent. I knew that Jesus was compelling me to go and that he was not going to take "No" for an answer. So, I stood up and got into the Communion line.

I watched the people ahead of me in line so that I would know what to do. But when I received the Communion, all of my concerns and awkwardness just melted away. All I could feel was the loving energy of Jesus flowing through me. It was a beautiful feeling to be filled with this energy. I was overwhelmed by the power of it. After a few moments, my knees became so weak that I could hardly stand. I sat in the pew nearest me and just gave in to the blissful sensation.

That is when I realized that the Communion experience was already very familiar to me. It felt just like receiving *darshan* from Ammachi. This realization showed me the power of Jesus as a spiritual Master. I was in awe of what he was doing through the sacrament of Communion. In this simple yet very potent ritual, he was able to transmit his love, his energy, and his wisdom to me some two thousand years after leaving the body.

It was an awe-inspiring moment. I felt intense love and reverence for Jesus. Here was a Master who kept giving of himself not just for a lifetime but for millennia. He was carrying out his message of unconditional love in churches throughout the world. It was staggering to realize not just that one individual could command such extraordinary power, but that he would use it with the purest of intention to open the hearts and minds of spiritual seekers throughout the world.

Yogananda and Babaji. I was driving with a friend from San Diego to Los Angeles when she suggested that we stop in the beach town of Encinitas to visit a retreat center founded by the Indian spiritual teacher, Yogananda. I had known about Yogananda for several years. In my 20s, I had begun reading his classic book, *Autobiography of a Yogi*, but I guess the timing was not right because I only read a few pages before losing interest.

Years later, I came across the name of Yogananda when I learned one of the so-called "cosmic chants" that he had composed. This chant, which became one of my favorites, has the following words:

Listen, listen, listen to my heart's song.
I will never forget you, I will never forsake you.

Whenever I hear it, I feel that the Divine is chanting to me and not the other way around. The idea that I am not alone on my path, that some force in the universe is watching over me and listening to my heart, gives me great comfort. Even though I knew virtually nothing else about Yogananda, I admired him for having written this simple yet powerful chant. That alone was enough for me to accept my friend's suggestion and to pull off at the Encinitas exit.

We asked for directions to the retreat center and found it within minutes. It is a stunningly beautiful facility that sits on a cliff overlooking the Pacific Ocean. Walking on the path that winds along the edge of the cliffs and through the magnificent gardens below it, I felt a tremendous sense of peace. But I also had another feeling that was becoming increasingly familiar to me: the distinct sensation of being in the presence of a Master. I did not really give it much thought, however, and after a relaxing visit there, my friend and I got back on the road.

Two weeks later, I was browsing in a Tucson bookstore when I saw a copy of Yogananda's book on a sale rack. Unable to pass up the bargain, I picked up the book and opened it at random. The first page I saw was one that had a description of *kriya yoga,* the spiritual practice that Yogananda had introduced to the West in the 1920s.

From the moment I read about *kriya yoga*, I knew it was something I had to learn. Less than a week later, I had read Yogananda's book from cover to cover and enrolled in a one-year home study course in *kriya yoga*. By the time I finished the course, I had formed a strong connection not only with Yogananda but also with the other Masters in his lineage, most notably one named Babaji.

According to Yogananda's book, the practice of *kriya yoga* was introduced by Jesus himself, who had taught it to his disciples. The practice was lost for many centuries until Babaji reintroduced it in the 1800s. Supposedly, Babaji has been alive for hundreds of years. He is said to appear only on special occasions and to a select few individuals.

When I started practicing *kriya yoga*, I would receive messages on occasion that I knew were coming directly from Babaji himself. He would share with me the significance of the practice I was doing. *Kriya yoga* has the power to purify all types of negativity, including illness, pain and disharmony. Babaji showed me when and how I could use *kriya yoga* to help alleviate suffering. Through him, I began to discover that I could serve others—starting with my own friends and family—by acting as an instrument of healing. Babaji was the first Master to show me what it takes to be a healer, and the approach to *kriya yoga* that he taught me has become an invaluable resource in my spiritual life.

Babaji inspired me to write the following chant, which I have used in many healing ceremonies:

I found your grace and mercy,
You purify and heal me,
I'll die in peace in your arms.
Your heart is my heart,
Your mind is my mind,
I feel your light in me; let it shine.
You and I are one; we are one.

Saint Francis of Assisi. One day, I received an unexpected call from my former roommate, best friend and travel agent, Ben Silverman. He had just learned that British Airways was offering a bargain airfare from Phoenix to London. For years, Ben had been dreaming of going to Italy and he saw this as his chance to fulfill that dream. When he asked if I wanted to tour Italy with him, I thought, *Why not?* So I told him to go ahead and book the tickets.

We had made reservations months in advance, and so I expected that I would get increasingly excited about the trip as we got closer to the departure date. Instead, my enthusiasm seemed to wane. I had never really shared Ben's desire to see Europe, and so I was going mostly for his company—or so I thought.

To help build my interest, Ben came by my house one day and dropped off a copy of a well-known travel guide. When I opened the book, the first page I saw was one that had a description of Assisi, the birthplace of St. Francis. From the moment I read about Assisi, I felt drawn to it. Nonetheless, the idea of spending two days on planes and trains to get there did not appeal to me.

On our departure date, Ben and I drove from Tucson to his parents' house in Phoenix. Our flight was not scheduled to take off until 10 pm, which gave us plenty of time for dinner with his family and a leisurely drive to the airport. We arrived at the British Airways ticket counter at 7:45 pm, with plenty of time to spare.

The ticket agent looked at our paperwork and said, "You two must not be very excited about going to Europe." Ben and I looked at each other and laughed. We thought the ticket agent's comment was odd, to say the least. Ben replied, "Of course we're excited!"

"Then why are you getting here so late?" the man asked.

Ben had a puzzled look on his face. "The flight doesn't leave until 10 pm?" he said.

"No," said the ticket agent, "it leaves in 15 minutes."

We were in shock. Our reservations had shown the departure time as 20:00, which is military time for 8 pm. Ben had misread the time, and because of my indifference about the trip, I had never even glanced at our tickets. Now, our trip was in peril. I could see the look of pain and humiliation on Ben's face. He was upset with himself. I knew him well enough to understand that he was berating himself for his mistake. As we stood there in stunned silence, I could hear him wondering: *How could I have done this? I know how to read military time. Is this really happening, or am I just having a bad dream?*

Knowing that anything I said at that point would only make matters worse, I kept my mouth shut. In my mind, however, I felt a sense of relief. Now, I had the perfect excuse to bail out of the trip.

"What options do we have?" Ben asked the ticket agent.

"The next flight is tomorrow night at 8 pm," he replied. "You can leave then."

Ben turned to me. "We only lose a day. We can just spend the night at an airport hotel and take off tomorrow."

I was wondering why he would want to stay in a hotel when his parents lived only a few miles away. Then I realized the answer: He was too embarrassed to tell them about his error.

Overhearing us, the ticket agent added, "I can get you an inexpensive room at a hotel that is just a two-minute shuttle ride from here."

Ben jumped at the offer, without noticing my lack of enthusiasm. I just wanted to get in the car and drive back to Tucson, but that was not really an option because the car was parked at his parents' house and he did not want them to know we were still in Phoenix.

Finally I spoke up. "Maybe this is a sign," I said. "The timing doesn't seem right for this trip. Why don't we just postpone it and do something else instead? I would be just as happy getting in the car and taking a road trip around the Southwest for a few days."

Although I could tell he was disappointed, Ben tried to be gracious. "I can't force you to do something you don't want to do. If you decide not to go to Italy, I'll cancel the trip. All I ask, though, is that you sleep on it tonight before making a final decision."

I agreed. We checked into the airport hotel, talked for a while, and then went to sleep. In the middle of the night, I was awakened by a voice. At first, I thought Ben had come over to my bed to talk to me. But the voice had the same quality and forcefulness as the one I had heard in Fiji years earlier. It said, "Go to Italy."

That was all I needed to hear. As soon as I heard the message, I knew that there was something important for me in Italy, although I had no idea what it was. When Ben awoke, I told him my news. "Get your stuff ready," I said. "We have a plane to catch"

A few days later, we arrived in Assisi. As I stepped out of the train station, I felt an instant affinity for the place. Of course, it is not hard to fall in love with Assisi. The town is built into a hillside overlooking a beautiful lush valley in the heart of Tuscany. I imagine that it looks and feels very much as it did a thousand years ago, except for the cars and tour buses that try to maneuver around the narrow, winding cobblestone streets.

But it was not just the charm of the place that attracted me. Assisi had a special energy that I found compelling. After we checked into our hotel—a beautiful old villa on the edge of town—I literally ran up the hill to the Basilica of St. Francis, which was drawing me like a magnet. Ben ran behind me, surprised at my sudden burst of energy.

The Basilica holds the remains of St. Francis. Unlike the churches in Rome, the building is very modest. The basement, where St. Francis is entombed, is one of the least ornate sanctuaries I have ever encountered—a dimly-lit room with a few simple pews. From the moment I entered the sanctuary, however, I knew exactly why I had come to Italy: to sit in that room.

I told Ben that he would be on his own for the next three days because I planned to spend as much of my waking time as possible in the Basilica. Although this made little sense to him, he was a good sport about it and set out to do his sightseeing and exploring. I, on the other hand, sat in the sanctuary, closed my eyes, and just immersed myself in the energy of St. Francis.

As I sat in contemplation, an Italian man in his 70s tapped me on the shoulder and handed me a bookmark with an image of St.

Francis. Then he left the sanctuary and I never saw him again. But when I looked at the image he had handed me, I could hear St. Francis speaking to me.

His presence was so sweet and loving that I felt honored to be acknowledged in any way by this great man. I had not yet realized that the encounter was no accident. It was St Francis who had summoned me to Italy, calling to me in the Phoenix hotel room.

For the next three days, he spoke to me steadily about the next stage in my spiritual life. I am fortunate enough to say that I learned about compassion, simplicity, and selflessness from St. Francis himself. He talked to me a great deal about Global Chant and the importance of keeping the chanting circle going. I was touched and amazed that such a great Master would even notice this little group.

He invited me to chant with the Franciscan monks. Each morning, I would wake up at dawn and climb the hill to the Basilica for the morning prayers. The only people in attendance at these services were the monks and a few local nuns. Like everything else associated with St. Francis, these services were utterly simple and heartfelt. The chants, sung in Italian, were heartbreakingly beautiful in their expression of yearning and devotion. Somehow, I managed to learn the words, even though I could speak virtually no Italian and the words to these chants were not written down anywhere. As I chanted along, I felt a powerful connection with the monks and the nuns. I became aware of them as my spiritual brothers and sisters. We were bonded together by our love of St. Francis.

On the morning of the second day, St. Francis said, "Go and find the image of me that is on the main floor of the Basilica." He was referring to the image that I had seen on the bookmark the old man had given me the day before. I walked around the Basilica for nearly an hour without spotting it. I even asked for directions from one of the security guards, who just pointed me to the front of the Basilica. That gave me little help because the walls there were covered with images of saints.

After a while, I went outside to get a drink of water. When I returned to the Basilica, I entered through a door that I had not used before. There, directly in front of me, was the image I had been seeking. I stood in front of it for a long while, just admiring the depiction of the odd-looking little monk.

Then I noticed something really strange. In the image, St. Francis is shown as having three hands. Two of them are holding a book and the third is grasping the garment of his robe. I knew from the moment I made this discovery that it was the reason St Francis had instructed me to look at the image.

At that instant, I heard him say, "If you offer your two hands in service to the Lord, He will provide you with a third." I understood the significance of this statement immediately: By offering whatever resources you have—no matter how limited they may be—in the spirit of selfless service, you will find that they grow exponentially.

St. Francis himself was the ultimate proof of this statement. The charitable works of the order he founded continue to proliferate long after his death. He offered his entire being in the spirit of selfless service and was given not one but a limitless number of extra hands, like the thousand-armed Chenrezig depicted in Tibetan Buddhist art.

Tuning In

I consider myself very fortunate to have had experiences in which I came to know a few of the Masters and to interact with them directly. But even before these encounters, I knew that someone was guiding me in my spiritual life. Almost from the beginning, I could feel a presence in the room during Global Chant. Several other members of the circle reported having the same feeling.

Although it took me years to discover the identity of the Masters who were guiding me, I rarely questioned the value or authenticity of their guidance. I always knew that I would end up on the right path if I just followed my intuition. From the beginning of my journey, I have had a sense that if you follow your intuition, you will "put yourself on a kind of track that has been there all the while, waiting for you, and the life that you ought to be living is the one you are living." These words, spoken by Joseph Campbell, have great resonance for me. They correspond to my own feelings about the importance of intuition on the spiritual journey.

The wisdom offered by the Masters and by your other inner guides gives you the best chance possible of getting on track. For us as Chanters, this guidance is especially crucial. Our mission, which is to bring healing and enlightenment to the planet through the power of chanting, is too enormous and too challenging be mastered on our own.

After my first wake-up call from Dr. Singh, I began to hear the Masters as a single, concerted voice. They gave me specific suggestions about every aspect of my spiritual life. Sometimes, they told me things I did not want to hear. For instance, they instructed me to keep my distance from certain people because my relationships with them were not conducive to my spiritual development. Although I knew in my heart that this information was accurate, I had a hard time letting go of the relationships.

When I would listen to what the Masters would tell me, though, I was able to free myself from my attachments in a way that allowed me to make dramatic gains in my spiritual life. Before the trip to Oaxaca, for example, the Masters insisted that I end a love affair I had been having with a woman named Gloria.

Beautiful, intelligent and graceful, Gloria had charmed me from the moment I met her. To say that my relationship with her was passionate would be an understatement. The attraction I felt for her bordered on obsession. I just wanted to look into Gloria's beautiful eyes, touch her, and kiss her face. From the beginning of our affair, I went out of my way to pamper Gloria. If she wanted to eat at a certain restaurant, I would take her there. If she wanted to drink a certain kind of wine, I would get it for her. I liked being able to grant Gloria's wishes and to spoil her. This turned out to be a counterproductive impulse.

Her entire life, Gloria had been accustomed to special treatment. In her adolescence, she had been a debutante and a beauty queen. Gloria's taste was impeccable and she was no stranger to luxury. If anything, she had become dependent on the comforts associated with wealth, even to the point of living beyond her means.

At the same time, I could see that Gloria had a loving heart and a genuine desire for spirituality. For years, she had traveled to seminars and spiritual retreats throughout the country, in search of something that was missing from her life. But she had never really made the kind of progress she had hoped to make. I believe that her attachment to comfort and luxury became a stumbling block for her.

One day, the Masters told me, "This relationship is holding you both down. As long as you keep seeing her, you will not be able to advance on your path." At first, I was not ready to accept this message. I could not imagine how my affection for Gloria could be detrimental to either of us. But the Masters were insistent, and as the departure date for Oaxaca drew nearer, they pushed me even harder.

I began to realize that something important was going to happen to me in Oaxaca, but only if I was in the proper frame of mind to receive it. The Masters made it clear to me that the only way to prepare myself for the experiences I would have in Oaxaca was by becoming detached. The concept of detachment is hard to grasp and even harder to practice. It does not mean that you have to stop loving the people, places, and things in your life, but it does mean that your love has to be free of dependence. If you cannot walk away from something, then your attachment will hold you back and keep you from any real awakening.

The passion that Gloria and I felt for each other had grown into an addiction. I needed to immerse myself in her beauty and sensuality, and she needed the attention I gave her. The Masters let me know in no uncertain terms that I had to stop clinging to the relationship. Less than a month before the Oaxaca trip, I came upon the following Rumi verse:

> *How long will we fill our pockets*
> *Like children, with dirt and stones?*
> *Let the world go. Holding it,*
> *We never know ourselves, never are airborne.*

When I read these words, they cut to the core of my struggle. My desire for Gloria had blinded me to my priorities. By holding on to her, I had become enslaved to the relationship, just as she had. My spirit wanted to fly but I was keeping it grounded, trading in my wings for a pocketful of dirt and stones. As much as I cherished Gloria, I was beginning to see the obvious yet very painful reality of why I was drawn to her: Being in the presence of her elegance and beauty was a boost to my ego. Being able to please her was even more of a boost. It made me feel powerful.

With pain in my heart, I ended the relationship. As difficult as it was to let go of Gloria, I also felt liberated. Once again, the focus of my life became my spiritual path. The Masters rewarded me amply for my difficult decision. They shared their wisdom with me every day, preparing me for the next stage in my path. Now that I was in a more receptive frame of mind, I could really benefit from their wisdom. I was becoming increasingly excited about the trip to Oaxaca.

The Inner Temple

The day after the Monte Alban adventure described in the Introduction, Dr. Singh took us on an excursion to another archaeological site—the ancient temples of Mitla. An hour outside of the city of Oaxaca, Mitla is a village of a few thousand people. The temples sit in the middle of the village, surrounded by homes and businesses.

As soon as we entered the temple grounds, we heard a series of firecrackers going off. The explosions lasted a few minutes and sounded like a 21-gun salute. I knew that the Masters had orchestrated this greeting for us. As I looked at my fellow Chanters, I could tell by their reaction that they had come to the same conclusion. The Masters were telling us: "At last, you made it!"

Dr. Singh told us that these temples were designed to facilitate multidimensional travel. Inside the temples, he explained, the ancient Chanters would open up portals to other dimensions through their chanting. We walked along the temple grounds until we reached a set of stairs leading to an underground chamber. After descending the stairs and inspecting the chamber, Dr. Singh returned and instructed us to go down into it and to just allow ourselves to feel the energy of the room.

Carmina, Harper, Ricardo, and I were eager to experience the inside of this temple for ourselves. When we entered the chamber, the four of us gathered in a circle and chanted the sacred Sanskrit syllable, OM. This syllable is the sound of pure consciousness. We chanted it spontaneously; it just felt right to us. In doing so, we merged our consciousness momentarily with the Big Beautiful Spirit.

There was not much to see in the chamber, which was dark and empty. So I closed my eyes and within seconds, something amazing happened: I could see a portal. It was opening right in front of me, and even though I had my eyes closed, I had a clear sense of what it looked like, as if I were seeing it right through my eyelids.

The portal was circular with a dark center and luminous edges. It also produced a sound that I can only describe as a low-pitched hum. I wanted to jump into it but I heard the Masters say, "No, not now. You are not ready to fly yet." They were so emphatic that I knew it was not safe for me to enter the portal. Plus, Dr. Singh had instructed us not to stay in the chamber too long. The others were ready to leave, and so I climbed back up the steps, although I did so reluctantly.

When we met up with Dr. Singh, he did not bother to ask us how our time in the chamber had gone. He could see its effect on us just by looking into our faces. Our tour of the temples continued, but I was no longer able to pay attention to any of the sites that Dr. Singh was showing us. Every time I closed my eyes, I could see the portal, and so all I wanted to do was to close my eyes. I had finally reached the threshold—the jumping-off point into other dimensions—and I wanted to savor the experience.

Later, the Masters would explain a great deal more about the nature of the portal I had encountered at Mitla. Just as Dr. Singh was a mirror for me—an outer reflection of my inner teacher— the temples at Mitla and Monte Alban were an outer reflection of my inner temple. For Chanters, the temples serve one primary function, which is to open portals into multiple dimensions of reality. But the portals themselves reside inside the Chanter.

If these portals exist within our own consciousness, I wondered, *then why were the temples built in the first place?* After all, it would be much easier to open a portal from wherever you are rather than having to enter a temple to do it. But the Masters explained how invaluable these temples really are. They serve as a source of inspiration for anyone who enters them, even individuals who have no intention of pursuing a spiritual path. For those individuals, a visit to one of the temples can be a catalyst for change. Just experiencing the energy found inside the temples is enough to nudge someone gently in a spiritual direction.

For the novice Chanter, the temples are a training ground. I had never been able to open a portal into other dimensions until I entered the temples at Mitla. Inside the underground chamber, though, it just happened effortlessly. Of course, the Masters had prepared me for that moment. If I had not tuned into their guidance, I would not have been in a frame of mind that was conducive to the experience.

Perhaps the most important function that the temples serve is as a focal point for multidimensional travel. By holding an image of one of the temples in their awareness, Chanters can open portals with relative ease. In a sense, the temples serve as *mandalas*—visual images that inspire alterations in consciousness. A *mandala* can be a powerful tool for meditation, drawing the practitioner into a meditative state. An image of the temples at Mitla or Monte Alban has an analogous effect on me. Since the journey to Oaxaca, such images have helped me get my first real taste of what it feels like to fly.

Sometimes I think that our mission as Chanters is to rebuild, renew, and restore our inner temples. Just as the ancient temples in Oaxaca had been sealed and forgotten for centuries, so too have the temples within our own hearts, minds, and spirits. Now is the time to reclaim the power and the wisdom that have always been our birthright. The planet has never needed it more.

Connecting with the Masters

The project that we are undertaking together is enormous. You and I are seeking to free our spirits completely, to access the profound wisdom of the universe, and to offer ourselves in service to our brothers and sisters. This may seem like a monumental enterprise—and it is—but now you know that you are not operating blindly or in isolation. You already have the wisdom of the great spiritual Masters at your disposal. The connection to these Masters has always been there, whether or not you have been aware of it. At this point, you can choose to tune into their guidance and to let them direct you in your spiritual life.

To do this, first you have to learn to listen to your inner voices. There are voices inside our heads speaking to us all the time. They have been with us our entire lives. If you pay attention, you will find that there are many such voices and that they are involved in an internal dialogue. Some of them belong to the people in our lives: our parents, grandparents, teachers, spouses, and children. Others include the voices of our mind and our spirit. Sometimes, we tune into the voices that hold us back, reinforcing our doubts, fears, worries, resentments, and disappointments. At other times, we hear the voices that propel us to new heights in our quest for joy, freedom, peace, and connection.

The voice of the Masters is distinct from all others. For me, it has an inspiring quality. The Masters communicate in ways that are authoritative yet compassionate, emphatic yet gentle, urgent yet tranquil. They also tailor their messages specifically to you—to your personality and your communication style. I happen to be someone who loves words and ideas. That is why the Masters speak to me in a conversational tone. For someone who is less verbal, the Masters' guidance may come in other forms: symbols, omens, ambient sounds, animal messengers, or seemingly random occurrence. The Masters may communicate in subtle and unexpected ways, but they will find a way to get through to you by using a language you understand.

For example, my beloved friend and spiritual sister, Cassady, was driving through a large Mexican border town completely lost, trying to find her way back into the U.S. She knew very little Spanish, had hardly any money with her, and was short on gas. In a moment of concern, she asked for intuitive guidance and within seconds, she saw a sign for a restaurant that literally had her name on it. The restaurant was called Club Cassady. Taking this as an omen, she decided to go inside the restaurant and ask for assistance. One man in the place knew enough English to understand her request. He directed her to the border crossing, which turned out to be only two blocks away.

Being able to receive the intuitive signals that the Masters send you is not enough. On your spiritual journey, you will also need to take action. Genuine receptivity includes the ability to trust the Masters' guidance enough that you can apply it to the choices you make. There is a natural tendency, especially for those of us raised in cultures or societies that do not value intuition, to question the authenticity of our inner guidance. We may simply dismiss it as the product of our imagination. I have found, though, that if the Masters have an important message to deliver, the intuitive signals will keep recurring like a persistent knock on your door. Eventually, you will need to answer it or the knocking will stop.

I have had people ask me, "How do you know that the intuitive guidance you are receiving is really coming from the

Masters?" This turns out to be an important question because the possibility of deception does exist. When I first started following my intuition, I discovered the occasional presence of an imposter. Sometimes, the voices that seek to undermine us pass themselves off as our real guides. The good news is that this occurs rarely and can be prevented with relative ease. Here is what I do:

I begin the day every morning by thanking the Big Beautiful Spirit, my own spirit, and the Masters for their guidance. Then, I close any connections from the previous day and open new ones. Before I actually re-connect with my inner guides, however, I set the following three-fold intention:

I demand that any connections I make today be with the entities I request and not with any imposters.

I demand that any connections I make today be free of outside interference.

I demand that any connections I make today be opened the moment I ask that they be opened and stay open and clear until I ask that they be closed.

These demands have never failed. Since I began using them, I have not encountered a single incident in which I have been duped by an imposter or in which I have experienced noise or interference in any of my intuitive connections.

Once I have set this intention, I re-open my connections to the three sources of guidance upon which I rely. In doing so, I refer to my spirit as Akshay, the name given to me by Ammachi. It means "the immortal One."

I love you, Big Beautiful Spirit. Thank you for everything, Big Beautiful Spirit. I invoke your strength and your presence, Big Beautiful Spirit.

I love you, Akshay. Thank you for everything, Akshay. I invoke your strength and your presence, Akshay.

I love you, Masters. Thank you for everything, Masters. I invoke your strength and your presence, Masters.

This is my own way of preparing myself to receive intuitive guidance. I am not sharing it with you because I want or expect you to follow my approach. Every Chanter has a unique relationship with the Masters. The way you choose to make your link to them is really up to you. But you can see that the process needs to be a very deliberate and mindful one. If you want to receive the guidance of the Masters, you have to make yourself an open vessel through which their wisdom can flow. Once you do, you will be amazed, as I was, to discover how much of their wisdom the Masters are willing to share. It is like an all-you-can-eat buffet, limited only by your own capacity to digest it.

Just as a pilot would never attempt to fly a plane without some kind of navigation system, it makes no sense to attempt any spiritual path without the proper guidance. In fact, I could not imagine that I ever would have made any headway on this path without my connection to the Masters. That is why I feel that this is such an important and fundamental step in the process of renewing your inner temple and assuming your rightful place as a Chanter. Once you are receptive to the guidance the Masters have to offer you, the sky is the limit.

CHAPTER 3

Beyond the Bubble

Once I jumped into my spiritual life as a Chanter with both feet and opened myself to the guidance of the Masters, I began receiving my first lessons in multidimensional travel. Dr. Singh showed me how to use the power of chanting to propel my awareness into other dimensions of reality. The ability to travel across dimensions, which he calls "flying," requires a major shift in consciousness. Chanting is the perfect vehicle for creating this shift, but it only exerts its effect under the proper conditions. No matter how much chanting we do or how intently we do it, the shift does not happen overnight—at least not for those of us whose consciousness is already shaped by a lifetime of experience. This shift happens in increments and only when the Chanter is ready to surrender certain ways of thinking and interacting with the world.

From the beginning, I was excited to make the shift because I was dying to experience the sensation of flying. I knew that this was going to be the single greatest adventure of my life. But I did not realize that it was going to change everything about me. My identity would be shattered and reassembled more than once, and I would come to value this aspect of my training as much as anything else I would learn on this path.

Early in my apprenticeship with Dr. Singh, I was driving him somewhere in my car when we passed a street called Don Juan Boulevard. He told me that the street had been named for Don

Juan Mateus, the Yaqui sorcerer whose wisdom Carlos Castaneda shared in his series of bestsellers starting with *The Teachings of Don Juan.*

"Don Juan was a genuine Master," Dr. Singh said. "His teachings were very powerful. It is such a shame that Carlos never really got it."

These comments puzzled me. I had read Castaneda's books when I was in my 20s and felt that they had influenced my spiritual life in significant ways. His descriptions of mystical experiences, in particular, had let me know that such things were possible. Dr. Singh must have known that he was baiting me with his words.

"What do you mean?" I asked. This was exactly the reaction Dr. Singh was expecting from me.

He replied, "Carlos missed the point of the teachings. He got caught up in the phenomena and failed to see the most important part of Don Juan's message."

My inquisitive mind was now ready to burst. "What phenomena?" I wondered.

"Don Juan taught Carlos how to fly, and Carlos was so drawn to the experience that he never realized that flying is just a tool—a means to an end. The purpose of flying is not to have a good time or to feel inspired. We use it as a way of serving others. Carlos never even mentions that in his books."

Dr. Singh was giving me a gentle warning, although I may not have realized it at the time. A new world of experience was about to open up for me, but I had no idea what was coming or the ways that my life was going to change. In retrospect, I see the value of our brief conversation about Carlos Castaneda.

Like Carlos, I had been a spiritual thrill-seeker. My first mystical experiences had happened under the influence of psilocybin mushrooms. During these experiences, I would get a sense of perfect clarity and connectedness. It was as if all the superficial layers of my mind had been stripped away until I had reached the core of my identity. These were among the most beautiful experiences I had ever had, and I wanted more. But I also knew that my body was having a toxic reaction to the mushrooms that would become increasing severe if I kept taking them.

That is when I decided to try to generate these types of experiences on my own, without having to depend on any drug. I began practicing meditation and became almost obsessive about it, collecting and sampling as many different meditation techniques as I could find. Then I discovered that chanting had a similar effect on me. I also studied hypnosis and began recording self-hypnosis tapes for myself and my friends. By the time I was in graduate school studying psychology, I was experimenting with a number of mind-altering techniques, including biofeedback, guided imagery, lucid dreaming, and sensory deprivation.

Although I had moments of inspiration, I was never able to sustain the intensity for any length of time. In retrospect, I can see that my search was misguided. I was so caught up in the phenomena that I had missed the point altogether: Mystical experiences are the direct consequence of an inner transformation. By the time I met Dr. Singh, I was beginning to understand that the focus of my attention needed to be on the transformation itself rather than on the experiences arising from it. Still, I was hooked on the phenomena.

From the beginning, Dr. Singh would talk to me about a process he called "popping your bubble." He used the term *bubble* to refer to our self-concept. As humans, we play an active role in defining ourselves. We choose to embrace a set of qualities or traits that make us distinct and that determine our identity. Basically, the bubble is the sum of everything we have come to know and believe about ourselves. It is the framework that shapes everything about our lives, including our thoughts, behaviors, attitudes, and emotions.

Dr. Singh helped me see that the bubble is a prison. It limits how we view and experience everything. If you are living in your bubble, you can only know the world in relation to yourself, and you can only experience whatever is consistent with your own expectations and judgments. You can make your bubble as beautiful as you want; I had spent a lifetime cultivating a self-concept that was very appealing—at least to me. But no matter how beautiful you make your bubble, it is still a prison.

By the time I met Dr. Singh, the phenomena themselves had become a big part of my bubble. I had become a connoisseur of mystical experiences. Instead of allowing myself to have them, I had become adept at collecting and studying them. I knew hundreds of meditation techniques and had sampled them all, but in truth, I was not much of a meditator. I only pretended to meditate. There is a big difference between the technique of meditation and the experience of it. I could give a series of lectures on technique but I had rarely known the feeling of what it is like to really meditate. That situation changed once I started spending time with Dr. Singh.

A Flash of Holiness

The second time I visited the Conservatory, Dr. Singh asked me to help him build a fence on the edge of the property. He instructed me to treat the fence-building process as a meditation, allowing myself to connect fully with the experience and with my surroundings, free of all analysis and judgment. It was a warm, sunny morning in Sonora, with perfect views of the mountains and the high desert of Northern Mexico. I tried to immerse myself in the experience of this beautiful place, but all I felt was a sensation of dull heaviness. The more I tried to do as Dr. Singh had asked, the worse it got.

I felt that my weaknesses had been exposed. With the all the years I had spent studying consciousness and teaching about it, I had made little progress in being able to alter my own conscious experience. Sensing my frustration, Dr. Singh came up to me and pointed at two lavender-colored butterflies that were gliding past us. "Can you feel the connection to our two friends here?" he asked.

I breathed a sigh of frustration. "Conceptually, I know there is a connection," I replied. "But I can't make myself feel it."

Dr. Singh gave me a puzzled look. "This connection is not conceptual. It really exists, whether you feel it or not," he said. "Stop thinking about it, and don't try to feel it. Just do it, my friend. Just melt."

I wanted so much to heed Dr. Singh's instructions because I knew he was helping me make a critical leap. But I had no idea how to go about it. Just melt, I repeated to myself. Just melt.

As he observed me, he added, "Act like a piece of cheese toast in the oven. The cheese starts out as hard little squares, but then it softens and loses it edges. Once the cheese melts, it can take any shape. It no longer has to be square."

OK, I thought, I am supposed to melt like the cheese on a piece of cheese toast. I felt a little ridiculous even thinking about it, let alone doing it. Then Dr. Singh looked at me with a hint of amusement and said, "If you don't know how to do that, just fake it 'til you make it." He encouraged me to keep practicing and then walked away.

As I continued working on the fence, I would stop occasionally to remind myself: *Just melt…like a piece of cheese toast.* After a while, I began to hear a Hindu chant in my head. This was a simple chant consisting of two Sanskrit words: *Hare Om.* The word *Hare* has many meanings, among which are "to take away" or "to end," and *Om* refers to the pure, infinite consciousness of the Divine. Together, they serve as a reminder that there is an infinite consciousness permeating all things, and that this consciousness can only be experienced when something is taken away. That "something" is the bubble.

The chant kept repeating in my head until I began to notice something happening to me. A shift was taking place in my awareness. It was subtle at first but definitely noticeable. For just a few moments, my mind would go silent. There was a gap between the end of one thought and the beginning of the next, and this gap was expanding.

I would later discover that Dr. Singh had a term for this type of experience: He called it *holiness.* This is when your mind turns off and you literally lose yourself. The boundaries that define and distinguish you dissolve like sugar in warm water. In brief flashes, I was merging into the plants, insects, rocks, and myriad aspects of nature surrounding me. For an instant, I existed only as part of the energy or consciousness that permeates all things. The more I moved in and out of this state of holiness, the more I started to feel high, as if a gentle drug were beginning to take effect on me.

In the early afternoon, Dr. Singh invited me to join him in a tiny covered courtyard he called the Garden of Tears. The courtyard was surrounded by a living fence made of ocotillo, a desert plant that looks like a set of spokes radiating out from a single point in the ground. Each spoke is covered with small angular leaves that drop in the winter. By cutting the spokes, burying them in the ground, and tying them together with wire, the volunteers at the Conservatory had created a space that had privacy, shade, and some greenery.

As we sat on a short bench that reminded me of children's furniture, Dr. Singh asked me to describe what I had been experiencing. I gave him as much detail as I could about the phenomena—the feelings and sensations I had been undergoing—including my analysis of the situation. In response to a simple question on his part, I had given him a scholarly treatise. He did not seem especially pleased with what I was telling him.

"Be careful not to get too linear," he told me. "That is going to be a big challenge for you."

"I don't understand," I said.

"In school, you are rewarded for linear thinking. You master rules of logic: *If x, then y.* You are encouraged to take things apart, to dissect them, and to ask questions about how they work and why they exist. But in the spiritual realm, this linearity will hold you back."

Dr. Singh's words stung me. After spending much of my life in school, cultivating my ability to think and reason, I did not want to hear that my intellect was a liability rather than an asset. So, I challenged him. "How is my mind holding me back?" I asked, with a hint of rebellion in my voice.

Showing no emotional reaction to my comments, he simply explained, "If you want to really experience holiness, your mind has to let go of all linearity: no thoughts, no judgments, and no analysis."

"And how do I do that?"

He smiled. "You are the one who knows all the meditation techniques," he said. "I have no doubt that you could give a much longer and more thorough lecture on how to meditate than I can. All I can tell you is to melt. Just melt. That's it. Let your mind become like that of a chicken or a lizard, without any linearity at all. If you can do that, then you will know what it's like to be limitless."

As I sat on the short bench and tried to absorb his teaching, Dr. Singh remarked, "This is not something new for you. I taught you all of this hundreds of years ago, the last time we were together. You just forgot—that's all. Now let yourself remember."

Taken aback, I asked, "Were we together before?"

"All of us were," he replied. "We were gypsies. Our little band of musicians and healers went from town to town, offering our services to the local people."

I felt like a small child listening to a bedtime story, filled with wonder and amazement. Dr. Singh knew that I wanted to hear more of our story but he had no intention of sharing any more of it.

He said, "You are just going to have to remember the rest of it yourself. I know you have forgotten who you are, but maybe it will help you to remember who I am."

With complete innocence, I wondered aloud, "*Who* are you?"

Dr. Singh chuckled. Then his demeanor changed completely. His eyes became intensely focused, and he spoke to me in a solemn tone. "In our lineage, there is the shaman. The one who teaches the shaman is called a nagual. Then there is the teacher of the nagual. This is someone who no longer needs to be in the body but is here only to serve. That is who I am."

Awe-struck, I looked down at the ground and asked myself,

Could I really be in the presence of such power? My question was answered immediately. When I raised my head to glance at Dr. Singh, he was no longer there. In his place stood an enormous figure, perhaps 20 feet tall, that was half man and half bird. As I stared in awe at this mythical-looking creature, it spread its wings, and once they were open, its entire body became engulfed in flames. When the fire subsided, I was once again face-to-face with the image of Dr. Singh that I knew and loved— his round face, Aztec features, and unmistakable smile.

Although I was stunned by what I had just seen, I had no trace of doubt or disbelief. There was no question this was real—as real as anything I had ever seen. Dr. Singh had just given me a glimpse not only of his own power but also of the rich, multidimensional reality that exists beyond the limits of linearity. After that experience, the melting started to happen on its own, without any effort on my part.

The Conservatory sits on a hillside overlooking the town of Sonora. Later that afternoon, I climbed up the hill to a rock outcropping that Dr. Singh named after Quetzalcoatl, the feathered serpent of Aztec mythology. I wanted some time alone to digest everything that had happened that day, and so I sat on the rock ledge in silence. Amidst the silence, all I could hear was *Hare Om*, which had been running through my head all day.

Within moments, I was no longer just hearing *Hare Om*; I was actually seeing it. For years, I had heard about the experience of synesthesia, in which the senses merge in unusual ways. This experience happens most commonly under the influence of hallucinogenic drugs, and it can take various forms. For instance, you might taste a color or see a texture. In my case, I was seeing a chant.

Sitting on the ledge, I noticed that my surroundings were beginning to glow. At first I thought it was a trick of the light, but then I realized that what I was seeing was an inner radiance. It was like looking at one of those 3-D images that slips into view when you relax your gaze in just the right way. The world was being transformed before my very eyes. I was seeing and experiencing the light of divine consciousness in everything around me.

Then as I directed my gaze at my own body—at my hands and feet—I could see that I too was glowing. The more I looked at myself, the less solid I became. Within moments, all I could see was light. I was merging into the divine light that engulfs all things and makes them shine. I no longer had a distinct consciousness of my own. Rather, I was swept up in a current of pure consciousness that drew me into everything—the plants, birds, rocks, and insects. I was inside of them as much as I was inside my own skin.

That is when I understood what it really means to be in love. I now realize that love is the binding force of the universe. It is an ongoing flow that unites all of creation. When you are *in love*—in the flow of love—you literally melt into everything that exists or that has ever existed. Space and time have no meaning; you are not bound by them. You can penetrate the consciousness of anyone or anything, because there is nothing in the universe that is impermeable to the flow of love.

As I sat on the rock ledge, my consciousness moved fluidly through every level of spatial reality, from subatomic particles to galaxies and nebulae. I could experience the point of view of a single-celled organism, a soaring vulture, or a mesquite tree. The entirety of existence came alive for me in ways that it never had before, because for the first time I could immerse myself in it and adopt the perspective of even its smallest component.

The moment I became aware of something, I would flow into it as pure love and my consciousness would merge with it. The sensation was so blissful that I could not imagine ever wanting to experience the world in any other way. The more absorbed I became in the experience, the more I began to get a feeling that something or someone was calling out to me, seeking my attention.

As I tuned into this call, I discovered that it was not comprised of just one voice but of millions. There were entities in various dimensions of reality that wanted me to flow into them and merge my consciousness with theirs. I had never realized that these other dimensions even existed, let alone encountered any of the entities that inhabited them. There were angels, nature spirits, fairies, demons, and the spirits of the dead. I was meeting them for the first time, and I just flowed through them as pure love.

All of these entities were open to me, receiving my love as a genuine blessing. I felt honored to be welcomed in this manner by my brothers and sisters in other dimensions. I also wondered how I ever could have allowed myself to feel alone in the universe. At this moment, the loneliness I had experienced at different times in my life seemed pointless. I knew that I would never have that feeling again, because now I was surrounded by loved ones. Even if I stopped being aware of their presence, from this point forward I would always know they were there.

I did not want the experience to end. Somehow, my conversation with Dr. Singh had opened an escape hatch through which I could step out of my bubble and get a taste of the multifaceted reality that exists just beyond its limits. But I had no desire or intention of going back. The very thought of having to return to the tiny little world in which I had been locked away upset me so much that I became almost frantic. I kept saying to myself, *I am not going back. I refuse to go back.*

But inevitably, I did go back. I was not ready yet to pop my bubble completely. In fact, I had no idea how to function in a permanent way without it. My mind was filled with questions that I had no way of answering: *Who would I be? How would I present myself to others? Would it even be possible for me to function in the world if my bubble no longer existed?*

I did not even know how to escape from my bubble, let alone pop it. The only reason I was able to have this profound experience is that Dr. Singh had facilitated it for me. He wanted me to have a taste of what it is like to exist outside the bubble. But if I had any intention of returning there in the future, I understood that I would have to get there on my own.

To return to my everyday life after such a profound experience felt like a fall from grace. I missed the freedom and the connection with my brothers and sisters in other dimensions. Mostly, I missed the sensation of being in the flow of love. I suppose that I was hooked on the phenomena, exactly the way Dr. Singh had warned me not to be. I knew that I had to let go of that attachment if I ever wanted to escape my bubble again.

The Masters' Gift

For the next several months, I had only an occasional flash of holiness. My journeys outside the bubble were brief and not very intense. At times, I wondered if I had veered off course. After years of seeking enlightenment, I had finally gotten a taste of it, and now I was back to square one. Or so I thought.

Without even realizing it, I was gaining the skills I needed to be able to exit my bubble in a lasting and complete manner. For a Chanter, the experience of being outside the bubble is not an end in itself. You have to be able to escape the bubble if you want to fly, and the only reason you fly is so that you can serve others. It was not enough to have an occasional glimpse of life beyond the bubble. I had to learn how to function out there, in a realm where I could not fall back on any of my preconceived notions or judgments about the world—not even my own self-concept.

Dr. Singh had given me a sense of what it is like to break through the bubble, but I had a great deal of training to do before I could return to the beautiful multidimensional reality that I had encountered that day in Sonora. I had to learn how to live as a Chanter, how to align my life more fully with my spiritual values, and how to be more effective in serving others, before I could really sustain the level of intensity that I had experienced there.

For the next few months, I just kept plodding along, practicing the things that Dr. Singh was teaching me. At times, my life felt relatively uninspired. I knew what I was missing, but I tried not to dwell on the sensations I had felt when I had been liberated from my bubble. There was no doubt in my mind that my attachment to the experience was the very thing keeping me from having it again. If I was ever to have any success in escaping my bubble, I had to let go of my desires and expectations.

This seemed painfully ironic to me: Wanting something so much that I ached for it was the very reason that I could not have it.

Then, something unexpected happened. The date was May 13, 2005. I was sitting in meditation as I do every morning. I keep a little altar in an alcove of my bedroom, where I sit facing images of the Masters. On that particular morning, my meditation practice felt more intense than usual. I could feel my perspective shift, and then I started to have the same sensation I did that day in Sonora. I knew that the 3-D image was about to slip back into view again, after all that time.

As I looked at the altar, the images of the Masters began to glow. There was a soft golden light radiating from their faces. Time stopped as I basked in this radiance. After a while, I heard the voice of the Masters speaking to me. They said, "Prepare to receive an important teaching that is not just for you but for all of humanity."

Overcome by a sense of awe, I could hardly believe what the Masters were telling me. I felt just as the Biblical prophets must have, questioning my own worthiness. *Why me?* I wondered. The Masters responded, "Why *not* you?" Then, they let me know that the message that was about to be transmitted to me was too long and intricate to commit to memory. So I reached for my journal and a pen. After that, it became simply a matter of taking dictation.

I wrote down everything the Masters told me that morning. They said: "When you are the flow of love, you are nothing. And when you are nothing, you are free. Everything that you are, that you have, that you expect to be, must be released. This is hard to do, and yet at some level it is not hard at all.

"You have had moments when you lose yourself in the very things that you are doing or feeling. Just extend those moments. Then things will start giving themselves up for you so that you can become nothing. They will disappear from your life and from your mind.

"The very things you love will disappear, and you may think that you will never get this far again without them, but you have already become your future self, which does not need these things to feel love. You ARE love. And so the tendency of the 'present you' to protect the things you love for the 'future you' does not matter because the 'future you' does not need them. That version of your Self is already a stream of pure, enveloping love."

Through this teaching, the Masters showed me how to find the experience of holiness that I was seeking. For now, I could allow everything I love—the people, places, animals, plants, rocks, sounds, images, and activities that inspire me—to draw me out of my bubble and into the flow of love. But to stay in that flow, I had to let go of my attachments to all of those things. In the long term, it is far more satisfying to be love than to feel love. More importantly, that is our ultimate destiny.

If that was all the Masters had to offer me that day, it would have been more than enough. But then they gave me an extraordinary gift: a chant that had the power to dissolve the walls of my bubble and to help me become a permanent resident of holiness rather than just a tourist. The words of the chant are:

DO YOU KNOW YOU ARE LOVE?
ONE THING—FLOWING THROUGH EVERYTHING

From the first moment I heard it, this chant began to have a profound impact on me. By merely hearing it, chanting it, or even seeing the words in writing, I can experience at least a taste of holiness.

Many of the world's spiritual traditions have mantras—sacred utterances that allow you to make contact with the infinite. Some Zen Buddhists use riddles, called koans, to help silence their minds. A classic example is the question: What is the sound of one hand clapping? The chant that the Masters shared with me combines the powers of both a mantra and a koan. It has two parts, beginning with a question:

DO YOU KNOW YOU ARE LOVE?

This question cannot be answered without facing the reality that you are love. Even if you answer the question with a "No," all you are saying is that you do not know you are love. The task of answering this question has a completely different effect than simply hearing the statement: You are love. The Masters designed the question in such a way that it cannot be avoided. If you take it on—as you inevitably must—it will melt you, opening holes in the walls of your bubble.

The second line of the chant is a paradox:

ONE THING—FLOWING THROUGH EVERYTHING

This phrase is impossible to grasp because it extends beyond logic. A logician would treat it as meaningless: If there is only one thing, then it cannot flow through anything other than itself. Within a logical framework, this makes no sense. How can the entity that flows be the same as the one through which the flow occurs?

Having said all of this, I can tell you that the question of how this chant works matters much less to me than the fact that it does work. My pragmatic side tells me that the proof is in the pudding: If something works for you, then use it. Otherwise, move onto something else.

I have incorporated this chant into virtually every aspect of my life, and it has been an important catalyst in my spiritual development as a Chanter. For one thing, the experience of holiness, which used to be so elusive for me, is now a regular occurrence in my life. My bubble is still there—that is not an easy thing to eliminate—but its walls are much more porous than they used to be. I move more freely beyond its boundaries than I ever imagined I would.

Entering the Inner Temple

Whenever I slip out of my bubble, I find my inner temple. This is where the wisdom of the universe resides. When I enter this inner temple, I am free of all limits. There are none of the restrictions of space or time here. I am not bound by linearity or by anyone's expectations of what or how things should be. All of the things that have held me back are stripped away, including my fears, doubts, worries, and concerns. In my temple, I have no possessions, not even a body or a mind. I have no distinct identity, either. Everything that I associate with my self—the traits, habits, and patterns that make up my personality—must be left outside the temple doors.

You can only enter your inner temple when your spirit is completely naked. There is nothing behind which you can hide, nor is there anything to hide. Safety is not an issue inside this temple. The version of you that exists here cannot be harmed in any way. It cannot be destroyed because it was never created. This *you* is simply the flow of pure love that has always permeated the universe—always. As you immerse yourself in this flow and allow yourself to be what you really are, you experience holiness.

Just to have this experience is enough. When you have arrived at your temple, there is nowhere else you need to be. Here, you are complete and you are free. This is perfection beyond all limits—even beyond the very concept of perfection. And yet, there is something more that needs to be done. You cannot keep this perfection to yourself. It is the birthright of every single being in the universe.

As long as there are those who suffer, who are lost and unable to reach their inner temple, I know that I have work to do. My mission as a Chanter—in fact, this is the mission of every Chanter—is to help all beings find healing and enlightenment. The primary reason we seek the experience of holiness is that it empowers us to carry out our mission. We identify with the intention made by Buddhists every day when they recite the Refuge Prayer: "May I attain Buddhahood in order to benefit all sentient beings." From our inner temple, we draw the energy and wisdom that allows us to serve our brothers and sisters.

Our inner temple is our launching pad into other dimensions. We venture into these dimensions for two reasons: First, we can access resources in these dimensions that can help those who are suffering. These resources include the wisdom and technology of the most advanced civilizations in the universe, as well as the direct aid of the beings who reside in those dimensions. A second reason we fly is that suffering is not limited to the human realm. There are beings in other dimensions whose despair, fear, and confusion is greater than anything we can experience as human beings. We have as much of an obligation to them as we do to anyone in our own world.

At first, I was content to just bask in the experience of holiness. Once I discovered that I could connect with my inner temple on a regular basis, I was delighted. This was something I had sought my entire life. As far as I was concerned, I had made it. The only thing that really mattered was to take that experience of holiness and expand it so that it would permeate every moment of my life.

It never occurred to me that this experience was a stepping stone in my training as a Chanter. Whenever I had heard Dr. Singh talk about flying, it aroused my curiosity. I wondered what it would be like to experience multidimensional travel. But it never seemed real to me. I just assumed that someday, in the distant future, I would get a chance to journey into other dimensions. My thoughts about flying were fleeting daydreams—nothing more. I did not realize how integral a part of my life's work flying would become. I had to learn how to journey into other dimensions if I wanted to be an effective healer and servant.

Everything that had happened up to this point was merely preparation: my experience of holiness in Sonora, the teachings that the Masters had shared with me, and my access to the inner temple. I had made an important transition in my training, no longer just exploring my inner temple but actually settling into it. Now, I was ready for the next step.

Flying to Monte Alban

Two months after returning from Oaxaca, I had my first real experience of flying. It was a quiet Saturday night in Sonora. We had no visitors that day—only Dr. Singh, Harper, Carmina, and I had made the trip down from Tucson. We had just finished our evening meal in the dining room of the Conservatory and started to reminisce about our time in Oaxaca. At one point in the conversation, I said something about how much I was missing Monte Alban. Dr. Singh did not say anything at first, but a while later, he told me, "Tonight, some Chanters are performing a ceremony there, and I have made arrangements for you to join them."

Then he gave me the following instructions: I was to lie down, close my eyes, and just let go of everything. In order to fly to Monte Alban, I had to detach completely from my life, which meant that I had to assume an attitude of complete passivity, almost to the point of indifference. I needed to get to a point where nothing in my life mattered. From this perspective, it no longer mattered if I ever returned to Tucson, if I were to lose all of my friends, if I were never to experience another kiss, or if I never finished writing this book. For all intents and purposes, I no longer existed, except as the flow of love through the universe.

He said, "Find a chant and immerse yourself in it until everything else falls away. If you do this, you will fly to Oaxaca, not just in spirit but taking your body with you. When you get to Monte Alban, look for the man who sold us the hats outside the main gate. His name is Nacho and he's one of the Chanters involved in the ceremony tonight. Tell him that Pablito sent you."

I was excited about the opportunity to try this. Dr. Singh had told me many stories about materializing in other places, but I had never experienced it for myself. An hour later, I was lying in bed, reviewing the instructions he had given me. Within moments of closing my eyes, a Jewish chant came to mind. The words of the chant, which are *Eheyeh Asher Eheyeh*, mean "I am that I am." As soon I started chanting it, I began to have the experience of moving through clouds. I had the unmistakable sensation of flying, quite literally, as if I were aboard a jet. Then I caught a glimpse of Monte Alban through the clouds. At first, I was looking down on the main plaza but the scene shifted and I found myself face-to-face with one of the pyramids.

I began to hear a drum rhythm. It followed a 1-3-5-3 pattern—a distinctive rhythm that I had never heard before. I then had the sensation of playing the rhythm myself. The pattern of my hand movements on the drum went like this:

L RLR LRLRL RLR (repeat) L = left hand R = right hand

I am sharing these details because the rhythm had such a powerful effect on me that I want you to have the chance to experience it for yourself. Since that time, whenever I play or hear the rhythm, I start to fly.

Along with the rhythm, I could hear voices chanting in unison. The sound they were making astonished me. They seemed to be chanting *Eheyeh*, or "I am." Could this be possible? I was hearing a group of strangers do a chant very similar to my own. *Maybe I'm dreaming*, I wondered. But the entire experience felt unlike any dream I had ever had.

Suddenly, I came in contact with a few shadowy figures. I knew these individuals were the Chanters who would be performing the ceremony. Although I could not see them clearly, I could speak with them. I said in Spanish, "Pablito sent me." One of them said, "Yes, we know." I could not say for sure if the Chanter who addressed me was Nacho, but I followed him to one of the pyramids.

The pyramid we were facing was a significant one for me. During my first visit to Monte Alban, Dr. Singh had told me that this was my pyramid—a place where I had performed ceremonies in the past. The archeologists call it System IV, not a particularly charming name but one that at least gave me a point of reference when I would look at maps or pictures of Monte Alban.

At the time, Dr. Singh had asked me to climb up to the top of the pyramid and to feel what it was like to be there. I was nervous because the pyramid was fenced off, and I had some concern about being thrown out by security guards. But Dr. Singh reassured me. "This is your place of power," he said. "Nobody is going to stop you from being here."

So I climbed over the fence and began to walk up the steps, which were steep and narrow. I could barely put the ball of my foot on each one. This meant that I had to either tiptoe up the pyramid or climb the steps sideways. As I ascended, I began to tremble. My first impression was that my body was shaking from fear. The combination of doing something illegal and looking down at the ground from my tenuous perch were definite fear factors for me, but I also knew that I was not afraid. It was something else that was causing my body to vibrate: a sense of incredible familiarity and reconnection with the past. I knew I was coming home to a place that I had never been before—at least not in this lifetime.

After I rejoined Dr. Singh and the rest of the Band, he asked me to describe what I had felt at the top of the pyramid. Although I was still trembling, I tried to find words for what I had just experienced. Then, as I began to speak, I burst into tears. Waves of emotion rushed through my body. To rediscover an important part of your identity the way I had that day is an indescribable feeling. All I can say is that I have rarely been so moved or felt so much like myself as I did standing on that pyramid.

Now, I was returning to System IV but under very different circumstances. My body was standing in front of the pyramid and lying in a bed in Sonora at the same time. Both experiences were equally vivid—or equally unreal. It was as if I were having a dream within a dream. Just as before, I found myself climbing up the narrow steps, along with my fellow Chanter. When I got to the top, I could see other Chanters atop the other pyramids. They were dressed in white and holding torches, which they set on designated nooks in each pyramid.

This whole time, the drum rhythm kept playing continuously. In unison, the Chanters began moving their bodies. They performed a dance that I had seen once before, in a vision I had had of Dr. Singh one night while he was visiting relatives in Mexico City. Intuitively, I knew that the Chanters were gathering energy from the moon and directing it towards someone in need of healing.

After the ceremony ended, I woke up in my bed in Sonora, but the feeling was not like awakening from a dream. I knew that I had been to Monte Alban physically, and the only way I could have done that was by moving through other dimensions. In retrospect, I am happy that my first journey as a Chanter was to a place as familiar and sacred to me as Monte Alban. Although I traveled outside the dimensions of space and time to get there, I spent most of the night in dimensions that I already knew how to navigate. It turned out to be a perfect introduction to flying.

Of course, this was not particularly surprising to me. With Dr. Singh as my guide, I knew that the timing and manner of my exposure to new experiences would always be perfect for me. My training had followed a clear plan from the beginning, though I may not have been aware of it. Before I could fly, I needed to become adept at stepping out of my bubble and into the inner temple. This meant letting go of my attachments— especially to the phenomena associated with the experience of holiness. But even before I could do that, I had to know the nature of those phenomena first-hand. This meant that I had to learn, in the words of Dr. Singh, to "just melt like a piece of cheese toast."

I believe such a plan works for anyone pursuing this path. Before you can fly, first you have to melt. That means opening yourself to the universe completely, with no fear, judgment, or questioning of any kind. Just let the boundaries of your bubble dissolve, even for a few moments, so that you can know the silent, limitless beauty that exists beyond its walls.

From the start, Dr. Singh warned me not to rely on any technique for doing this. The biggest danger of a technique is that it becomes mechanical. A technique for melting would be like a technique for falling in love. In this age of *How To* books, I would not be surprised to find a shelf full of paperbacks at my local bookstore, all containing elaborate instructions on the art and science of falling in love. But you and I know that falling in love is a matter of opening our hearts, and ultimately this is something that no book can teach us. When the conditions are right, it just happens.

A Daily Dose of Holiness

With the process of melting, I have found that there are a few things I can do to help create the right conditions. Before I share them with you, I want to reiterate Dr. Singh's warning: Please do not treat these suggestions as a set of techniques you need to use if you want to melt. You already know how to melt; this knowledge resides in the core of your spirit. I am just describing some things that have been helpful to me. It would sadden me to find anyone turning my observations into a formula for melting. There really is no formula that works for everyone all the time. If there were, I suppose spiritual life would be much easier, but it would also be much less interesting.

I begin with something that inspires me. That changes from moment to moment. I can usually count on chanting to put me in the right frame of mind, although I will choose different chants for different occasions, based entirely on my mood. Regardless of the chant that I choose, however, I know that the act of chanting will pull me out of my bubble if I can immerse myself in it. For me, chanting has become the ultimate vehicle for attaining holiness. But it is certainly not the only one.

Being a visual person, I may look for something that inspires me in my field of vision. Right now, I am enjoying a flower bed filled with bright pink petunias in my neighbor's front yard. The vibrancy of these flowers contrasts with the muted colors of a rare gray day in Tucson. As I look at these beloved plants and appreciate their stunning beauty, I literally take them in. I welcome them into my heart and into my consciousness.

In this, I take a lesson from St. Francis, who treated the entire world—including plants, rocks, insects, stars, and the elements—as his brothers and sisters. His "Canticle of the Sun" captures the essence of melting as beautifully as anything I have ever encountered:

Most high, all powerful, all good Lord! All praise is yours, all glory, all honor, and all blessing. To you, alone, Most High, do they belong. No mortal lips are worthy to pronounce your name.

Be praised, my Lord, through all your creatures, especially through my lord Brother Sun, who brings the day; and you give light through him. And he is beautiful and radiant in all his splendor! Of you, Most High, he bears the likeness.

Be praised, my Lord, through Sister Moon and the stars; in the heavens you have made them, precious and beautiful.

Be praised, my Lord, through Brothers Wind and Air, and clouds and storms, and all the weather, through which you give your creatures sustenance.

Be praised, my Lord, through Sister Water; she is very useful, and humble, and precious, and pure.

Be praised, my Lord, through Brother Fire, through whom you brighten the night. He is beautiful and cheerful, and powerful and strong.

Be praised, my Lord, through our sister Mother Earth, who feeds us and rules us, and produces various fruits with colored flowers and herbs.

Be praised, my Lord, through those who forgive for love of you; through those who endure sickness and trial. Happy are those who endure in peace, for by you, Most High, they will be crowned.

Be praised, my Lord, through our Sister Bodily Death, from whose embrace no living person can escape. Woe to those who die in mortal sin! Happy those she finds doing your most holy will. The second death can do no harm to them.

Praise and bless my Lord, and give thanks, and serve him with great humility.

When I want to melt, all I have to do is to take in the beauty and magnificence of this world and of all the creatures that fill it with their splendor. As I breathe in, I draw the entire universe into me. Then, as I breathe out, I release myself entirely into the universe. In no time at all, any sense of separateness I have just dissipates, and I find myself outside the bubble. At these moments, my bubble cannot contain me, because I am as light and expansive as air.

The experience of holiness just arises from there. It really is that simple. I have spent much of my adult life trying to figure out how to experience holiness, and now I know that the struggle to figure things out is antithetical to the experience. You simply relax into holiness the way you would a warm bath. How much analysis do you need to do or how much understanding do you need to have in order to immerse yourself in a bathtub filled with warm, soothing water? Of course, the answer is: None at all. You know how to do it perfectly fine. Nobody has to give you any instruction whatsoever.

To escape the confines of my bubble, I had to unlearn rather than learn. I had to let go of all the tendencies I had been cultivating through years of academic training, including my ability to reason, analyze, evaluate, and judge. In my pursuit of holiness, these mental abilities just got in the way. I found it more useful to cultivate an entirely different set of tendencies within myself, including detachment, serenity, and compassion.

As a Chanter, I have found a new and profoundly satisfying way to live. Holiness has become part of my day-to-day life. Although I have not yet reached the point in which every moment of my day is infused with holiness, I am allowing fewer moments to get past me without at least an attempt to experience and savor them. When I think of how I want to live my life, I am reminded of a game I used to play when I was a little boy. I would blow on the puffy head of a dandelion until all of the seeds would float into the breeze. Then I would chase down the seeds and try to catch as many of them as I could. Each seed was precious to me, and I just wanted to be able to touch it.

I still play a version of that game, with only one slight change:

Now, the moments of my life are the seeds that I am seeking to touch. Each one floats by so quickly, and it is so precious, that I just want to jump and reach for it with complete abandon. And when I manage to catch one, the last thing I want to do is just to keep it for myself. What would be the fun of that? Any joy or delight that I have in my life, I want to share with you.

There is enough holiness to go around. The inner temple that you and I seek is not a hermitage. There is nothing secluded or exclusive about it. Everyone is welcome there. We just need to know how to open the doors. For that, we need a set of keys.

CHAPTER 4

Keys to the Temple

The first time I brought my new love, Cassady, to the Sound Circle at the Tabernacle, Dr. Singh asked her to introduce herself to the group. He said, "Tell us all about yourself."

Cassady went silent for several seconds. It was a difficult task, to summarize one's life in a few sentences. After a long pause, she said, "I have been closing doors in my life, letting go of things that no longer work for me. And now that I have met this special person in my life"—she looked over at me and smiled lovingly— "I know that new doors will begin to open, but I don't know yet what those doors look like or where they will take me."

Dr. Singh nodded his head in approval. "The keys that unlock those doors are not made of brass or of steel," he observed. "They consist of the actions you take in your life. Just practice detachment, humility, serenity, and compassion. Show forgiveness and unconditional love, and serve others without expecting anything in return."

In a simple statement, Dr. Singh had shared with Cassady the set of values by which every Chanter seeks to live. If you are looking to open the doors of your inner temple, these are the only keys you will ever need. They will lead you to holiness and propel you into new dimensions of reality. For a Chanter, the practice of chanting is a vehicle for healing and enlightenment, and this set of values is the rocket fuel that powers the vehicle.

The values identified by Dr. Singh have the potential to cut through your bubble, freeing you from all of your beliefs, thoughts, attitudes, and judgments. They can counteract all of the aspects of your mind that limit your experience to the dimensions of time and space. Although there is no formula or recipe for enlightenment, the closest you will ever find is the set of seven values that Dr. Singh teaches. If you live your life by them, they will provide the lift you will need in order to glide effortlessly into new levels of awareness.

For Dr. Singh, the life of a Chanter is one of action. It is not enough, for instance, to read this book and to understand it at a conceptual level. To be a Chanter, you have to be willing to take action—to "walk the talk." This means aligning yourself with the Seven Keys, as Dr. Singh calls them. By putting them into action, you become a Chanter. It is really that simple. How you act in the world determines who you are.

I am reminded of the book *Mother Night* by Kurt Vonnegut. The protagonist is a U.S. spy who infiltrates the Nazis during World War II and becomes one of the leading propagandists in the Nazi war machine. The only other person who knows his cover is his commanding officer, who dies in the days following the war. Because there is nobody who can vouch for him, the protagonist is brought back to the U.S. and put on trial for treason. Even though he thinks of himself as a patriot, his work for the Nazis is anything but patriotic. The point of the story is that if you act like a Nazi, you are a Nazi. Conversely, if you act like a Chanter, you are one.

This sounds simpler than it is. If you think of your life as a sheet of paper, the seven values I will be discussing in this chapter must be perfectly centered on that page. To live the spiritual life of a Chanter, you will need to make a commitment to align yourself with these values. Everything you do is driven by them. You will need to ask yourself constantly, "Are my actions in keeping with my values?" If the answer is "No," then you will need to make the necessary adjustments to your course of action.

This is like steering a boat. You set a course and then point the boat in the direction it needs to go. But you have to account for the winds and currents that are likely to pull you off-course. As soon as you find that you are veering away from your intended destination, you take the rudder in hand and adjust the steering.

Being around Dr. Singh is like watching a master yachtsman. The most impressive thing about him is that his boat never veers off-course. I have never seen him waiver from his values—not once. That sets an extremely high standard for those of us who aspire to live the spiritual life of a Chanter.

Just keep in mind, when you begin to hold yourself to such standards, not to punish yourself for your "failures." This is something I had to learn the hard way. When I began my apprenticeship with Dr. Singh, there were many times when I would find myself reacting to a situation in ways that were inconsistent with the values he was teaching me. These reactions were part of a behavioral pattern that had become habitual for me. Breaking a habit is never easy, but it is especially hard when you criticize yourself.

At first, you are going to have lapses. Trying to put values such as humility or unconditional love into practice may be relatively unfamiliar ground for you. Even though you have heard about these values all your life, you probably have never attempted to live them. The process of learning to align your actions with your values represents a major transition. By subjecting yourself to harsh criticism and disapproval—as I did at first—you will only make the transition more difficult.

I would lose my serenity, for example, and then become angry at myself, which would only make me less serene. When you react in a habitual and imbalanced way to a situation, your initial reaction is never as damaging as your reaction to the reaction. The judgment you impose on yourself sends you spiraling downward into a cycle of what Dr. Singh would call unproductive thoughts and emotions. The main thing to keep in mind, as you learn about the Seven Keys, is that the best way to align yourself with values such as compassion, forgiveness and unconditional love is by practicing them first on yourself.

Whether or not you choose to incorporate them into your

daily life, please do not treat the Seven Keys lightly. They have power to transform lives on a global scale. Even if only one person were to adhere to these values, a lasting ripple effect would be felt throughout the world. Just consider the impact of such individuals as Gandhi, Mother Teresa, or Martin Luther King Jr.

Now, imagine an entire political and economic system based on the Seven Keys. The result would be a revolution the likes of which the world has never seen. A society based on these values would have no choice but to create entirely new models of commerce, health care, technology, environmental policy, and education. Every institution, starting with the home and family, would have to be modified to yield a completely peaceful and sustainable way of life.

This all may sound like a pipe dream, but it is actually the destiny of human civilization. As Chanters, a large part of our mission is to facilitate the transition to a world built on the Seven Keys. The best way to begin carrying out this mission is by applying these values to ourselves.

Key #1: Detachment

Everything you will experience or accomplish in your spiritual life as a Chanter will stem from your ability to let go of your attachments. The people and things to which you are attached hold you back and prevent you from experiencing holiness. When you enter into this path, you quickly discover how strong these attachments really are.

How do you know you have an attachment? The answer is simple: Just look for something that you value or depend on so much that you cannot imagine living without it. Discovering your attachments is actually pretty simple because they are everywhere. The hard part is finding a way to let go of them.

When you strip away one layer of attachments, you will find that there are many more layers buried beneath it—the bottomless onion. I have had to deal with all kinds of attachments on this path, including my attachment to financial security, friends, social status, sex, intellect, television, youth, spiritual beliefs, health, comfort, order, and privacy.

It may not sound like much fun to surrender these attachments, but as strange as this may sound, it has been one of the most enjoyable experiences of my life. When I release something that I never thought I could do without, I feel an incredible sense of freedom. It is like dropping a lead weight that you have been carrying for miles.

In preparing for my South Pacific journey many years ago, I remember the day when I put my few remaining possessions in storage and turned in the key to my apartment. It was liberating to move through the world without the responsibility of a house, a job, a car, or bills. I felt as light as a feather.

This same sense of lightness is what it takes to enter your inner temple and to experience holiness. If you are detached, you cannot be confined to your bubble. The walls of your bubble are made of attachments. The very things that you care about the most can turn into the prison cell that keeps your spirit from soaring. Once you are able to detach from them, your spirit will begin to fly without any effort on your part.

To become detached, you do not have to jettison everything and everyone you love. That is not the point. What matters is that your happiness not be dependent on something that cannot last. You will only find lasting happiness in the flow of love. This is the essence of who you are. When you are in that flow, you are fully connected with the Big Beautiful Spirit and with the vast multidimensional universe that surrounds and envelops you.

From a linguistic perspective, the term detachment is synonymous with disconnection, indifference, and apathy. But from a spiritual perspective, detachment is just the opposite. When you are detached, you are fully engaged in the world and immersed in the experience of this moment. Dr. Singh is living proof of that.

He has many different responses to the simple question, "How are you?" All of them are accurate indicators of the intensity with which he lives his life. As I have already mentioned, Dr. Singh likes to say, "I am in love," which lets you know that he is immersed in the flow of love. At other times, he will answer, "Life is so good," "What a wonderful day," or "I feel so pretty, my friend." These replies reflect his genuine joy and his sense of playfulness. They let you know, beyond a shadow of a doubt, that this is someone who is enjoying life to the fullest.

Dr. Singh is constantly reminding us that the point of life is to be happy—and to share our happiness with others. He once told me, "Happiness is contagious. When you go around being happy, other people will notice. They will want to know why you are so happy, and they will also want to know how they can be as happy as you."

Dr. Singh's recipe for happiness is actually quite simple: "You can be in heaven, if you choose, or you can be in hell." Although you may not be able to change the events of your life—and Dr. Singh would argue that you can—you certainly can control how you interpret and react to these events.

It is easy to get used to living on a roller-coaster, letting your emotional state be determined by the ups and downs of your life. If you win the lottery, you are overjoyed, and if you lose all your winnings on a bad investment, you are miserable. But when you are detached, you see both of these events equally as divine grace. Everything that happens in your life brings an opportunity for spiritual growth and transformation. From the perspective of genuine detachment, the tendency to label some events as "good" and others as "bad" seems arbitrary.

Soon after I began working with Dr. Singh, a woman named Lynn came to see him in search of healing. Lynn had had what many would call a hard life. She had been sexually abused as a child, disowned by her parents, and gang raped as a teenager. Also, she had lived through homelessness, drug addiction, alcoholism, cancer, obesity, arthritis, and diabetes.

When she first started coming to Dr. Singh, he simply told her, "Rewrite your story." He was trying to get Lynn to see the events of her life from an entirely new perspective. If she could look at these events with detachment, she would be able to discover their spiritual significance.

Dr. Singh was seeking to unlock Lynn's spiritual power by liberating her from the heavy baggage associated with a lifetime of suffering and victimization. By restructuring her life story, he would help her use it as a tool for transformation. Stripped of all the labels she had assigned to it, her story would be a testament to her passion for life and her determination to find holiness.

But Lynn had a hard time detaching from the perception of her life as a series of setbacks. She had grown accustomed to seeing herself as a victim and to defining her life in terms of the suffering she had experienced. For Lynn, the traumatic events of her life had become the bricks and mortar that made up the walls of her bubble. If she were to reinterpret these events from a detached perspective, the bubble would collapse, and Lynn had no intention of allowing that to happen. Too much of her self-concept and her belief system was tied to her misery.

When you try practicing detachment, you will find that it is hard to let go of even the things that make you miserable. It is easier to stick with patterns that are old and familiar, even if they are unfulfilling. I have seen firsthand how much courage is required to really let go of attachments. One of the most courageous—and detached—people I have ever met is my dear friend and spiritual sister, Carmina.

At age 18, Carmina found her calling when she read *Be Here Now* by Ram Das. That is when she realized that she needed to devote herself to her spiritual path. This path led her to several of the great spiritual Masters, including Yogananda. For many years, she practiced his teachings and was an active member of the organization he founded.

From the beginning, Carmina embraced the idea of detachment, especially with regard to material possessions. She learned to live frugally and worked just enough to be able to pay her bills. The only jobs Carmina would take were ones that she felt were of service to others. For years, she worked in a nursing home caring for Alzheimer's patients and in a ward for sick and abused children.

Although she had lived in the South for much of her life, Carmina was drawn to the Arizona desert. After a long-term relationship ended, she packed all of her belongings into her car and drove to Tucson with only a few hundred dollars to her name. Several months later, she met Dr. Singh.

From their first meeting, Carmina recognized Dr. Singh as her spiritual teacher. He offered her the chance to devote herself entirely to her spiritual practice, and she jumped at the opportunity. Carmina quit her job and at one point was sleeping on someone's floor. Having virtually no material possessions, no home, and no job, she felt a sense of freedom and fulfillment.

By the time I met her, Carmina was living in a dilapidated trailer on a parcel of land in the desert. Dr. Singh had obtained the land for the purpose of constructing a temple there. Largely designed and built by Carmina, this temple will be used for healing ceremonies when it is completed.

Most days, you will find Carmina somewhere around the temple, pouring floors, putting up walls, plastering, or tending to the gardens that surround the structure. Although she has told me that she had never had much interest in construction work prior to the start of this project, Carmina seems perfectly happy building a temple in the desert. Like everything else she touches, the structure has a peaceful and comforting quality. It feels like a true sanctuary; you can tell just by stepping inside that it was built with loving hands and an open heart.

Key #2: Compassion

When I had my first experience of holiness in Sonora, I made contact for the first time with sentient beings whose existence I had never even considered. Some of these beings inhabit dimensions that are much closer to heaven than the human realm. Others reside in dimensions that the Tibetan Buddhists call *hell realms*. These beings experience a level of suffering far beyond anything you and I will ever know in this lifetime.

As I connected with my brothers and sisters in other dimensions, I could feel the pain and misery of beings in the hell realms. Their cries of despair touched my heart. I was taking on their suffering as if it were my own. In a way, that was not particularly hard for me to do. At various times in my life, I have known the despair that comes from disconnection. In fact, this has been the single most consistent source of pain in my life. When you are alienated from your own spirit, when you feel no sense of kinship with anyone or anything, and when it seems as if your existence has no purpose, you can become so consumed with despair that it can become the focal point of your life.

For me, nothing captures that feeling better than the Robin Trower song, "Bridge of Sighs." In my most despondent moments, I would listen to this song repeatedly and sink into the misery and hopelessness conveyed by the lyrics:

The sun don't shine,
The moon don't move the tides to wash me clean.
The cold wind blows,
The gods look down in anger on this poor child.
Why so unforgiving and why so cold?
Been a long time crossing Bridge of Sighs.

Even at the time, I knew that my use of this song was self-indulgent; it was a way for me to wallow in my own despair. But I also had a sense of how important it was for me to feel this despair as fully as possible. My sense of disconnection turned out to be a powerful driving force in my spiritual life. It also was the key that unlocked my feelings of compassion, because I could always relate to the alienation and despair of others, even if I could not identify with them in other ways.

The term compassion means shared suffering. You develop compassion by knowing what it is like to suffer. The Buddhists claim that life and suffering are inextricably linked. You cannot live without knowing suffering or causing others to suffer. The food we eat, for instance, comes at the expense of another being.

One of the prayers that I say every day, which comes from Tibetan Buddhism, has a line that states, "May there not arise in my mind, even for an instant, the thought of harming others." But even without the thought or intention of harming others, your actions still may result in harm.

As Chanters, we seek not just to minimize our negative impact on others but to counteract it with positive action. This action begins with compassion. To alleviate the suffering of other beings, first you have to feel it. Another line of the same prayer says, "May I take upon myself the great burdens, the difficult to endure sufferings of beings in hell and the other realms, and may they be liberated." You can become so sensitive to the suffering of others that you feel it as strongly as you would your own pain. When you get to that point, you have no choice but to take whatever action is needed to alleviate that suffering.

I have found that my own sense of compassion has developed in stages. I began by allowing myself to feel my own pain. Rather than run from my despair, I faced it and even immersed myself in it. As I did that, the feelings shifted, and eventually I began to understand the source of my despair.

I realized fully what was missing from my life when I heard the chant, "Door of My Heart," written by Yogananda. One of the verses asks, "Will my days fly away without seeing Thee, my Lord?" This question is very poignant for me because it expresses a concern I have had my whole life, which is that I might never discover my connection with the Big Beautiful Spirit.

Until I met Dr. Singh, I felt a void—a sense that the most important pieces of the puzzle were missing for me. In spite of all my efforts, I had no idea how to find my inner temple or what it takes to live in the experience of holiness. When I began to locate these missing pieces, I discovered a growing sense of obligation within myself. Suddenly, I felt accountable to those beings that were experiencing the same sense of emptiness I had known. I could not keep my newfound happiness to myself, knowing that others were suffering from the kind of despair that had plagued me for so long.

At that point in my spiritual life, I began to take on the despair of others as if it were my own. I think the reason I could feel someone else's pain so directly is that my own pain was no longer getting in the way. The more I was able to step outside of my bubble, the more open I became to the experience of compassion.

As surprising as it may sound, this is a beautiful sensation. When you experience the suffering of another being as your own, you feel a true sense of connectedness. My own happiness derives from this awareness that I am connected to all things, and there is no way to have that awareness without feeling the suffering of other beings. As I take on their suffering, I have to remind myself to remain as detached from it as I would from my own. Just as I would not define myself by the despair I have felt in my life, I cannot identify with someone else's despair.

As long as I do not hold onto the suffering of other beings, I can transform it into something very pure. One of the things I have discovered in my apprenticeship with Dr. Singh is the power of catharsis, which is the purification of an emotion. At its core, every emotion is just pure energy. Think about what happens in your body when you experience an emotion. If it has enough intensity, the emotion may cause your heart to race, your palms to sweat, and your breathing to accelerate. These are the symptoms of the intensely aroused state that is characteristic of your body's fight-or-flight response. Your body is simply reacting to a large, sudden jolt of energy.

How you interpret this jolt determines your emotional experience. At a purely energetic level, your body cannot distinguish fear from joy or anger from excitement. Your mind has to draw these distinctions, and it does so by looking for emotional cues in the environment. It asks: *What is happening right now? Is there something going on that would cause me to feel a certain way?*

Sometimes, the jolt of energy you experience is not your own. As a Chanter, you may take on the emotions of others—especially unproductive emotions such as fear or despair. You do this because your compassion opens you up to their suffering. Once your sense of compassion gets heightened, you will find it increasingly difficult to walk away from someone else's pain. In a very real sense, it becomes your responsibility.

The term catharsis comes from a Greek word meaning "to cleanse." As Chanters, we can take another individual's emotional pain, strip it of all judgment and interpretation, and transform it back into its original form—a stream of pure energy that can be sent out into the universe to benefit all beings. To pull this off, we have to empty ourselves of all attachments, including any conditions or judgments we might tend to impose on the emotions we are experiencing.

When you become adept at catharsis, people will seek you out to help heal their pain. Dr. Singh takes part in thousands of healings every year. I once saw him treat a woman in her 50s who had come to him with pain in her arthritic left knee. Dr. Singh was so committed to taking this woman's pain from her that he spent nearly a month limping on his own painfully swollen left knee. In a more recent case, Dr. Singh asked the Band members to assist in a healing ceremony for a man who had just been diagnosed with throat cancer. Each of us who took part in the ceremony began experiencing soreness in our throats immediately afterwards and continued to have symptoms for several days.

This level of compassion is not for everyone. It requires a great deal of dedication to other beings. As Chanters, we do not act compassionately because of any benefit we may gain, but because our hearts become so receptive to the suffering of our brothers and sisters that we cannot ignore it. The irony, however, is that we benefit the most from our own compassion. It aligns us with the very core of our identity, not as isolated individuals, but as a continuous flow of love that interconnects all things.

Key #3: Serenity

Dr. Singh refers to certain emotions as unproductive because of the way that they hold us back in our spiritual development. These emotions are perhaps the most powerful forces keeping us from the experience of holiness. When we are caught up in them, they have the power not just to draw us into our bubble but to trap us there.

How do we know which emotions are unproductive? For me, my most unproductive emotions are the ones that take over control of my thoughts and actions. I find myself judging and reacting to my circumstances in a habitual, almost unconscious manner, and that is when my unproductive emotions pour out of me like a cascading fountain.

These emotions usually take the form of fear, anger, sadness, frustration, jealousy, worry, or resentment. Ultimately, they arise from a lack of detachment. I am overcome by these feelings when I am attached to a certain outcome. There are times when I want and expect things to be a certain way and the world refuses to cooperate.

The quality of serenity is based on letting go of expectations about how things should be. This attitude of surrender is conveyed in the Serenity Prayer made famous by Alcoholics Anonymous: "God grant me the serenity to accept the things I cannot change, the courage to change the things I can, and the wisdom to know the difference."

Acceptance is an important part of serenity. It is not enough, however, simply to accept the things we cannot change. For me, serenity comes from not having any investment in the outcome. If I am genuinely serene, then it will not matter to me whether things change or stay the same. Either way, I choose to be happy, and my happiness cannot be based on external factors. The kind of happiness I seek arises solely from my connection with the Big Beautiful Spirit.

My grandmother has a saying: "If you lean on a wall, it will crumble. If you lean on a man, he will die. Only lean on the Divine." The point is that if your well-being depends on anything other than the Big Beautiful Spirit, you are setting yourself up for disappointment because everything else is impermanent and therefore unreliable.

This condition of impermanence is reflected in the mythological symbol of the wheel of fortune. "There's the hub of the wheel, and there is the revolving rim of the wheel," explains Joseph Campbell. "If you are attached to the rim of the wheel of fortune, you will be either above going down or at the bottom coming up. But if you are at the hub, you are in the same place all the time."

When you find your spiritual hub, you are not susceptible to the mood fluctuations associated with changes in fortune. Regardless of whether you are rich or poor, healthy or sick, your happiness is unwavering. In fact, you are grateful for whatever life brings you, because you are aware that everything that comes your way is a gift.

Although you may not always want the gifts that you receive from the Big Beautiful Spirit—in fact, you may go out of your way to avoid them—it is important to recognize and acknowledge them for what they are. Even the most seemingly difficult circumstances in your life are an opportunity for spiritual development. In fact, the more difficult they may seem, the more powerful—and valuable—are the life lessons that they bring.

Dr. Singh likes to remind us that the Big Beautiful Spirit "will never give you more than you can handle." No matter how you may interpret something that happens in your life, you cannot lose sight of the fact that it comes to you as a gift from a benign source, and that this source always responds to your spiritual needs. As the Rolling Stones song points out, "You can't always get what you want, but if you try sometime, you just might find, you get what you need."

That is why gratitude is such an important component of serenity. Even when you are unable or unwilling to see the benefits of the gifts that the Big Beautiful Spirit brings you, those gifts are always addressing your spiritual needs. When you reject a gift or struggle against it, you are imposing a very narrow interpretation on what is happening. Caught up in the limitations of your own bubble, you are unable to see the vast beauty and perfection of the universe that is unfolding in and around you at this very moment.

Being grateful for what the universe brings you does not

mean that you stop trying to make things better. It is important not to confuse serenity with passivity. You can be at peace with things as they are and still take action to change them. For instance, even though you may accept suffering as part of existence, you can act in ways that alleviate suffering. The really intriguing question is: Why?

I know that the world is perfect as it is, and that there is nothing we can do to add to that perfection. Yet I have also said that we as Chanters have a mission to help reshape the future and to bring a new era of peace to the planet. This may seem like a perfectly senseless proposition. After all, if the world is perfect, then it is pointless to try and change it.

The reason this seems to make no sense is that it represents the kind of paradox the mind has a hard time grasping. The world is perfect, and at the same time, it is in a constant state of unfolding. This is also true for you and me. Our quest for enlightenment is really just a reconnection with something that already exists in us. In a sense, we are already enlightened.

Blaise Pascal, the French mathematician and religious philosopher, wrote, "Thou wouldest not seek Me if thou hadst not found me." The things we strive to attain, whether they be enlightenment, a peaceful world, or the end of suffering, already exist in certain dimensions of reality, and not just as potentiality. A Zen poem reads:

> *When you seek to know it, you cannot see it.*
> *You cannot take hold of it,*
> *But neither can you lose it.*
> *In not being able to get it, you see it.*
> *When you are silent, it speaks.*
> *When you speak, it is silent.*
> *The great gate is wide open to bestow alms,*
> *And no crowd is blocking the way.*

Serenity comes from knowing that the ideals to which we aspire are already here. We do not need to attain anything.

There is no need for struggle. We cannot find something that has never been lost. All we can do is to act in accordance with our ideals, and in doing so, these ideals are realized not just in some dimensions but in all of them.

Mahatma Gandhi created an entire social and political movement based on serene action. He called this movement satyagraha, which derives from the Sanskrit words satya, meaning truth, and agraha, meaning firmness. In explaining the origin of the term, Gandhi wrote, "Satya implies love, and agraha engenders and therefore serves as a synonym for force. I thus began to call the Indian movement satyagraha, that is to say, the Force which is born of Truth and Love or non-violence, and gave up the use of the phrase passive resistance."

For Gandhi, the ultimate point of satyagraha was neither social change nor persuasion. It was to realize the ideals of truth and love in such a way that your serenity would be conveyed through all your actions, including your interactions with so-called "opponents." You can see this emphasis on serenity in the code of conduct that Gandhi developed for individuals taking part in the satyagraha movement:

1. *Harbor no anger but suffer the anger of the opponent. Refuse to return the assault of the opponent.*
2. *Do not submit to any order given in anger, even though severe punishment is threatened for disobeying.*
3. *Refrain from insults and swearing.*
4. *Protect opponents from insult or attack, even at the risk of life.*
5. *Do not resist arrest or the attachment of property unless holding property as a trustee.*
6. *Refuse to surrender any property held in trust at the risk of life.*
7. *If taken prisoner, behave in an exemplary manner.*
8. *As a member of a satyagraha unit, obey the orders of satyagraha leaders, and resign from the unit in the event of serious disagreement.*
9. *Do not expect guarantees for maintenance of dependents.*

In this code, you can see the various components of serenity: letting go of unproductive emotions such as anger; not getting caught up in someone else's emotions; acting in a calm and peaceful manner; and remaining free of expectations or attachments. This is what it takes to be serene. But what happens if you slip? How do you regain your serenity once you have lost it?

Since childhood, I have been aware of a part of me that seems to remain calm, no matter what is happening around me or how I am reacting emotionally. When I first came across the term higher self, I knew that it was referring to this aspect of our selves—the part that can view the events taking place in our lives from a very peaceful and detached perspective. It is as if the higher self is floating in the air above us, looking down at each situation with absolutely no judgment but perhaps a hint of amusement.

The reason your higher self might be amused by the circumstances of your life is that it perceives them all as a form of play. In Sanskrit, life events are referred to as lila (pronounced LEE-lah), which means "divine play." The assumption is that we are divine beings who have chosen to play the part of human beings. Our lives are simply the unfolding of this lila, in which the Gods play at being mortal. We can choose to take life very seriously, but at its core it is just play.

When I met Dr. Singh, I was consumed by worry. Having just walked away from a high-paying job, I was concerned about paying my bills and making ends meet. Ironically, I had more assets than anyone else in the Band, and yet I was the one most worried about money. To some degree, I know that I inherited this worry from my parents, who came to the United States as immigrants and struggled to survive their first few years in the country. In no way do I blame them for passing on their worries to me; that is not the point. But it was important for me to realize that my fears around money were not really my own.

One day, Dr. Singh gave me a sheet of paper and asked me to read it twice a day. The paper contained a silly little poem called "The Worry Monster" that had been written by a psychiatrist friend of his. Although Dr. Singh had lost contact with this friend years earlier, he continued to use the poem as a tool for fostering serenity:

Don't feed the worry monster,
His appetite is endless.
Juicy thoughts of disaster,
He likes with romaine lettuce.
Never feed the worry monster,
He'll only ask for more.
Thoughts of bankruptcy and cancer,
He especially adores.
Feed not the worry monster,
Don't share with him your wealth.
Don't let that shady character
Use up your time and health.
Don't feed the worry monster,
Starve him 'til he dies.
Then you'll be the master
Of your planet and your skies.

The first time I read "The Worry Monster," I felt a little foolish. The poem seems cheesy, like something that Dr. Seuss would have written on a really bad day. And yet its power lies in its cheesiness. As I read it, I began to see my own worries as cheesy. They seemed so silly and unimportant that I was surprised I had ever given into them. I wondered: *Why had I been so willing to lose my serenity over something as trivial as money?*

If you have ever struggled financially, you may be thinking that there is nothing trivial about money. The saying goes that "money is only unimportant to those who have it." Although there is certainly some truth in this saying, it is also true that worries about money are not limited to the poor. In my heart, I knew that I was not even remotely in danger of homelessness or starvation. Dr. Singh had even assured me of that when he told me, "As long as I'm alive, you will always have food to eat and a roof over your head."

My worries were about security. I wanted to have enough money stocked away so that I would never have to face poverty. But I now understand that there is no real security to be had in this world. Financial markets can collapse tomorrow. An environmental crisis can affect food supplies. Our government may go bankrupt, leaving banks uninsured and bringing the Social Security system to a halt.

At some point, I had to surrender. I had to accept the fact that life is a wild ride—a divine soap opera that keeps taking new twists at every turn. All I really have in this life is my connection to the Big Beautiful Spirit. Nothing else matters. As long as I am living in the flow of love, I will know serenity. And that serenity cannot be shaken by anything that happens around me.

Key #4: Unconditional Love

Long before I met Dr. Singh, I came to a realization that all the love I had experienced from other people had come with strings attached. Even more startling, I discovered that my love for them had strings attached, as well. We had all set terms and conditions on our love. In my relationships, I had expected that my partner would meet my needs, at least to some degree. And I know that my partners had expected the same of me. When those expectations were not met, we would cut each other loose.

I even found that my parents' love for me was not unconditional. When I was in my late 20s, I reached a point in my life when I was lost. I had no money and no idea what my next step would be. That is when I landed on my parents' doorstep, moving back in with them for the first time in a decade.

Although they agreed to take me in, I knew they were not particularly thrilled with the arrangement. None of us were. The last thing I wanted to do was to sacrifice my autonomy, living by their rules and under their constant scrutiny. But I had no clarity, no direction, and nowhere else to go.

I fell into a mild depression. There were days when I hardly wanted to get out of bed. This was hard for my parents to witness. They wanted to see me gain control of my life and take some kind of action. Moreover, they were not all that pleased with me as a housemate; I did not take much interest in cleaning house or picking up after myself.

One day, I cancelled a meeting with a friend to stay in my room and read. My mother, assuming that I was gone, began talking about me to my father. The conversation was more like a tirade. She vented her frustrations and expressed genuine resentment towards me. Moreover, she said I was lazy, selfish, and manipulative. It was the most unflattering depiction that I had ever heard of myself—and it was coming from my own mother.

Hurt and angered by her words, I let her know that I had heard the entire conversation, and then I stormed out of the house. A few weeks later, I gathered my belongings and moved out on my own again.

My parents could not see that I was going through a phase—a difficult yet short-lived transition in my life. All they could see was my behavior, which was unacceptable to them. They assumed that this behavior was a permanent reflection of my character, and so I became unacceptable to them, as well.

At that point in my life, I felt that my parents' love for me—or at least their ability to accept me—was conditional. My love for them was no less conditional, however. I refused to love someone who would not accept me as I was. After that incident, I closed myself off to them emotionally for several years.

A few weeks after meeting Dr. Singh, I flew to Seattle to visit my family and attend a wedding. Before I left, Dr. Singh presented me with this challenge: He asked me to refrain from any judgment of my parents for the entire duration of my visit. To me, this seemed like a monumental task.

"What do I do if I start reacting to something they say or do?" I asked.

"Just chant," he replied. "You know so many beautiful chants. Just keep one ready at all times, and when you begin reacting, start chanting in your head. The chant will fill your mind so that there won't be any room left for judgment."

In a few words, Dr. Singh had offered me an important lesson in unconditional love: The ability to love unconditionally begins where judgment ends. As long as you are judging the people in your life, expecting them to be a certain way and evaluating them based on how well they meet your expectations, you will never know the experience of unconditional love.

Most of us keep score in our interactions with others. We award them points for saying and doing the things that meet with our approval and we deduct points when they "fail" us. Most of us are quick to penalize the behaviors that hurt us or that meet with our disapproval. We put the people in our lives on trial and assign ourselves the role of judge, jury, and executioner.

So I went to Seattle and even stayed in my parents' house— something I had not done in years. Every time I felt myself judging them or reacting emotionally to something they said, I sang a chant that I had recently composed. The words of the chant are:

You are in my heart,
Living in my heart,
Always in my heart.

I had composed it after coming across a bracelet I had been given at a meditation retreat years earlier. On the bracelet was a quote from Ammachi that read, "I have no special place to dwell; I dwell in your heart." When I saw the bracelet after all those years, I was touched by the idea that there is a source of pure love residing in every heart. Even though this love has no agenda—"no special place to dwell"—we try to keep it locked away in our hearts. By unlocking our hearts, we release this love into the world, where it can be shared with others.

When you let love flow unconditionally, it multiplies. Dr. Singh once told me, "In the linear realm, three minus two equals one. In the realm of unconditional love, three minus two can equal twenty-two." Not only does the flow of love keep growing, but something even more dramatic happens: You melt into that flow. And that is when you enter the inner temple, from which you can access all of the spiritual power and wisdom of the universe.

After my trip to Seattle, my relationship with my parents changed. Using the technique that Dr. Singh had taught me, I was able to break out of my old patterns and stopped judging them altogether. For the first time in my life, I could accept my parents exactly as they are, without wishing they were somehow different or imposing unrealistic expectations on them. Once that happened, we began enjoying one another's company more than we ever had. My parents found they could relax and be themselves around me. They liked the fact that I was completely open with them because I was no longer concerned about being judged by them. I took all the pressure off them by making my love for them unconditional. They responded to it with enthusiasm—and perhaps a sense of relief.

Through this transformation, I discovered something interesting: When you begin to practice unconditional love—even with one person in your life—you create a snowball effect. It gets harder to judge anyone because you feel how constricting it is to hold back your love. You even begin to react differently to the people who used to annoy you. Surprisingly, their behavior towards you changes. That is because everyone loves to be loved.

Unconditional love is the most powerful force in the universe, beyond question. Even those who fight it cannot resist it. There is not a single point in the entire universe that is impermeable to the flow of love. The men who assassinated Gandhi and Martin Luther King Jr. had unconditional love locked away in their hearts. So did Adolph Hitler and Charles Manson. Nobody is devoid of love or immune to its touch.

That is why Jesus told his disciples, "Love your enemies, bless those who curse you, do good to those who hate you, and pray for those who despitefully use you." His teachings on unconditional love are perfectly beautiful and profound in their simplicity. They demonstrate the transformative power of love. For someone who applies them fully, there is no such thing as an enemy. Jesus had no enemies—not even his crucifiers could be called that.

One summer day in Sonora, I had a small taste of what can happen when hatred is transformed into love. My entire life, I have had an aversion to insects. When I was four, I was stung in the foot by a bee. Within minutes, my foot had become so painfully swollen that I had to be taken to the emergency room. It turned out that I was allergic to bee stings, as I am to insect bites in general.

My physical reaction to some insect bites is so intense that I have to carry antihistamines in my backpack when I go hiking. Perhaps because of this negative association, my emotional reaction to insects has been almost as strong. I used to become nauseated at the mere sight of a housefly or cockroach. And if a bee or wasp would buzz near me, my entire body would tense.

While sitting in the kitchen of the Conservatory on a hot Saturday afternoon, Harper said to me, "Last week, when you were in Seattle visiting your family, Dr. Singh talked about our role as caretakers of the plants and animals. He said that each of us has an assignment to look after certain species, to send them love and blessings, and to act as their protectors."

"What is your assignment?" I asked.

"I'm supposed to look after the birds," Harper replied.

Hearing her response made me think aloud. "I wonder what my assignment is going to be."

"Oh, we know that too," she said. "Dr. Singh mentioned your assignment while he was talking to all of us."

"What is it?"

"You may not like it, Omar."

"Of course I'm going to like it. Tell me."

Harper paused and gave me a sympathetic look. "You are in charge of the insects," she said, with a hint of a smile.

"The insects? This has got to be a mistake!" I exclaimed. "I think Dr. Singh may have picked the wrong man for the job."

Her look became a little sterner, like that of a mother about to scold a petulant child. "I don't think he picked the wrong man at all. Maybe you need to sit and reflect on this assignment."

That night, as I was preparing to go to bed, I did exactly as Harper had suggested. I asked the Masters why I, of all people, would be asked to take care of the insect species that I so thoroughly detested. The Masters did not answer me. Instead, I found myself thinking about something that had happened a week earlier.

I had walked outside my back door, only to find a long line of ants zipping along my patio deck, overrunning my back yard the way they did everything else. I remember wondering why we needed so many ants and if the world would not be better off without them. In a moment of frustration, I began stomping on ants with the soles of my shoes. I knew this was a pointless act, even at the time. Ants make up an endless army with plenty of reinforcements. I had no doubt that the line would be back in full force the very next day. I also knew that even a single ant bite would send me racing to the medicine cabinet for my Benadryl, and that I would be sleeping off the effects of the medication an hour after taking it. In spite of that knowledge, I just kept stomping. I must have killed ten thousand ants that day.

After recalling that incident, I called again to the Masters, but they still did not answer me. Instead, the spirits of the ants I had killed came to me. There were thousands of them, speaking in a unified voice. As they faced me, they asked, "When are you going to see?"

Startled and uncomfortable being interrogated by these dead ants, I responded to their question with one of my own. "What do you want me to see?" I asked awkwardly.

"We want you to see us for what we are."

"And what are you?"

"You know exactly what we are." That was the last thing they said before disappearing. As soon as they left, I realized what it was they wanted me to see: The insects that repulsed me so strongly are souls on a spiritual journey—no different than human beings. They too are seeking enlightenment. And they want to experience holiness as much as we do.

Insects lead short yet challenging lives. They are in a constant struggle for survival, searching for their next meal while trying not to become someone else's. Besides playing a critical role in the ecosystem—each insect species has an important niche to fill—they are also spiritual messengers for human beings and other animal species.

Insects have always served as models of spiritual attributes such as persistence, cooperation, and selflessness. They also like to test our adherence to the Seven Keys, especially the ideals of serenity and detachment. It is always fascinating to watch grown men and women lose their composure because of the presence of a single bee or cockroach in the room. I have reacted to insects in this way myself, and so I can relate. Yet, it is still compelling to recognize and observe the psychological power that insects have over us. Just think back to your own reaction the last time you discovered the sound of a mosquito that had snuck into bed with you—or worse yet, your tent.

As I began to understand the spiritual role that insects play, I gained new levels of compassion and respect for them. Lying in bed that night, I vowed to give my brothers and sisters in the insect realm the unconditional love they deserve. I also vowed to protect them from harm whenever I could. These vows were put to a test immediately the next morning.

A few minutes after awakening, I went to the kitchen, where I prepared a cup of tea for myself. Soon, Harper came in and joined me. As we sat and enjoyed our tea, we noticed that there were bees gathering outside the window next to us. Looking around us, we realized the same thing was happening at all four kitchen windows. Their numbers seemed to be growing by the minute, along with their determination to find a way inside the kitchen.

Harper remarked, "I have never seen anything like this in all the years I've been coming to Sonora."

I wondered, "What are they looking for?"

"I don't know, but I think they are here for you, my friend," she replied.

Just then, Ricardo opened the door and entered the kitchen.

A bee flew into the kitchen behind him.

"What's with all the bees?" he said.

"I think they came to bring a message for Omar," replied Harper.

"Oh yeah, that's right," Ricardo remarked. He turned to me with a gleam of mischief in his eye. "You're supposed to be the King of the Bugs."

"They prefer to be called *insects,*" I replied. "*Bug* is a derogatory term."

Ricardo laughed. "OK, Mr. Insect Man. You need to talk to your friends before Dr. Singh's patients start arriving. If those bees are still out there at 9am, we are going to have to start spraying them."

The waiting area for Dr. Singh's patients was in the courtyard just outside the kitchen door. As we looked out the window, we could see a large swarm of bees circling around the courtyard. This swarm would alarm the patients and could even pose a threat to some of them. Obviously, we had to do something.

At that moment, the bee that had snuck into the kitchen buzzed past Ricardo's head. Suddenly, he stopped being amused by the situation and began focusing his attention on the bee. Everywhere it went, his eyes followed. I could see that the bee was making Ricardo very uncomfortable, and so I offered to trap it and take it outside.

After catching the bee in a glass jar, I opened the kitchen door carefully so that no more bees would get in, and then once I got outside, I took the lid off the jar to let the bee escape. No matter what I did, though, the bee would not leave the jar. I heard the spirit of the bee say, "I want to be close to you."

That is when I realized what was happening: The bees were recognizing me as their friend and guardian. Somehow, they could sense the transformation I had undergone the night before, including my newfound commitment to love insects unconditionally and to protect them from harm whenever I could.

Now, tens of thousands of bees were surrounding the kitchen. They had come to acknowledge me, and I was honored by their

display. At the same time, I could not allow them to put themselves in danger. I went to each of the four kitchen windows and,
nearly touching the bees, tapped on the glass to get their attention. Then I said to them, "Thank you for being here. I offer my
blessings and my love. But I must ask you to leave. Please
disperse by 9 am. If not, you may get sprayed with poison."

I felt that the bees had understood my request and were willing to comply. So, I returned to the kitchen, only to be greeted
by surprised stares.

"Wow!" Ricardo exclaimed. "That was so unlike you. I never
imagined I would see you walk into a swarm of bees like that.
You didn't even seem scared."

"I wasn't," I replied. "Those bees had no intention of hurting
me."

Harper still had a look of concern on her face. "How are we
going to get them to leave?" she asked.

"They will be gone by 9 am," I explained. "I got them to
agree to that."

Just then, Dr. Singh entered the kitchen for the first time. He
said, "It looks like the bees have come out to visit Omar."

"Yes," said Harper, "but he promised that they will all be
gone by 9 am."

"That sounds about right," he replied. "It is good to hear that
Omar has it all under control." Then he poured himself a cup of
coffee, walked out of the kitchen and into a swarm of bees. Dr. Singh
was unperturbed by this. For him, having a cloud of bees buzzing
around his head seemed perfectly normal—even enjoyable.

By 8:30 am, the swarm had not dispersed. There were still
thousands of bees congregating in the courtyard and on the
kitchen windows. Twenty minutes later, I could see that the
swarm was thinning. At 9 am, a few hundred bees remained. I
was relieved that their numbers had decreased but disappointed
that there were still enough of them to create a problem for
anyone walking into the courtyard.

Fortunately, though, no patients had arrived yet. I was
getting concerned for the remaining bees, knowing that we

would have no recourse but to spray them. By 9:10, the last of the bees had gone.

A few minutes later, Dr. Singh came back into the kitchen to refill his coffee cup. "What happened to the bees?" he asked. I knew that he knew the answer to this question, but he just wanted to hear it from me.

"They all took off," I replied, "but they were a little late. I asked them to disperse by 9 am but they didn't leave until 9:10."

He gave me a big smile. "You have to understand that these are Mexican bees," he said. "They always run a few minutes late."

Key #5: Humility

The first time I sat down to talk with Dr. Singh, he asked me, "What is the biggest obstacle or challenge in your spiritual path?"

I was not sure how to answer. As I considered possible responses, I realized that I had several choices. Finally, I narrowed it down to two. After that, it was basically a coin flip.

Finally I replied, "I guess I would have to say my big ego." I chose this one because in the previous month, two different people had called me egotistical. One of them was my former employer, who claimed that I had too much ego investment in my work. The other was a member of Global Chant who was pushing her agenda—as others had done before her—trying to take the chanting circle in a direction that did not feel right to me.

Dr. Singh looked at me with surprise. Later, I would come to realize that it was mock surprise. Nothing ever seemed to catch him off guard.

He said, "I prefer to say that you have a big eagle." Then he added, "Your spirit is like an eagle waiting to spread its wings and soar, but you have been holding it down. It's time to let it fly."

"And how do I do that?" I asked.

"Oh, that's easy. Just keep reminding yourself every day of the one thing that you and I both know about ourselves, which is that we are nobody."

At the time, I did not realize the profound nature of the teaching Dr. Singh had just shared with me. It took me months to uncover the significance of his words: *We are nobody.*

It may sound like a degrading statement, but it is just the opposite. There is a great deal of freedom in those words. To be nobody means to have no attachments, no expectations, and no room for unhappiness.

Trying to be somebody makes us miserable. I had spent much of my life building my bubble, creating an identity and then defining myself by it. In doing so, I put a lot of pressure on myself to be a certain way, to attain personal goals and to establish my reputation. That is why I had such ego investment in everything I did, including my work and the chanting group.

The misery comes when things stop going according to plan: Your big project fails. Someone in a position of authority questions your reputation. Your spouse asks for a divorce. If your identity is linked to success in any aspect of your life, then any outcome that you perceive as a failure is going to be devastating to you.

When you realize that you are nobody, life becomes much easier—and happier. You no longer need to keep score because the quality of your life is not something that can be measured in terms of your accomplishments. Your happiness becomes a matter of being rather than of doing. "All you need to do to be happy is to just melt," as Dr. Singh would say. You enter your inner temple, merge into the flow of divine love, and share yourself and your love with others. There is nothing more you need to achieve.

The more you allow yourself to be nobody, the more it transforms you. You step out of your bubble enough to see that the core of your identity has nothing to do with achievement, status, or wealth. Rather, it stems from your connection with others. The impulse to set yourself apart, to rise above the crowd, and to be a winner, is replaced by a sense of love, compassion, and humility.

Practicing humility means putting others first. This goes against our basic impulses, especially for those of us who have grown up in a culture that emphasizes individualism. The attitude of *me-first* has been engrained in many of us from earliest childhood. We are led to believe that happiness comes from making our own needs and desires our highest priority. But you just have to look at the lives of those who have adopted this strategy to know that it does not work.

The problem with the *me-first* approach is that it traps you in a frame of mind inherently devoid of happiness. Psychologist Abraham Maslow captured this problem perfectly in his distinction between deficiency motivation and being motivation. When you are operating from within your bubble, your needs and desires have to do with deficiency—with the things that you lack. You assume that you will find happiness by obtaining something you do not already have: a nicer house, a prettier body, a faster car, or a larger bank account.

When you move beyond the bubble, your priorities change. You are motivated by being—by the experience of holiness. And this experience cannot happen in a vacuum. It requires an awareness of your interdependence with all beings and all things. As you let go of your individual identity and merge into the flow of love, your happiness becomes linked to that of others.

After my first few visits to the Conservatory in Sonora, I asked to be served last at every meal. The idea of receiving my food ahead of someone else just felt wrong to me. If one of the other people seated at the table was experiencing the discomfort of hunger, I would not be able to enjoy my food.

This was a new sensation for me. I had always had the ability to feel empathy for others, just as every human being does, but I had chosen to disregard these feelings when they were inconvenient for me. Once I began to experience holiness on a regular basis, I had no choice but to pay attention. It was no longer easy for me to focus on my own needs while ignoring the needs of another.

One morning when we were in Oaxaca, our hosts served us a local delicacy for breakfast: a sauce made of pork rind. Dr. Singh had instructed us to be polite guests and to eat whatever we were served. At the time, I was maintaining a strict vegetarian diet, but he asked me to ease my restriction on meat for the duration of our visit, given that our hosts were likely to serve us meat dishes as a show of respect for us. I was prepared to avoid mentioning anything to them about my vegetarianism, but during our first breakfast with the host family, Dr. Singh told them about my dietary restriction. Although I felt a little embarrassed to be singled out in this way, I also realized that this was a test for me.

My fellow Chanters were carnivores but their meat intake was limited to fish and poultry. Each one of them found the prospect of eating a sauce made of pork rind as repulsive as I did. Yet none of them uttered a word when this concoction was set in front of them.

When the hostess approached me, she inquired, "I am assuming you can't eat pork rind sauce because of your vegetarian diet. Is that right?"

After three days of answering persistent questions about my eating habits, I finally saw an opportunity to use my vegetarianism to my advantage. "Yes, that's right," I nodded politely. "As much as I would like to try it, I can't eat it."

When Ricardo heard these words, he practically flew out of his seat. He asked Dr. Singh, "Hey, how come Omar doesn't have to eat the pork rind sauce?"

I turned to him, shrugged, and smiled. After months of enduring Ricardo's teasing and his constant maneuvering to get the upper hand, I found the situation amusing. But then I noticed that he was not amused. In fact, he seemed angry that I was allowing myself to get away with special treatment.

As I watched him, Harper, and Carmina choking down as much of the vile sauce as they could handle, I felt ashamed. I had put myself ahead of them. At the very least, I could have been courageous enough to let the hostess know that none of us could tolerate the sauce. Or I could have accepted a serving of it. In any case, I wondered how I could subject the people I care about to a hardship that I was unwilling to endure myself.

Meanwhile, Dr. Singh took some of the pork rind sauce off the other Band members' plates and ate it calmly. Although there was no expression on his face, I knew that he was not enjoying the sauce any more than the others. Yet, he was going to do every-thing in his power to ease their discomfort. In his quiet way, Dr. Singh was showing us the real meaning of humility.

After the meal, I watched as Harper went upstairs and quietly took her Pepto Bismol. This really had been an unpleasant experience for her, and yet she never said a word about it. Being as connected as I was to her, I could feel how much the food had sickened her. I realized that I needed to do more to protect the people I love, even if it meant putting their interests ahead of my own.

As a Chanter, you realize that the list of people you love is pretty big. In fact, it has to include everyone. There is nobody who lacks the divine spark. Even the most annoying or mean-spirited person is an embodiment of the Big Beautiful Spirit. As such, they are worthy not just of your love but of your honor.

In India, a stranger might say "Namaste" when greeting you. In essence, this person is acknowledging the divine within you, greeting you as a visiting deity. To practice humility, all you need is the answer to this simple question: *How would I treat a deity who came to visit me?* Once you have that answer, you will know exactly how to treat everyone you meet.

Key #6: Forgiveness

When Dr. Singh speaks about the importance of practicing forgiveness, he is referring to something much deeper than the concept of forgiveness most of us have come to understand. The type of forgiveness that he teaches involves going back in time and reshaping destiny.

As I mentioned earlier, Dr. Singh often gives the following instructions to people who come to him for healing: "Rewrite your story." The purpose of these instructions is not just to help these individuals see the events of their lives from a more detached perspective. In rewriting their story, they actually reshape the past.

"We say that certain events are in the past because we are caught up in the idea of linear time," Dr. Singh once told me. "When you realize that time is actually circular and not linear, you discover that the events of the past are still unfolding. Saying that these events are in 'the past' does not even make any sense because they have not passed at all."

Hearing this, I wondered about the relationship of the past and present. "Can we change these events?" I asked.

"Yes," he replied. "That is called forgiveness."

I had always thought of forgiveness as something you do for yourself. If you are hurt by something that happened to you in the past, then you are perpetuating the pain, replaying the events of the past so that they continue to exert an effect on you in the present. In essence, you imprison yourself in a cycle of pain that continues to play itself out endlessly.

By forgiving those who have hurt you with their words and actions, you free yourself from that prison. Your memory of the past no longer controls you. When you are able to forgive, you regain power over your emotions. You stop reliving the pain and reopening old wounds. Forgiveness lets you revisit the past without being attached to it.

Although this transformation is beneficial, Dr. Singh would say that it is not enough. The kind of forgiveness that Chanters seek to practice is intended to create balance in the hearts and minds of both the injured and the injurers. Those who hurt others, especially with the intention of doing harm, end up hurting themselves in much more serious ways. As Chanters, it is our responsibility to minimize or even eliminate the damage created by such actions.

From a karmic perspective, every action is linked to a consequence and vice versa. The things that happen to you in the present are the consequences of your past actions. When you are harmed or injured, you are repaying a karmic debt. Any individuals who set out to harm you are taking on your karma. They are acting as healers, albeit accidental ones. Without realizing it, they are sacrificing their own spiritual well-being for yours.

Forgiveness minimizes the destructive repercussions of past

actions. At a karmic level, the past is not set in stone; it is more like cooling lava. Even years after a volcanic eruption, lava continues to cool. Although it may seem solid on the surface, the underlying layers are still molten. If you drill down far enough, you will see hot red lava that is still flowing.

The forgiveness we practice acts like a torch, radiating an intense heat that keeps the past from solidifying into a particular version of the present. By forgiving even those who have perpetrated the greatest atrocities against humanity, we can save them—and everyone else—from the devastating consequences of their actions. It is as if we have strapped ourselves into our time machines, traveled into the past, and altered the course of world events.

Imagine having the power to rewrite history. Forgiveness as taught by the Masters and practiced by spiritual people throughout the world has been the single greatest tool for averting planetary disasters. When offered in the spirit of love and compassion, the quality of forgiveness acts like an enormous karmic eraser that minimizes the impact of past actions.

That is why the Prayer of St. Francis puts such great emphasis on forgiveness. The prayer reads:

Lord, make me an instrument of your peace.
Where there is hatred, let me sow love.
Where there is injury, let me sow pardon.
Where there is doubt, let me sow faith.
Where there is despair, let me sow hope.
Where there is darkness, let me sow light.
Where there is sadness, let me sow joy.
O, Master, grant that I may not so much seek,
To be consoled as to console.
To be understood as to understand.
To be loved as to love.
For it is in giving that we receive.
It is in pardoning that we are pardoned.
It is in dying that we are born to eternal life.

St. Francis understood that forgiveness is the key to creating peace, both in oneself and in the world. This is why he prays, "Where there is injury, let me sow pardon." But he also states, "It is in pardoning that we are pardoned." This shows that there are two aspects of forgiveness. Although the ability to forgive others is important, the ability to seek forgiveness is equally important.

Two months after meeting Dr. Singh, I had a dream in which three of my ex-girlfriends confronted me seeking an apology for the pain I had caused them. When I described the dream to Dr. Singh, he asked, "Did you apologize?"

"Oh yes," I replied. "I am very sorry for any pain I caused them. It was never my intention to hurt anyone."

He smiled but his words were stern. "It does not matter what you intended to do," he said. "The fact of the matter is that you hurt them. Now, you need to take the blame."

In the short time I had known Dr. Singh, I had heard him use that phrase on several occasions. "Take the blame," he would tell us, "even if you feel that you were not at fault."

I had tried doing this once. A visitor who had come into our kitchen at the Conservatory to help clean up after a meal had broken a glass coffee pot accidentally. I knew that the coffee drinkers, including Dr. Singh himself, would feel the loss of this particular coffee pot, which went with the only working coffee maker we had in Sonora. Rather than letting our visitor take the blame, I apologized to Dr. Singh for having broken it and offered to buy a replacement. He accepted my apology and my offer without saying a word, but I knew that he understood what was happening.

Afterwards, I began to realize why Dr. Singh was so insistent that we take the blame. By doing so, we create a climate in which forgiveness can take place. Many people find the practice of forgiveness especially challenging because they have a hard time letting go of their pain. Knowing the importance of forgiveness, we Chanters must do what we can to facilitate the process.

When I told him about my dream, Dr. Singh suggested that I contact my ex-girlfriends and apologize to them. By taking the blame for what had gone wrong in these relationships and by forgiving them completely for any pain they may have caused me, I would be able to remove some of the karmic burden from these women. Even if they were never able to forgive me or to own up to anything they had done, they would reap the benefits of my actions.

The word forgive means to "give away." If it were spelled foregive, it would mean to "give beforehand." In a way, both of these meanings are implied in the spiritual concept of forgiveness. You give away your love and compassion freely, and you do so before it is asked of you. If you practice true forgiveness, nobody will ever need to ask you for it because there will be no temptation for you to hold anything back. After all, why would you want to withhold something as powerful as this? If you have a tool at your disposal that can improve the quality of life in the present by minimizing the negative impact of the past, you are going to want to use it.

Key #7: Selfless Service

When patients come to see Dr. Singh at the Conservatory, he often asks Band members to conduct ceremonies that will support and augment the healing work he is doing. In these ceremonies, we direct our love and compassion to the patients in service not only to them but also to the Big Beautiful Spirit acting through us. Each of us realizes that we are not healers per se but simply instruments through which healing may occur.

The first healing ceremony in which I ever participated was for a patient named Doña Carmen, who had suffered a massive heart attack three weeks earlier. She and her family had been coming to see Dr. Singh for years and had developed strong ties to all of the Band members. When Doña Carmen arrived at the Conservatory, she was so weak that her family had to carry her into Dr. Singh's office. The grayish pallor of her skin revealed the severity of her condition. There was little doubt in my mind that she was dying.

Dr. Singh told us that Doña Carmen was at risk for a second heart attack, which her body would not be able to withstand. He said that if we did not take action immediately, she would be dead in a matter of weeks. The only way to help her, he claimed, was to perform a miracle.

"Through our love for Doña Carmen, we can heal her," Dr. Singh said. "The way we are going to do this is by taking the pain and damage from her heart into our own."

When I heard these words, I began to panic. Although Doña Carmen seemed like a nice person and I could see how my fellow Chanters loved her, I was not ready to sacrifice my health for hers. *What if I succeeded at doing what Dr. Singh had asked of us? I would end up damaging my own heart to help save the life of a perfect stranger.*

I took Dr. Singh aside and asked, "How do I protect myself?"

He gave me a puzzled look. "What do you mean?"

"I don't want to injure my heart," I whispered, with some embarrassment. I wondered why I felt so uncomfortable admitting that I was concerned about my own welfare. Maybe it felt a little selfish. Instead of asking how I could help Doña Carmen, I was worried about myself.

Then Dr. Singh said something that took me by surprise. "For healing to occur, we have to be willing to lay down our lives for the other person," he said. "This may be the first time you have ever met Doña Carmen, but that doesn't matter. She has come to us for help, and we have to be willing to serve her."

"But can we serve her without killing ourselves?" I questioned.

"The only purpose of our lives is to be of service," he replied. "This means giving ourselves completely to those we serve, even to the point of sacrificing our lives for theirs."

This challenged my most basic assumptions about how the world works. From earliest childhood, I was taught that my life was the most precious possession I have, and that it should be protected at all cost. My parents taught me that caution is a virtue: looking both ways before crossing the street, keeping metal objects out of electric outlets, and turning down offers of candy from strangers. Now, it seemed that Dr. Singh was asking me to throw caution to the wind.

Eventually, I realized that Dr. Singh was saying something much more subtle. He was letting me know that caution has to have a reason. It is not enough to keep yourself alive simply for the sake of being alive. The point of protecting yourself is to live long enough to do some good.

According to Dr. Singh, the biggest waste of life happens when you keep it to yourself. A life that is not of service to others is not worth living—or protecting. Such a life is empty and unfulfilled. As a human being, your life is not yours to keep. By the time of your death, you will be stripped of everything you have anyway, including your life. That is why it is better to give your life away than to have it taken from you.

What is the difference? Either way, it seems, you lose your life. But that is not the case. You cannot lose something you never owned. Life is a gift. It comes from a mysterious source and returns to that source eventually. Each of us is granted the opportunity to experience and enjoy life for a brief period of time. When the time comes, you and I will have no choice but to let go. That is the nature of death.

You can either struggle with death or you can make peace with it. Those who view death as an adversary to be battled are doomed to fight a pointless war that they will eventually lose. The news media reflect this viewpoint in the way they report death: "The famous movie star lost his battle with cancer last night at the age of 76."

Dr. Singh offers a very different perspective on death. To him, death is to be embraced as a friend and ally. He refers to "Sister Death" as a beautiful yet enigmatic entity that has great wisdom to share. Through her, each of us learns the meaning of selflessness. Sister Death demands that each of us approach her only after we have been stripped of all our attachments, including our attachment to life itself. If we can do this while we are still living, rather than waiting until we have taken our last breath, we can create a partnership with Sister Death that allows us to serve the needs of others.

As Chanters, the primary service we provide involves the process of healing. Our partnership with Sister Death facilitates this process in a number of ways. In the case of physical illness, only Sister Death can determine who will live and who will die, but there is much more to healing than that. Chanters can have an effect on the quality of death, as well as the quality of life. A dying person can be healed and die nonetheless. In fact, this is not uncommon.

Healing and death can coexist because healing is not the same as curing, which is simply the restoration of an original state of health. Healing goes far beyond that; it involves the creation of wholeness and balance. The word heal comes from the same root as whole. When we take part in healing, we create a sense of wholeness in ourselves. This requires stepping out of our bubble and into the flow of pure love, where there is nothing but wholeness.

All healing is self-healing because we cannot impose wholeness on anyone but ourselves. To facilitate healing in someone else, all we can do is to empty ourselves of all our attachments so that we are like a hollow pipe through which pure love can flow. This is our act of selfless service. We become a hole so that someone else can become whole. By letting go of everything we have and everything we know, we experience a form of death. In essence, we are sacrificing ourselves for the benefit of others.

When you allow yourself to die in this way, you will find that death is not such a bad thing after all. In fact, it may be the best thing that has ever happened to you. Not only do you get to experience holiness; you also get the opportunity to act as an instrument of healing for those in need.

"There is no other way to exist," Dr. Singh told me recently. "If I could not give my life in service to others, I would not want to live. What would be the point?"

No matter what you decide to do with your life, you end up devoting it to something. You can choose to devote your life to your work, your family, recreation, politics, travel or any number of things. If you are unable to choose, then you devote your life to indecision.

Some choose to devote their lives to a cause. "I only regret that I have but one life to give for my country," said American patriot Nathan Hale as he was about to be hanged by the British. Others, like Jack London, devote their lives to the spirit of adventure: "I would rather be ashes than dust; I would rather that my spark should burn out in a brilliant blaze than it should be stifled by dry-rot; I would rather be in a superb meteor, every atom of me in magnificent glow than in a sleepy and permanent planet; the proper function of man is to live, not to exist."

As Chanters, we choose a path of selfless service. D. H. Lawrence wrote, "Life is ours to be spent, not to be saved." I can think of no better way to spend my life than in helping those who seek healing. To me, the ultimate form of healing is enlightenment. I am happy to devote my life to the enlightenment of others. If I can be an instrument through which another entity experiences enlightenment, then my life's mission will be fulfilled.

Opening the Temple

The more you apply these Seven Keys to your life, the more you will free yourself from your bubble. Eventually, everything you feel and do will be imbued with a sense of holiness. And if your destiny is to pursue the path of a Chanter, you will find that your chanting practice will become supercharged. Every time you chant, you will gain access to your inner temple and to the power locked away inside of it. Within this temple, healing and enlightenment are more than just ideals to which you aspire; they become the fundamental realities of your existence. So does the multidimensional universe that will open itself to you.

There is one catch, though: You have to leave your identity behind. The power contained in the inner temple belongs to the Big Beautiful Spirit, not to you. To access this power, you have to merge your consciousness—at least temporarily—with the Big Beautiful Spirit. This does not mean that you become the Big Beautiful Spirit. It is actually the other way around.

One of the chants that I sing on a daily basis has the following words:

I know God knows I know,
That I am a wave on this ocean.
I am a wave on the ocean of God.

This chant puts things in perspective for me. Modern spiritual writings are filled with affirmations such as: "I am God." But these statements are subject to misinterpretation and can actually reinforce the bubble by feeding our ego. By chanting the words, "I am a wave on the ocean of God," I remind myself that I am simply a vessel through which the Big Beautiful Spirit moves. In truth, it would be more accurate to say that "God is me" rather than "I am God."

When you live your life in accordance with the Seven Keys, there is nothing but God in you. Through the practice of detachment, compassion, serenity, humility, forgiveness, selfless service, and unconditional love, you let go of everything that has ever kept you from really knowing and experiencing the Big Beautiful Spirit within yourself. You surrender to the Big Beautiful Spirit so that it can work through you. And that is when you step effortlessly into your inner temple.

Among the many chants that Yogananda composed throughout his life, one of my favorites is entitled, "Who is in My Temple?" This chant describes the process by which one gains access to the inner temple:

Who is in my temple?
All the doors do open themselves;
All the lights do light themselves.
Darkness like a dark bird,
Flies away, oh, flies away.

There is a reason this chant begins with the question: *Who is in my temple?* This question assumes that whoever is in my temple is not me. I cannot enter this temple—at least not the "I" that is defined by my bubble. To enter, each of us has to leave our entire self-concept at the door. This includes everything we have come to know and believe about ourselves. If we succeed at leaving our entire identity behind, then the question remains: *Who is in my temple?*

Someone or something in us will manage to reach the inner temple if we practice the Seven Keys and use chanting as our vehicle. That, of course, is the Big Beautiful Spirit within us. To melt into the Big Beautiful Spirit and to allow our consciousness to merge with it is the best feeling in the world. All of our striving stops. As the chant states, "All the doors do open themselves; all the lights do light themselves."

According to Yogananda, the doors that open are the chakras, which are the centers of divine consciousness in our bodies and the gateways to enlightenment. The lights that light themselves are the pure energy and consciousness that move through our chakras, creating the experience of enlightenment in us. By immersing ourselves in our chanting practice and living by the Seven Keys, we pull ourselves out of the bubble. Once we do that, the process of enlightenment happens on its own. All we have to do is to allow ourselves to melt into the flow of divine love that is the Big Beautiful Spirit.

When that happens, "Darkness like a dark bird flies away." We begin practicing the Seven Keys in order to free ourselves of all the things that have weighed us down, including our attachments, our unproductive emotions, and our sense of separateness. Eventually, the process builds enough momentum that all of these things just fall away. They leave us like a dark bird flying away from us.

Through the power of our intention, we can initiate this chain reaction, not just in ourselves but in everyone we encounter. The life of a Chanter is really a charmed existence. Imagine living in a way that fulfills your true spiritual purpose, which is to bring enlightenment and healing to everything you touch. What does this way of life look like? How do you fulfill your spiritual purpose while meeting the responsibilities of the "real" world? When you find the answers to these questions, you will take your ideal existence from the realm of imagination and transform it into reality. And this is exactly what you are about to do.

CHAPTER 5

24/7

There are different ways to pursue your spiritual path. You can treat it as a hobby, something at which you dabble in your free time. Or you can treat it as a job, something at which you work for a certain period every day. But for a Chanter, spirituality is a different matter altogether: It is who we are. That is why Dr. Singh likes to talk about it being "24/7."

For him, this is not merely talk. Dr. Singh lives his spiritual path every moment of every day. I have called him in the middle of the night with one personal crisis or another, and he has been there for me. When I apologize for disturbing him, he says, "My friend, I am honored and happy to have this opportunity to serve you."

Through his actions and his words, Dr. Singh has taught me that the Seven Keys are not just a set of pie-in-the-sky ideals but rather the roadmap for a truly spiritual life. The trick is to put these ideals into practice in everything you do. You only become a Chanter by walking the talk, living as consistently as you can in accordance with your spiritual ideals.

That is not an easy thing to do. Once you jump into this path, you are faced with the constant question of how to live a truly spiritual life. The reason this question never ends is that you have the challenge of transforming each minute of each hour of each day into something sacred. In a sense, every Chanter is an artist, and our lives are the art form we practice.

As I have taken on this challenge in my own life, Dr. Singh has offered very little input. He has only given me a few basic guidelines related to the specifics of my spiritual life. I have had to figure out the rest on my own. You will have to do the same. This means finding ways to align everything you do with your spiritual path. In your everyday life, you will need to become mindful of how you eat, sleep, exercise, have sex, earn a living, form relationships, spend money, and do even the simplest and most mundane things, like driving a car or cleaning a bathroom. Each aspect of your life must have a spiritual purpose and must benefit others in some way.

Nobody can tell you how to do this. Every Chanter's life is different. All I can do is to share with you the decisions I have made in my own life. I hope that you know enough about me by now to realize that I am far from perfect. Some of what I will be sharing here are my mistakes and the distractions that have kept me from living this path 24/7. In no way am I trying to set myself up as a role model for you. There are far better role models out there. Just look at the life of a true spiritual Master such as Jesus or Gandhi.

I have given a great deal of thought to the details of my daily life, which include everything from the time I wake up in the morning until I go to bed at night, and even what happens while I am asleep. My intention is to make sure that everything I do has a spiritual purpose. Those are high standards, and I do not always live up to them. But when I veer off course, I manage to find my way back. I will describe for you the elements of my typical day in order to show you how I have chosen to integrate the guidelines that Dr. Singh has taught me and how I deal with the obstacles and distractions that I have had to face at times. In sharing these details, I offer merely a starting point from which you can begin shaping your own life as a Chanter.

Starting the Day

As I discussed in Chapter 2, I begin the day every morning by thanking the Big Beautiful Spirit, my own spirit, and the Masters for their guidance. Then, I close any connections from the previous day so that I can open new ones. Once I re-open my connection to my sources of guidance (see p. 88), I am ready to begin my morning exercises and meditation.

Dr. Singh has recommended that I begin the day with yoga and Tai Chi. If done properly, both of these practices have the power to facilitate the experience of holiness. Besides their spiritual significance, they have other benefits as well: Yoga maintains physical flexibility, and Tai Chi insures a smooth flow of energy throughout the body.

When I began looking for a yoga routine that I could do, I consulted with Carmina, who has been practicing yoga for many years. She recommended starting out with the set of postures taught by Ram Das in his classic book, *Be Here Now* (you can find these postures in the section entitled "Asanas," at the back of the book). This turned out to be an excellent recommendation. Although I have altered the routine at times to keep things fresh and to tailor it to my own physical and spiritual needs, the postures taught by Ram Das are as good a starting point as any.

I have yet to learn Tai Chi, but I do perform a set of exercises designed to move and to build energy in the body. These are the Energization Exercises developed by Yogananda and taught by his organization, the Self-Realization Fellowship. The primary purpose of the exercises is to recharge the body with energy, although they also have the effect of strengthening the muscles and purifying the bloodstream. When doing these exercises, you alternate between tensing the muscles, one at a time, and then relaxing them.

An additional benefit of the Energization Exercises is that they are an effective form of muscle relaxation. When you apply tension slowly to a muscle and then release it, the muscle relaxes. It compensates for the tension you apply to it by returning to a more relaxed state than the one in which it started.

The more relaxed your muscles are, the easier it is to sit in meditation. That is why I begin my morning meditation practice immediately after doing these exercises. Dr. Singh's only prescription for meditating is to "just melt." He maintains that techniques can get in the way of the experience of holiness that happens during genuine moments of meditation. And yet, I must admit that certain meditation techniques have been extremely helpful in facilitating such experiences for me. The important thing for me is not to become too attached to any one technique or to let my meditation practice fall into a monotonous routine.

I remind myself constantly that meditation should be a joy and not a chore. It is my opportunity to experience at least a taste of holiness every day. What could be better than that? As I become more adept at it, I find that I am able to penetrate deeper and to stay longer in my inner temple. I also am able to receive clearer signals from the Masters during meditation. Plus, the experience of holiness that I have when sitting in meditation carries over to the rest of my day.

In my mind, there is an important distinction to be made between the practice of meditation and the experience of it. If you can just melt at will, then every moment becomes a meditation, permeated with a sense of holiness. But chances are that you have not gotten to that point in your spiritual development yet. I can tell you quite honestly that I have not, although I feel myself creeping ever closer.

I have invested a great deal of thought and care into the design of my meditation space. In my bedroom, I have an alcove that was once a closet. There, I have built a small altar on which I keep the following items: images of the Masters, a bundle of sage, two candle holders, and a number of objects that have spiritual significance for me, including shells, feathers and rocks. Rather than sitting on a cushion, which is too soft to support my back properly, I use an old tape deck covered with a piece of carpeting. I find this to be the perfect meditation bench. It has just the right amount of firmness to allow me to sit for extended periods of time if I choose. The height, which is five inches, creates just the right angle to take pressure off my lower back.

I begin my meditation practice each morning by smudging myself and my meditation space with sage. You may be familiar with the practice of smudging as a way of cleansing or purifying a space, but the burning of sage goes much deeper than that. The smoke released by the sage reminds us of the impermanence of physical reality. As the sage burns, it is transformed from a solid into a sweet-smelling smoke. This smoke is symbolic of the Big Beautiful Spirit. It blends into everything it touches, thus turning the entire space into something sacred. Of course, the space was never anything but sacred, except perhaps in our minds. The only thing that the sage transforms is the consciousness of those who burn it.

Immediately after smudging, I chant each of the following Sanskrit syllables one time: OM, AH, and HUM. In Buddhist teaching, these syllables have the power to purify our actions, speech, and thought, respectively. When I chant OM, I place my ring finger on my third eye. For AH, I touch my throat chakra, and for HUM, my heart chakra.

I follow this with two prayers that Dr. Singh has encouraged us to use in the various ceremonies we perform. He refers to the recitation of these prayers as "opening the Four Corners." In Native American tradition, the Four Corners or Four Directions represent the four great powers of the Medicine Wheel. To the North is found wisdom. The South symbolizes innocence and trust. The West corresponds to our introspective nature, and the East is the place of illumination. In opening the Four Corners, we invoke each of these powers and invite them into our circle.

First, I recite a variation of a traditional Native American prayer:

Oh Big Beautiful Spirit, whose voice I hear in the wind, and whose breath gives life to all the world, hear me. I come before you, one of your children. I am small and weak; I need your strength and wisdom. Let me walk in beauty and make my eyes ever behold the red and purple sunset. Make my hands respect the things you have made, my ears sharp to hear your voice. Make me wise so I may know the things you have taught my people, the lessons you have hidden in every leaf and rock. I seek strength— not to be superior to my brothers and sisters but to be able to fight my greatest enemy: myself. Make me ever ready to come to you with clean hands and straight eyes so when life fades, as a fading sunset, my spirit may come to you without shame.

Those of us involved in healing work can add the following lines to the prayer:

Of course, it was not I who healed, but the powers from the outer world, and the visions and the ceremonies had only made me like a hole through which the power could come to the two-legged and the four-legged. If I thought it were myself doing the healing, the hole would disappear and no power would come through it.

In the past year, Dr. Singh has asked us to add a Buddhist prayer to our opening invocation. This prayer, which is called "The Eight Thoughts of a Great Being," was brought to our attention by my dear friend and spiritual brother, Mr. Bone. It reads:

Through the power of the compassionate truth of the Supreme Refuges, and through the root of virtuous action, and through pure noble motivation, may I alone, by my own efforts, dispel the sufferings of all beings who pervade space.

Through the excellence of virtuous activity in this world and beyond it, may I fulfill the hopes and desires of beings just as they conceive them.

May my body, flesh, blood, skin and all the rest of me benefit all sentient beings in appropriate ways.

May the sufferings of beings, my old mothers, dissolve into me; may my happiness and virtue be obtained by them.

As long as the world remains, may there not arise in my mind, even for an instant, the thought of harming others.

May I exert myself diligently in benefiting beings, not letting up for even a moment because of sadness, fatigue or anything similar.

May I be able to give effortlessly whatever enjoyment is desired by all beings who are thirsty, hungry, needy, or poor.

May I take upon myself the great burdens, the difficult-to-endure sufferings of beings in hell and the other realms, and may they be liberated.

In the first stanza of this prayer, the phrase "Supreme Refuges" refers to the Three Refuges of Buddhism, which are: the Buddha, the Dharma, and the Sangha. As a Chanter, I have my own interpretation of these Refuges—an interpretation that may not coincide with the tenets of Buddhism. For me, the Buddha refers to the Big Beautiful Spirit that resides in each of us. The Dharma is the set of teachings that make up our spiritual path. And the Sangha is our spiritual community. For me, that community includes members of Global Chant, the Sound Circle, and all of my fellow Chanters everywhere.

Dr. Singh has told us that the "Eight Thoughts of a Great Being" is one of the most powerful prayers we can say because it aligns us with our true spiritual purpose as Chanters. Just by reciting or hearing the words of this prayer, we become accountable because it holds us to the highest standards in terms of how we live our lives. Dr. Singh would say that if we can live up to these standards, we are carrying out our mission as Chanters.

Once I have completed my invocation by reciting the appropriate prayers, I am ready to begin meditating. As I have already mentioned, Dr. Singh offers no formula or technique for the practice of meditation. He has never given me any instruction except to "just melt." Sometimes, I can carry out this instruction just by closing my eyes and remaining silent. At other times, I need a little more help than that.

One of the most effective tools I have found is the simple Hindu mantra: MA OM. In Hinduism, MA is divine love and OM is the divine light of consciousness. You can use this mantra by chanting MA to yourself as you breathe in and OM as you breathe out. As you breathe in, you envision the entire universe entering through your heart chakra and filling you; and as you breathe out, you envision your consciousness being ejected from your body through your crown chakra at the top of your head and being dispersed into the universe.

When you use this technique, you are emptying yourself so that you can be filled by the divine love that permeates the universe. This is how I understand the process of melting. The mantra and the breathing are just aids in this process. They are training wheels for those of us learning to "just melt." As soon as we learn to do it on our own, the wheels can come off.

I want to stress to you that there is nothing special about this technique. If you become attached to it, you miss the point. Rumi wrote:

Test your love-wings and make them strong.
Forget the idea of religious ladders.
Love is the roof. Your senses are waterspouts.
Drink rain directly off the roof.
Waterspouts are easily damaged
and often must be replaced.

The idea is to open yourself up to the flow of divine love and then to merge with that flow. This is where holiness resides. As Rumi reminds us, anything we use that gets us to that point is a mere tool or crutch—even our own senses. Ultimately, we have to make the connection in the most direct way possible. If love is the roof, then we need to drink rain directly off the roof, which means that we have to find holiness without depending on anything to get us there except our own hearts and spirits.

I continue to chant MA OM until I can feel the melting start to happen. Or I may use another chant in its place. Here is a chant that I use on a regular basis and that I find particularly effective:

I am Love, I am, OM,
I am Love, I am.
Dancing in the sky,
Melting in a stream.

After chanting it for a few minutes, I sit in complete stillness and silence, just soaking up the experience of holiness that washes over me. There is no minimum or maximum time limit on the meditation. I stay in that experience for as long as my heart desires and my body is able to sit still. Then I shift to the next phase of the meditation, in which I share the blessings that I am receiving.

One of the ways that I do this is through the practice of kriya yoga, which I learned through the Self-Realization Fellowship. Because this organization has a policy of swearing students to secrecy about the practice, I cannot share it with you. To learn it, you will need to contact the Self-Realization Fellowship directly. This organization offers a one-year home-study course that culminates in kriya yoga initiation.

A similar practice that is just as effective and less secretive is that of Tonglin. This Tibetan Buddhist technique, which was taught to me by Mr. Bone, combines breathing with visualization. The essence of the practice is to breathe in the suffering of others and to breathe out healing, compassion, and unconditional love.

When I have completed my kriya yoga or Tonglin practice, I am ready to close the meditation. At this point, I offer a prayer of thanks to the Big Beautiful Spirit for all the blessings that have been bestowed upon me, including the guidance of the Masters and the other entities looking out for me. Then I set the following intentions:

Bless everyone in my life.

Let me be an instrument of healing for those with whom I come in contact today, directly or indirectly. Let me be a conduit, Big Beautiful Spirit, through which you give them what they need and take from them what they don't need.

Fill my heart so that I may know you in every moment and everything.

Let me attain enlightenment in this lifetime and let me help others on their path of enlightenment.

Give me the clarity to find my mission in life, and the courage and focus to carry out that mission.

Remove any obstacles on my path so that I may help others remove obstacles from theirs.

I close the meditation with the Hindu chant: OM SHANTI SHANTI SHANTIHI. The word shanti simply means "peace." This chant is a call for peace to prevail throughout the universe, starting with ourselves.

Exercise and Nutrition

As Chanters, we understand the importance of taking care of our bodies. The body is the vehicle through which we serve others. Although it is a beautiful and sacred vehicle, it is also limited in terms of how much it can do and how much energy it can hold. We try to expand those limits so that we can be more effective teachers, healers, and spiritual servants.

One of Dr. Singh's favorite sayings is, "Give your body more exercise than it wants and less food than it wants." This saying holds the basic principles upon which I have built my own exercise and nutrition plan. If you want to increase your physical health, you simply exercise more and eat less. Of course, the kind of exercise you do and the types of food you eat make a difference.

For me, exercise has always been a matter not just of physical health but of mental health. It relaxes me, increases my energy level, helps me sleep well, dissipates any stress I may be feeling, and keeps my mood consistently high. In the last few years, it has also become a form of meditation for me. When I am exercising, I sometimes lose myself in the physical movements I am performing.

Although I am not a fitness expert, I am aware of the three main physical health benefits of exercise, which are: strength, flexibility, and heart health. I try to address each of these in my exercise program, making sure that I stretch and do yoga every day to increase flexibility and that I do aerobic workouts and weight training on alternating days to strengthen my heart as well as the other muscles of my body.

Many people—especially women—are resistant to weight training. All I can say, in response to this resistance, is that the benefits are too great not to do it. First of all, if done properly, weight training is an opportunity to become more attuned to the muscles of the body, which are wondrous in their capacity for adaptation and growth. Dr. Lawrence Golding, an exercise physiologist at the University of Nevada, describes this capacity as follows: "If you have a 10-horsepower motor and you subject it to a 12-horsepower load, it will burn out. But when you have a human body that is the equivalent of a 10-horsepower motor and you subject it to a 12-horsepower load, it eventually becomes a 12-horsepower motor."

Weight training can also increase longevity, lower stress levels, prevent back pain, improve posture, and even reduce the risk of mood disorders and dementia. Many of the physical health problems associated with old age can be attributed to muscle atrophy. Loss of muscle strength and flexibility is probably a contributor to a number of ailments, including respiratory problems. As the muscles that surround the ribcage become weaker, the capacity of the lungs to expand and fill is reduced. This means less oxygen to the body, which also means that our organs are being deprived of nourishment and—ultimately—life.

If we are going to take our mission as Chanters seriously, we need to be healthy enough to carry out the demands of our assignments, whatever they may be. As the "Eight Thoughts" prayer reminds us, we cannot let up "for even a moment because of sadness, fatigue or anything similar." This means maintaining high energy levels in the body. To do this, we may need to push ourselves to do more exercise than the body wants. This is a matter both of discipline and of patience. The patience comes in knowing that once we start to exercise—even if we have to go against our own inertia to do it—the process becomes enjoyable. Ultimately, the human body appreciates movement, activity, and pushing against resistance, as long as it is not being injured or damaged by these activities.

The second factor in energizing the body is proper nutrition. As you know, the modern diet offers a deadly combination of too many calories and too little nourishment. This produces a body weighed down by excess fat, and at the same time, depleted of basic nutrients. In his instruction to "give the body less food than it wants," Dr. Singh is not suggesting that we starve ourselves. We are already doing that if our diet consists of food that comes out of a box, a can, a freezer, or a drive-through window. When the body fails to get what it needs, it craves more food.

Lowering your food consumption is simple: Just eat fresh fruits and vegetables, whole grains, legumes such as peas and beans, and raw nuts. Replace processed foods with ones that are either raw or freshly prepared, and make sure that as much of your diet as possible is organic or at least pesticide-free. If you do this, you will find that you just eat less.

This is not that surprising, really. There is only so much organic broccoli that I can eat, for instance, and I actually like broccoli. The body does not require very much of the foods that provide the nourishment it needs. On the other hand, many people can consume a bag of cookies, a quart of ice cream, or a half-gallon of soda in a sitting because their bodies are not satisfied. In binging on these foods, they are responding to their body's call for nutrients that the foods themselves lack.

Ultimately, what our bodies seek is life force. We can obtain it from the foods we eat, but there are more direct sources. All the plants and animals that we consume have derived their vitality—directly or indirectly—from the sun. A few minutes of sensible sun exposure every day can increase the energy levels in our bodies. So can spiritual practices, such as the Energization Exercises mentioned earlier, that connect us to the ultimate source of our life force: the Big Beautiful Spirit.

Throughout history, there have been documented cases of Masters who have lived without eating. These Masters have found ways to derive all their vitality directly from the source. Recently, Dr. Singh said to me, "Eating is so primitive, because digestion is slow and some foods contain toxins. At the same time that they nourish us, these foods also poison our bodies. But most humans rely on eating because it is the only option they know."

The point is not that you should forego eating altogether. It is to remember the reason we eat, which is to sustain our vitality so that we can improve the quality and extend the duration of our lives. In doing so, we become more effective in carrying out our mission as Chanters; we gain more energy, which allows us to tackle ever greater challenges in our spiritual lives and to be better servants for those who are suffering.

Sex and Relationships

One day, while the Band members were sitting around the table in Sonora having lunch, Dr. Singh dropped a bomb on us. Looking at each of us intently, he said, "Give your body as much sex as it wants." This message was so important that he made me repeat it. The reason I found this piece of advice so surprising is that it goes against spiritual teachings I have found from other sources. Most spiritual teachers seem to encourage the suppression of sexual impulses. For instance, Yogananda taught that the animal instincts—particularly the sex drive—interferes with our spiritual advancement.

When I asked him about it, Dr. Singh replied, "Many Masters end up modifying or adapting their teachings about sexuality when they come to the West because they know that people in this society have a hard time understanding the real relationship of sex and spirituality."

"What is that relationship?" I wondered.

"Sex has the power to create new streams of love," he said. "There is a reason that people use the term 'lovemaking' to describe it. Sex is one of the few ways you can add love to the flow that is already there."

"How do you do that?"

"You make sure that you only have sex for spiritual purposes."

I walked away from that conversation confused. In my mind, I could not reconcile the two different pieces of information that Dr. Singh had given me. On the one hand, he said to give your body as much sex as it wants. On the other hand, he added that you should only use sex for spiritual purposes. I asked myself: *How can you do both?*

For me, this was much more than just a philosophical question. When I began to discover my sexuality as a teenager, I also found that my appetite for sex was practically insatiable. Although I lost my virginity relatively late, at the age of 20, I soon made up for lost time. Several of my ex-lovers have admitted to me that they found my need for sex overwhelming at times. At least a few of my relationships have ended because of what I can only term as "sexual incompatibility."

As I have gotten older, I have become a little less persistent but not because of any decrease in my physical desire for sex. I have had to tone down my sex drive because it began to feel like a wild beast that had broken out of its cage and run amok. Every aspect of my life has been impacted adversely at one time or another by this beast. Besides my relationships, it has had a limiting effect on my career, my community involvement, my social life, and—most importantly—my spiritual practice.

In truth, I have had a love-hate relationship with my sexuality. It is through sex that I first experienced moments of holiness. And yet, I also resonated with spiritual teachings that treated sex as a distraction. The more immersed I became in my spiritual life, the more strongly I believed that I needed to redirect my sexual energy. I would find myself thinking of a statement that the Indian spiritual teacher, Ramakrishna, once made to his students: "If you spent one tenth of the time you devoted to distractions like chasing women...to spiritual practice, you would be enlightened in a few years!"

It was just a matter of learning to harness this energy, I would tell myself. But when I tried to suppress my impulses, they only grew bigger. Every time I would even think about celibacy, I would end up going on a sexual binge of some sort. The intense pleasure of these experiences was always followed by an emotional letdown and feelings of self-recrimination.

Obviously, this strategy was not working for me. By the time I met Dr. Singh, my runaway sex drive had become the central issue in my life. During our first lengthy conversation, when Dr. Singh asked me to identify the biggest obstacle on my spiritual path, I was prepared to tell him about the "sex thing." At the last minute, I gave in to my feelings of embarrassment and talked about my ego instead. Based on the way he reacted to my response, I could tell that he knew the real answer without me saying it. But he never mentioned it until months later.

After Dr. Singh offered his paradoxical insights into the relationship of sex and spirituality, I tried to reconcile his two statements. How do I give my body all the sex it wants and still use sex only for spiritual purposes? Sitting in a quiet place, I asked the Masters for clarity. They told me that the body is a messenger. When it sends a signal of sexual desire, it lets you know that there is an opportunity at hand to serve a spiritual purpose. But just because the opportunity exists does not mean that you will make the most of it.

How you respond to sexual impulses depends entirely on your power of discernment. As a Chanter, you need to ask yourself, "Does this really have a spiritual purpose or is it just an excuse to gratify my desire?" Dr. Singh points out that the decisions a Chanter makes in these situations will only be valid if they are based on spiritual guidance.

I am learning how to tune into my guidance in these situations. The tricky part is that I have to be open to what the Masters tell me as opposed to just hearing what I want. Desire is such a powerful force that it can cloud judgment and breed attachment. I know that I can become so wrapped up in my own needs and desires that I am willing to overlook everything else— even to the point of deceiving myself into thinking that I am fulfilling a spiritual purpose when I am not.

For me, the task of creating detachment when it comes to sex and relationships is so enormous that it feels impossible at times. Dr. Singh has helped me see the ideal way to be in relationships, which is to enter them only when there is a clear spiritual purpose and to walk away from them when that purpose is complete, with no longing or remorse. By "spiritual purpose," he means that you are serving the needs of the spirit, acting in ways that move yourself and others in the direction of healing and enlightenment.

Three months after returning from Oaxaca, I experienced this sense of purpose in a relationship when I began seeing Cassady. This 31-year-old wanderer was everything I could ever want in a lover and companion: She was intelligent, sweet, beautiful, funny, thoughtful, and genuinely spiritual. From the first time I talked with Cassady, I felt intense love for her. This was not like anything I had ever experienced before. Every time I looked into her face, heard her voice, smelled her scent, or watched her do even the most mundane thing, my heart would open and I would just melt.

Being around her had the effect of drawing me into the experience of holiness. Although I was becoming increasingly familiar with holiness at this point in my training, I had mostly experienced it on my own, or at least independently of other people. In all of my relationships—even the most casual sexual flings—I had been seeking a connection with the Big Beautiful Spirit. There were always moments of holiness, but they were fleeting. With Cassady, I was connecting to the Big Beautiful Spirit virtually every time I was in her presence.

The second time we met, we were professing our love for each other. A month later, we started a sexual relationship, and two weeks after that, Cassady moved in with me. This was a significant move for me because I had not lived with anyone in years. But my love for her felt so pure and so intense that I never had a moment of hesitation.

When I asked the Masters for their guidance, they confirmed that there was a spiritual purpose to the relationship for both of us and that I could pursue it if I wanted. Of course, I wanted nothing more. Every night when we would go to sleep and every morning when we would awaken, I would let Cassady know how blessed I felt to be with her. We both fell into a dreamy state in which we would fantasize about a future that included marriage and children.

I did not realize that the spiritual purpose the Masters had in mind was not necessarily the one I had wanted. Through me, Cassady met Dr. Singh and the other Band members. In doing so, she found her spiritual calling and chose to jump into the path of a Chanter. The day she announced this intention to Dr.

Singh was the beginning of the end of my relationship with Cassady. Three days later, she moved out of my house and into the temple that Carmina was building on the other side of town.

The suddenness of this change caught me by surprise, and I was absolutely crushed. Here was this woman who had touched my heart in a way that no other woman had, and only six weeks into the relationship, she was gone. I had fooled myself into thinking that I was doing well in terms of creating detachment in my life. Since knowing Dr. Singh, I had let go of the vast majority of my concerns about money, status, my career, and almost everything else that I had ever cherished. But now I was up against the one attachment I had never been able to surrender: my need for a spiritual and sexual companion.

The question of companionship is tricky for anyone on a spiritual path—not just a Chanter. There is something so beautiful about having a partner with whom you can walk your spiritual path. For a few weeks, I felt that I had found that in Cassady. Everything we did together seemed to be in alignment with my spiritual life. But every spiritual path is unique. Although two people's path may cross in such a way that they walk side-by-side for a period of time, there is no guarantee of permanence.

I know in retrospect that Cassady's love for me opened her heart in a way that let her jump into her spiritual path. This love was so intense that it became the catalyst for a profound spiritual transformation on her part. In one of the poems that she gave me, Cassady wrote:

> *When I look at you,*
> *the light of a hundred thousand suns shines through my heart.*
> *I am consumed.*
> *And as we become portals,*
> *the light of our love expands*
> *and burns everything around us*
> *into its perfect, natural Whole.*

Cassady was beginning to realize something that it took me much longer to accept, which is that the love we were feeling was something we could not contain. It would be impossible—and pointless—for us to try and hold onto it. Rather than keeping it to ourselves, we had to let it flow freely and to share it without any attachment. Another one of her poems to me read:

I sat and looked out the coffee-shop window.
I saw the trees as I see you.
I saw the sky as I see you.
I saw the mountains as I see you—
My Dear Omar—
I never expected to see the world
through such a window as you.
When I see the world through you,
I see the world through love.

The day Cassady left, I cried for six hours. Dr. Singh invited me to the Tabernacle, where he comforted me and guided me through the blasts of grief that were detonating inside of me. On top of the sense of loss I was experiencing, I had to deal with the staggering blow to my self-concept. My reaction to Cassady's departure showed me that I was not as far along on my spiritual path as I thought I was—at least with respect to the question of detachment. It was a fall from grace the likes of which I had never known.

When Dr. Singh encouraged me to find serenity, I did everything I knew how to do, but nothing seemed to work. I was caught in an emotional whirlwind, grasping at anything I could in search of stable ground. But the force was too great, and it overwhelmed me. I was sucked into the giant void that Cassady's absence had created in my life. Her decision to leave was so sudden that she had not even packed her things or let anyone know what she was doing. Even though she was gone, I had to look at her belongings every day, which were spread all over my house. I also had to answer phone calls from friends and family who were unaware of her move. For the first few days, I would just tell everyone that she was on a spiritual retreat. I could not bear the pain of admitting that she was gone.

As I reflected on what had happened, I came to realize that the Masters had given me exactly what I had asked for. Two months before meeting Cassady, I had prayed that I would find someone with whom I could create spiritual partnership. This meant having a companion with whom I could walk my spiritual path. On more than one occasion, Dr. Singh had spoken to me about "having your cake and eating it too." I took that to mean that I could pursue a spiritual path and have a stable relationship at the same time.

Cassady possessed all of the qualities that I had envisioned in a spiritual partner. Until the very end, our time together was easy and joyous, without any real conflict or tension. It was the kind of relationship I had dreamed of having since childhood, and now it was gone. When I asked the Masters why this was happening, they said, "We gave you the spiritual partnership you were seeking, but we never promised you that it would last forever."

Dr. Singh told me that the only way a Chanter can be in relationship is without being attached to any particular outcome. "Every night when you put your head on the pillow and look at the other person, you know that this may be the last time you will ever see them. The only thing you can count on is this moment. There are no guarantees of anything else."

I knew that the pain I was feeling was not just about Cassady. When Dr. Singh asked me to run a small errand as a favor to him, I started having strange little reminders of past relationships. I walked into a supermarket and saw a woman standing in the checkout line who was the spitting image of my ex-wife, Catherine. Although I knew this could not be her— Catherine had descended into severe mental illness a few years earlier and was living in a nursing home in another part of the country—I moved as close to her as I could without drawing attention to myself.

Once I saw that the woman was not Catherine, I recognized her presence as a sign from the Masters. The rest of that evening, the signs just kept coming. I ran into a friend of

Catherine's that I had not seen in years. And when I returned from my errand, I had a phone message from an ex-girlfriend who would call me maybe once or twice a year. I realized that I was being confronted by all of the unresolved emotions from my past relationships. As soon as I had this realization, the phone rang. Dr. Singh was on the line.

He asked, "What is new and different, my friend?"

I told him about what I had just experienced, and then I said, "I need to do something to let go of my past relationships."

Dr. Singh instructed me to write down the names of all the women I had loved. Then, he told me to perform a ceremony in which I would acknowledge every one of my them individually, identifying the lessons I had received from them, thanking them for being in my life, blessing them, forgiving them if necessary, and letting go of any attachments I still had to them.

I stayed up much of the night going through the list. When I connected with the spirits of these women, I could see the qualities in each of them that had attracted me and that I continued to love about them. I found that I felt no remorse, regret or resentment towards any of them—only love. But I also discovered that I had created a relationship bubble with each one.

You are already familiar with the individual bubble. Basically, this is our self-concept—the sum of everything we have come to know and believe about ourselves. The bubble we create for ourselves shapes and limits the way we experience the world. As I mentioned in Chapter 3, our bubble can be our prison. Being able to break free of it is perhaps the biggest challenge in our spiritual lives.

The relationship bubble is a different kind of prison. We create it when we direct our love towards one person—or a small group of people—to the exclusion of everyone and everything else. It can be summed up by the phrase "you and me against the world." When we form a relationship bubble, we split the world in two. Those who make it into our bubble become our VIPs, receiving special status and treatment from us that nobody else can have.

In acknowledging my past relationships, I came to discover that I had been parceling out my love with incredible stinginess, directing it primarily to a select group of people. Even worse, the love I had been willing to share was conditional; a person had to love and accept me in order to receive it. When a relationship ended, the flow of love would slow to a mere trickle.

But that was not even the worst of it. I realized that sometimes I had not even given my love to an entire person. Instead, I chose to love only certain aspects of my "significant other." When I connected with the spirits of my former lovers, I found that I had only loved some of them for the qualities they possessed: their innocence, intelligence, sweetness, or grace. In a few cases, it was even more superficial than that: I was drawn to a particular woman because of her smile or her figure.

By the time I acknowledged all of the women on the list, I felt like I had closed the door on a relationship pattern that had never really worked for me. This was not how I wanted to love! I knew it was time to find a new way of loving that was much more generous and less exclusive. The moment that thought entered my mind, I heard a clear, powerful voice. It was the Big Beautiful Spirit.

"From now on, there is only one love in your life," the voice said, "and that is me. You can be free to open your heart with me, and to love me with total passion and abandon. In fact, this is your destiny. You can no longer love in any other way. But there is one condition: Your love for me has to extend to everyone and everything that comes into your life."

This was a critical moment in my spiritual training. I learned how to create a new kind of relationship, which is with the Big Beautiful Spirit. This relationship is not exclusive. You cannot love the Big Beautiful Spirit without loving all of creation equally. It makes no sense to direct your love to only a few small pockets of the universe because everyone and everything is imbued with holiness. Although other entities may not see the holiness in themselves, we must be able to see it in them. This is the core of our existence as Chanters.

At that moment, my relationship bubble burst for good. I do not know exactly what my future love affairs will look like. All I know is that there is no going back to the way I used to love.

After she left, Cassady told me, "I needed to learn how to love you without any attachment." Of course, I needed to learn exactly the same lesson, which turned out to be a very painful one for me. Letting go of her was one of the hardest things I have ever had to do. And I suspect that it was just as challenging for her. I commend her for the courage she has shown in pursuing her spiritual path, even though it meant walking away from her relationship with me.

You may be wondering why there is any need to walk away from a relationship that is as satisfying as ours was. The reason is simple: No matter how satisfying or beautiful, our relationship was limiting from a spiritual standpoint. Each of us became a window through which the other could experience holiness— and love. Less than two weeks before she left the relationship, Cassady had written this line:

When I see the world through you,
I see the world through love.

Then she discovered that it made no sense to depend on me to be her window into love. Anything can serve as that window: nature, reading, family, community, art, music, etc. The important thing is to realize that the flow of love comes from inside of us. Any emotional attachment that we form will impede that flow in the long run. The very people we love the most can become obstacles on our spiritual path if we are unable to let them go.

The Masters had already shared this lesson with me the day they taught me the chant:

DO YOU KNOW YOU ARE LOVE?
ONE THING—FLOWING THROUGH EVERTHING

That day, they also gave me the following message: "The very things you love will disappear, and you may think that you will never get this far again without them, but you have already become your future self, who does not need these things to feel love. You ARE love."

When I received this message, I understood it and felt it deeply in my heart. But caught up in the pain of losing my relationship with Cassady, I lost sight of it. When you witness the disappearance of the people and things you love, it is hard to remind yourself that you do not need them in order to experience love. But it is crucial that you do just that. Keep in mind that although the people and things you love may vanish from your life in an instant, the love does not. That is because you are the love. This flow of love is you, and it emanates from within your own spirit.

When you attach the flow of love to a specific thing, that thing becomes a pool in which love collects and eventually hardens into something joyless. The only relationships that are conducive to your spiritual path are the ones founded on detachment. If you choose to live the life of a Chanter, your love is something to be shared with everyone; it cannot be allowed to just sit and stagnate in a few small pools.

The other hard lesson about relationships that every Chanter must learn is that a relationship is only worth pursuing if it serves a spiritual purpose. Only the guidance of the Masters can let you know whether such a purpose exists. You may want to listen to just your heart, your body, or your mind, but none of these will lead you consistently in a productive direction. As Chanters, you and I are here to experience enlightenment and to serve the spiritual needs of others. We have an obligation to ourselves to make sure that everything we do is consistent with our mission. This means entering only into relationships that have a spiritual purpose and staying in them only as long as that purpose is being served.

If a relationship can radiate love out into the world, then it is serving this purpose and can be considered a true blessing in our lives. As Chanters, we come together with the intention of immersing ourselves in the flow of love and then of directing that flow to wherever it is needed. The power of two or more people acting in unison to fulfill this intention can be staggering. There is nothing more beautiful than a relationship that can channel love, energy, and blessings to others. To create this kind of relationship takes a great deal of focus and dedication. We cannot afford to lose sight, even for an instant, of the spiritual purpose of our union.

Job and Career

Whenever any of us uses the term work in front of Dr. Singh to describe what we do for a living, he corrects us gently: "Call it play. Only slaves work, my friend." In doing so, he is helping adjust our way of thinking about jobs and careers to bring it more in alignment with our spiritual lives as Chanters.

Although each of us as Chanters is very focused on our spiritual path, we still function in the linear world. In fact, we would not have it any other way. Dr. Singh is always reminding us of that. "We might like to be in a monastery, where we can sit and meditate all day," he says, "but that is not our mission." Chanters must be immersed in society because this way of life gives us greater access to the populations we serve. If we are genuinely committed to healing and enlightenment, then we need to live among the people who are most in need of both.

The primary reason that a Chanter holds a job or pursues a career is to be of service. Our concern is not financial. Because we practice detachment, our worries about paying the bills and surviving in the world do not control our lives. Recently, Dr. Singh told me, "As Chanters, we have no reason to want anything for ourselves. We know that the Big Beautiful Spirit will give us exactly what we need."

Earning a living is our excuse to do what Dr. Singh calls invisible healing. Just consider the number of people each of us encounters every day as a result of our jobs and careers. In our commute, we observe or interact with thousands of drivers, riders, and pedestrians. Throughout our day, we encounter colleagues, supervisors, customers, students, patients, and the people who provide services to our employers. During our breaks, we may find ourselves face-to-face with food servers, barristas, and store clerks. Every single person we come across stands to benefit from their contact with us.

Harper, who teaches at a high-school that serves a student population consisting primarily of juvenile offenders and home-less teens, uses invisible healing with all of her students, fellow teachers, and school staff. From my perspective, Harper is a master of the art. She was the first one to teach me this practice. When I asked her to share it with me, she said, "It's pretty simple, really. I just empty myself completely so that my own needs, desires and expectations won't get in the way. Then I ask the Big Beautiful Spirit to let me be an instrument of healing. In that moment, I become a conduit through which the Big Beautiful Spirit gives the person what they need and takes from them what they don't need."

There are many ways to practice invisible healing. The main thing is that the person to whom you are directing healing energy, love, and blessings not be aware of what you are doing. There is no need for anyone to know. Besides that, it is impor-tant for you to keep in mind that you are not doing it to stroke your own ego. Personal style does come into play, though. Each Chanter practices invisible healing in a slightly different way.

For instance, Ricardo shared with me recently a technique that he has been refining. When he identifies a suitable "target," he approaches the person and finds a way to touch him or her with his hand, as subtly and imperceptibly as possible. It could be as casual as the slight hand contact that occurs during the exchange of money at the checkout line, or brushing past an individual in a narrow aisle or hallway. At the moment of contact, Ricardo focuses his intent on sending blessings to the other person.

I am not quite as "hands-on" as that. My approach is to direct my gaze at people and to concentrate on transmitting loving energy to them. As I do that, I repeat the word "blessings" silently or I use my powerful chant:

DO YOU KNOW YOU ARE LOVE?
ONE THING—FLOWING THROUGH EVERYTHING

Sometimes, I raise my hand slightly, envisioning the healing energy shooting out of my palm and towards whomever I am blessing. I try to do this gesture as discreetly as possible to avoid drawing attention to myself. It is amazing, though, how little people will notice you when you move through your day practicing invisible healing. It is as if the Big Beautiful Spirit puts an invisibility shield around you.

Since the beginning of my training as a Chanter, my view of my career has changed completely. When I began teaching at the college level, my primary concern was to make sure that my students learned the concepts and skills that I was presenting to them. Now, the course content is secondary. I am in the classroom to serve the students' spiritual needs, first and foremost. This means sending them invisible healing. It also means that I make myself available as a source of support for them.

In the first college course I taught after meeting Dr. Singh, I told the students that I would stay after class to discuss anything they wanted, including personal and academic issues. At first, one or two students would come to see me. All I did was to listen without judgment of any kind and to send them blessings. They talked about their families, their relationships, and their struggle to find themselves. I offered my perspective only when they called for it. Otherwise, I was just there for them.

After a few weeks, more students started coming. An informal discussion circle started, and it kept growing larger every week. By the end of the semester, there would be at least a dozen students staying after class to talk about their personal issues and concerns. A powerful bond developed among all of us who participated in this circle. I came to realize that it was the most satisfying experience of my teaching career. In many ways, I was of more service to the students who stayed after class that semester than to any of the thousands of students whom I had taught in the classroom.

Dr. Singh had told me that the best way I could serve my students was by being happy and serene. These qualities draw people to you like a magnet because they want a little piece of what you have. When they discover that you are willing to share every bit of it, they relax and open themselves to you. That is when magic happens. Their openness allows you to transmit healing and blessings directly to them. And then invariably these people begin to find the qualities in themselves that they had originally sought in you.

If I were not teaching college students, I would be perfectly happy with a job as a cashier in a supermarket checkout line. I think of all the people with whom I would have contact each day. There would be so many opportunities to practice invisible healing. I would greet every customer as an embodiment of the Big Beautiful Spirit. And it would be so easy to be happy and serene in the presence of that much holiness!

What you do matters much less than how you do it. Of course, if you are doing a job you find unethical, such as building bombs or selling drugs to children, you are not aligned with either your spiritual mission or the basic values of this path. But assuming you have a job or career that is relatively harmless and that pays the bills but does not inspire you, it is up to you to bring the inspiration to what you do. Because each of us touches so many lives in the course of a normal workday, we can inspire ourselves by the very notion of bringing blessings, healing, and love into the lives of the people we encounter.

Martin Luther King, Jr., once said: "If a man is called to be a street-sweeper, he should sweep streets even as Michelangelo painted, or Beethoven played music, or Shakespeare wrote poetry. He should sweep streets so well that all the hosts of heaven and earth will pause to say, here lived a great street-sweeper who did his job well."

There is inspiration to be found in anything we do that is in keeping with our values and ideals. Even the most mundane job or commute is filled with opportunities to be of genuine service. When we seize these opportunities, we come into our own as Chanters.

Home Life

Ricardo and Harper share a home with Ricardo's mother, Tía Luz. When I first visited their place, I found a very modest little manufactured home out in the desert that looked and felt very much like any other American home. In the living room, the television was the centerpiece with a sofa and recliner on the opposite wall. The decorations consisted mostly of generic art and knickknacks that did not reflect the spiritual lives of the people living there.

Over the next year, that house would undergo a radical transformation. Today, we refer to it as the Temple of Song. What used to be the living room is now the altar room, where we perform weekly ceremonies. The TV and sofa are gone, replaced by a beautiful altar and a set of cushions on the floor. Everything in the room has a spiritual significance, including images of the Masters, candles, musical instruments, and other medicine pieces that have come into the hands of various Band members over the years.

The more committed Ricardo and Harper have become to their spiritual lives as Chanters, the more they have realized that their home has to reflect this commitment. They had no choice but to turn it into a true sanctuary—not just a place of refuge but of holiness.

For a Chanter, everything begins in the home. This is where we practice the Seven Keys and perform our private ceremonies for the healing and blessing of others. As Chanters, we want our homes to reflect our spiritual lives in such a way that visitors know they are entering a sanctuary the moment they walk in the door.

The décor alone does not make a sanctuary, though. What matters most is the way you live inside your home. If there is an air of holiness, then your home is a sanctuary. The only way to create holiness is by being mindful of everything you do inside those four walls. This means acting—and interacting—in ways that promote not only your enlightenment but also that of others.

Dr. Singh likes to talk about reverence. You set the tone for the kind of home you want to create. If you want your home to be a true sanctuary, then you have to treat it with the kind of reverence you would a church or temple. I remove my shoes the moment I step into my home, and I ask others to do the same. This is not simply a matter of cleanliness, although there is no denying that this practice has made it easier for me to keep my home clean. It also lets visitors know that they are leaving the mundane world behind and entering a sacred space. By taking off their shoes, they shed some of the baggage of that other world. The practice also fosters a sense of humility, bringing the person a little closer to the ground and removing a layer of protection.

Your attitude of reverence should extend to each person who enters your home. Whether someone else lives there with you or is just visiting, you have the responsibility to honor and welcome them. You create holiness by practicing the Seven Keys in every interaction that takes place in your home. The idea is simple: You acknowledge each person who sets foot in the home as you would Jesus, Buddha, or any other Master, because each one is an embodiment of the Big Beautiful Spirit. This includes children, spouses, parents, siblings, friends, acquaintances, and even solicitors. There can be no exceptions.

A second attitude that fosters holiness is gratitude. As Chanters, we realize that we must give thanks for everything that comes into our lives and our homes because each gift represents divine grace. The Big Beautiful Spirit is generous enough to give us what we need—and then some. But we cannot take these gifts for granted. For one, they are not ours to keep. Although I may refer to the place where I live as my home, I know this is just a trick of language. Our homes do not belong to us. We are just the temporary custodians of these sanctuaries—an assignment that one day will be passed along to someone else.

Even the food we eat does not belong to us. It is just the fuel we need in order to serve our brothers and sisters. The bodies that metabolize this food and transform it into new cells, tissues, and organs are not ours to keep, either. At best, these bodies are a "loaner." They provide a temporary vehicle for our spirits until we no longer need them.

At every meal, we give thanks for the blessing of vitality that we are receiving. Every Chanter has his or her own way of doing this. Here is the prayer I say at the beginning of every meal:

> *Thank you, Big Beautiful Spirit, for this abundant feast. Let me receive this food as divine love and let me transmit that love to others as your humble servant, remembering who I am, where I'm going, and how I'm getting there, today, yesterday, and tomorrow.*

I close this prayer of thanks, and any other prayer I say, with a hand gesture that Dr. Singh taught us. The gesture begins by placing the palms of your hands together in the traditional posture of prayer, with the fingertips up against your lips. You then kiss your fingertips, extend your hands a few inches from your face, creating a triangle in which your thumbs form the bottom side and the remaining fingers form the other two sides. After that, you let your hands and arms draw a circle, with the two hands separating at the top of the circle and then coming back together at the bottom. Finally, you spread your hands apart and point them upward while wiggling your fingers.

This sacred hand gesture is not merely symbolic; it is a tangible way to pull in energy as an instrument for the Big Beautiful Spirit and then to send it back out into the universe for healing purposes. First, you acknowledge your role as a servant. By folding your hands and then kissing your fingertips, you honor the Divine for the blessings you are about to receive and to share with others. The triangle you form with your hands opens a portal through which you can draw energy into yourself. The circular motion that follows is the circle of life. As you form this circle with your hands, you are bringing the energy you are receiving into an ever widening circle that begins with friends and family and extends outward to infinity. Finally, you propel that energy from your fingertips out into the universe from which it originated. Every time you use this gesture, you consecrate your intentions as a Chanter, showing your commitment to share the blessings you receive with the entire universe.

Finally, it helps to adopt an attitude of mindfulness. If you are interested in having a home life that is conducive to the experience of holiness, then everything you do has the potential of contributing to that experience. Even the most mundane household chores can turn into important spiritual assignments if you are open enough. Much of what I have learned in my training as a Chanter has come to me while I have been pulling nails, hauling rocks, or pouring concrete.

In one of Dr. Singh's favorite movie scenes, from *The Karate Kid*, the wise Mr. Miyagi teaches young Daniel the fundamentals of karate through a set of three routine tasks: painting a fence, washing windows, and waxing cars. A line from that scene—"Wax on, wax off"—has become Dr. Singh's way of referring to the hidden spiritual significance of the "routine" events and activities of everyday life.

In your own path, you will discover that there is no such thing as a routine task. With the proper intention, every action can be dedicated to the benefit and healing of those in need. Moreover, you have an obligation—at least to yourself—to put the Seven Keys into practice in everything you do. Otherwise, these Keys are just abstract concepts with no relevance to your life.

Dr. Singh likes to remind us that our path is not one of isolation and contemplation but of direct action in the service of others. Our commitment to being of service has repercussions that affect every activity we undertake—even the way we sleep. For a Chanter, each moment is packed with significance. The sound of a bird call or a jet flying overhead will have meaning for you. Even simple acts, like answering the phone or organizing a closet, are opportunities to advance on your spiritual path and to direct healing energy and blessings to those who need it. Nothing you do as a Chanter is purely for yourself. The benefit of living this way is enormous because you end up consecrating your life, transforming every moment into pure poetry.

The flip side of mindfulness is that you also have to be aware of the things you do that are not productive from a spiritual standpoint. For instance, television is an enormous distraction. A University of Michigan study showed that watching television lowers personal contentment levels by five percent for every hour watched. It can create unrealistic expectations and promote our attachment to material possessions.

"There is no time to waste," Dr. Singh has told me. "If you are doing something that does not have a spiritual purpose, stop doing it." This does not mean that you have to bend yourself out of shape or give up the things you love to do. It does mean that the farther you travel down this path, the more you will gravitate to activities that nourish your spirit by letting you experience holiness and by giving you the opportunity to be of service to others.

Sometimes, you merely need to make a minor adjustment to the things you already do in order to give them a spiritual purpose. For instance, I have loved singing and playing music since childhood. As I got older, I began to discover the spiritual power of music. Once I made this discovery, I became even more drawn to what I had always loved: singing, drumming, and playing music. I began my love affair with chanting, which opened up new doors in my spiritual life and ultimately served as the vehicle through which I met Dr. Singh. My passion for chanting was so strong that I started Global Chant, which has drawn hundreds of people over the past decade. In doing so, I have been able to provide an important spiritual service. For many of the people who have come to Global Chant, the act of chanting has filled a void in their lives that nothing else could fill.

Once I began my apprenticeship with Dr. Singh, he showed me how to maximize the spiritual power of the chanting circle. Now, we begin the chanting with an intention: Each of us dedicates our chanting in such a way that we direct the energy we are creating together to someone or something that needs it. When we close the circle, I remind each member that the love, the healing energy, and the blessings we create for ourselves when we chant together are something that we can take out into the world and share freely with others.

Now, making music brings me more joy than it ever has. Not only is the music beautiful and heartfelt; the experience of creating it has a profound spiritual purpose. It lets me flow as divine love and contribute—even in some small way—to the healing and enlightenment of my brothers and sisters throughout the universe. There is nothing more satisfying than that.

The Ultimate Role Model

As Chanters, we aspire to live out each day of our lives in a manner consistent with our spiritual mission. This is an ambitious standard. Fortunately, we have role models: The spiritual Masters whose wisdom guides us are perfectly congruent in the way they exist. If you spend enough time in the presence of true Masters such as Ammachi or Dr. Singh, you will notice that they are immersed in holiness all the time. There is never a moment when they slip up, lose their composure, mistreat someone, or show anything less than complete reverence for the people they encounter.

Sometimes, I have dismissed this observation by telling myself that the Masters are not mere mortals; that they have an extraordinary character that the rest of us lack; or that it is somehow easier for them because they do not need to live in the same dog-eat-dog world that the rest of us have to navigate each day. Of course, none of this is true. Dr. Singh, for instance, has a family, a career, and a mortgage. He even commutes to his job every day. In no way is he cloistered in some mountain retreat, spending the day in silent meditation. He is engaged in the same kinds of everyday activities as the rest of us, only he moves through his day with perfect equanimity and happiness.

You do not have to be a Master—or even a Chanter—to lead an exemplary life. Two months ago, a student of mine named Jeremy contacted me on a Friday to say that he would be missing class that day because both his parents were in the hospital. Jeremy's mother, Donna, was recovering from a heart transplant and his father, Paul, was having complications related to diabetes. Jeremy asked to meet with me, and so I scheduled a meeting for the following Monday.

When Jeremy walked into my office, I could see he was in shock. His father had died just a few hours earlier. From the moment he told me of Paul's death, I felt an intense connection to this man whom I had never met. I inquired about the time and location of the memorial service, which I attended the following Saturday.

As soon as I arrived at the church, I knew that Paul had been a special man. The parking lot was filled to overflowing, and there were cars lining both sides of the street for several hundred yards. The church was packed, and there were even people standing in the back. All of them had come to honor this unique man.

The minister began by describing Paul's intense passion for his church. Paul was the self-appointed greeter who would welcome visitors and new congregation members. As far as Paul was concerned, the minister said, there was no such thing as a stranger. He enjoyed being able to help people feel comfortable in an unfamiliar setting.

After the minister spoke, the testimonials began. The first person to stand and speak was Paul's brother, who talked about the way Paul had rescued him from severe alcoholism. He cried as he admitted that Paul had saved his life.

Then Paul's former employer, the owner of a small nursing home, explained that Paul had chosen to devote his career to nursing home administration because he wanted to make sure that every resident would be treated the way he would want his own parents treated if they were institutionalized. A number of people whose parents had lived in Paul's nursing home confirmed that he had done just that.

Paul's neighbor told the story of his own wife, who was paraplegic and spent much of her day at home. After Paul was forced to retire because of his declining health, he would pay daily visits to his neighbor's wife to bring her lunch and watch soap operas with her.

Jeremy and his brother cried as they talked about their father. For them, he was the ultimate role model. He would listen to his sons' problems without offering any judgment or advice, and he would teach them simply through his example. The way his sons described him, Paul always seemed to make time for them, taking them fishing on the weekends or sharing silly jokes with them.

Even though Paul's wife, Donna, was still weak from her surgery, she said a few words about the way she had met her husband. Paul had been her co-worker and had offered her support when her first marriage ended suddenly and painfully. Whenever things would break down in her house, he would come over and fix them happily and without any expectation of even a word of thanks. Although there were age and ethnic differences between the two of them, her admiration for this man who showed so much compassion and unconditional love for others was so great that she realized she wanted to spend her life with him. They became not just husband and wife, but best friends and spiritual partners.

Their partnership ended up touching thousands of lives, as the stream of testimonials showed. Almost everyone in the room had a story about the way Paul had helped them in a crisis, cared for their loved ones, made them feel at home, or simply brought a smile to their face. When one of his friends got up and sang Paul's favorite song, "Amazing Grace," nearly everyone in the room cried. But for the most part, these were not tears of sadness. They were an expression of people's appreciation and love for an extraordinary man.

Since that day, I have felt Paul's presence in my life on a number of occasions. When I grieved the loss of my relationship with Cassady, his spirit was there, offering gentle words of support. Paul's commitment to being of service did not end with his death. I did not need to ever meet him to know that Paul walked his spiritual path 24/7.

I think of Paul often. He is a continuous source of inspiration for me, having set a standard that keeps me focused on what I need to do every day to live in alignment with my own spiritual purpose. In his modest way, he has shown me that a truly spiritual life does not need to be grandiose. It can be simple, quiet, humble, and invisible. You simply create beauty in the little circle of influence directly surrounding you, starting with your own heart. This is simply a matter of treating everyone you encounter, including yourself, with sweetness, compassion, and unconditional love. Eventually, your circle of influence spreads, because nothing is more compelling than love. Through your love, you can make miracles, which is something that every Chanter has the ability to do.

CHAPTER 6

Making Miracles

In May 2006, my 71-year-old mother was driving her little Honda Civic on a quiet residential street when a miracle happened. As she pulled into an intersection, a van barreling down a hill going at least 40 miles per hour rammed into the passenger side of her car. The impact was so severe that her car rolled three times before landing upside down on a nearby sidewalk. Neighbors who heard the crash and saw the demolished Civic assumed that the driver was either killed or seriously injured.

For nearly half an hour, my mother dangled awkwardly from her shoulder harness as a team of firefighters cut into the driver's side door and pried her free of the wreckage. An ambulance rushed her to a local trauma center, where she underwent every possible test for head trauma, internal injuries, and fractures. Amazingly, all the tests came out negative. She was kept at the hospital overnight for observation and then released the next morning.

When I told Dr. Singh about what had happened, he said, "Yes, I know. I was there."

"What do you mean?" I asked.

"A few days ago, Carmina told me that she was feeling deep sadness," Dr. Singh replied. "She had a premonition that someone we love was about to die."

"Did she know that it was my mother?"

"No, but I felt it as soon as I came home and saw the painting your mother had given me," he remarked.

Since her retirement, my mother had taken up painting, immersing herself in it with total passion. Within months, her art works covered the walls and filled the closets of her house. When she met Dr. Singh, she asked me to find out his favorite colors so that she could create something just for him. On one of my visits to my parents' home, she handed me a carefully-wrapped painting that she instructed me to frame and to give to Dr. Singh the next time I saw him.

Of course, I followed my mother's instructions, and when I presented the painting to Dr. Singh, he had tears in his eyes. He said, "I love your mother so much. She has a beautiful, loving heart. I am going to keep this painting in a place where I can look at it every day and connect with her spirit."

At the time, I was touched by the way Dr. Singh had accepted my mother so completely, as if she were a member of his own family. But I had no idea that the painting she had given him would save her life one day. Through that painting, Dr. Singh was able to intervene in the accident and to protect my mother from physical trauma that could have killed her easily.

When I asked Dr. Singh how he was able to do that, he told me, "I had a conversation with Sister Death, in which I used the painting as a sign of your mother's vitality and of her loving heart. I told Sister Death that your mother is a good servant whose spiritual mission in this body is not complete. It seems that Sister Death agreed with me, because she let me take action."

"And what kind of action did you take?" I inquired.

Dr. Singh paused for a moment and took a deep breath before continuing. "I flew to where your mother was and made a shield around her body. By putting myself in the way of any impact her body would receive, I took the blows from the accident so that she would not be hurt."

At one time, I would have found Dr. Singh's story to be unbelievable. But by this point, not only had I observed these types of astonishing interventions on a regular basis; I had taken part in a number of them. On several occasions, Dr. Singh would call me to tell me of healing ceremonies we were going to be doing and would preface his remarks to me by saying, "We are going to make a miracle."

The irony is that Dr. Singh knows that making a miracle is impossible. First of all, the term miracle has no meaning to a Chanter. It only makes sense from the standpoint of the linear mind. A miracle is an extraordinary event that occurs through supernatural intervention. But nothing we do as Chanters is either extraordinary or supernatural in origin. In fact, the healing ceremonies we perform are quite ordinary in the sense that they happen on a weekly—if not a daily—basis. And the source of the healing that takes place is the Big Beautiful Spirit, which is nature itself. There is nothing supernatural about it.

More importantly, we do not make anything happen ourselves. Any healing that takes place is a matter of Divine Will. We Chanters merely serve as instruments through which the Big Beautiful Spirit acts upon the universe. That is why we include the following words in the invocation we say at the beginning of each ceremony we perform:

Of course, it was not I who healed, but the powers from the outer world, and the visions and the ceremonies had only made me like a hole through which the power could come to the two-legged and the four-legged. If I thought it were myself doing the healing, the hole would disappear and no power would come through it.

In our capacity as healers, we are nothing more than a conduit through which energy moves. As such, we allow ourselves to be used as a vehicle through which the Big Beautiful Spirit gives others what they need—on a spiritual level—and takes from them what they do not need. In no way do we make any decisions about what is needed. That is not up to us.

The healing work that Chanters do is not just about alleviating suffering. We are not averse to certain types of suffering. Sometimes, individuals suffer because there are spiritual lessons to be gained from the experience. Nor are we here to rescue anyone from death. Chanters see physical death as inevitable—an outcome we do not fear or dread. And so, if our role is not merely to prevent suffering or to delay death, then what is the purpose of our healing work?

Dr. Singh once told me, "The healing work we do is just an excuse. It is our foot in the door. Our real work as Chanters is to address the needs of the spirit."

Every being in the universe is moving in the same direction. Call it what you will: enlightenment, liberation, release, or self-realization. It is the merging of the individual spirit with the Big Beautiful Spirit. As Chanters, we look to facilitate that process. This is not to say that we are in any rush to bring about enlightenment. It will happen for each individual when the timing is right. But this lifetime is as good an opportunity as any and cannot be squandered. If we can extend the opportunity by maximizing both the duration and quality of a life, then we can increase the chances—even a tiny bit—that the individual will experience enlightenment in this lifetime. Every bit matters, because the enlightenment of even a single individual has an impact that can be felt throughout the universe.

The Flow of Miracles

The first time Dr. Singh asked me to take part in "making a miracle" was with Doña Carmen, the woman who was dying of heart disease when she came to see us at the Conservatory (p. 150). As she was lying on the floor of the Song Chamber, Dr. Singh asked each of us to chant the Latin prayer, *Dona Nobis Pacem*, which means "grant us peace." This chant served to heighten our sense of serenity so that we could serve Doña Carmen more effectively.

Dr. Singh also instructed us to approach her, one at a time, placing a hand on her arm and envisioning ourselves giving her something from our own hearts that would help in healing hers. When I placed my hand on Doña Carmen's forearm and closed my eyes, I envisioned myself shrinking to microscopic size. Then I entered her body through the skin of her arm and flowed into an artery. As I began to move closer to her heart, my momentum increased. I was determined to give her every bit of my strength and vitality at the moment I penetrated her heart. And that is exactly what happened.

After the ceremony, Doña Carmen's family took her home and we did not hear from them for several weeks. I assumed that she had probably died within a few days of coming to see us. This was not the case. In fact, the next time I saw Doña Carmen, about three months later, she looked like an entirely different woman: vibrant, robust, and happy. You would never know by looking at her that she was recovering from a life-threatening heart attack.

A few weeks after that, I was involved in one of the strangest interventions I could ever imagine. One clear, beautiful day in Sonora, Dr. Singh asked me to get up on a high ladder with a wire brush and to scrape paint off an old wooden beam. For me, this was a particularly challenging task because of my fear of heights. Dr. Singh stressed that I needed to remain serene throughout the day, and that if I became nervous or anxious, all I needed to do was to look out at the clouds and start chanting. As soon as I got up on the latter, I began chanting the Sikh prayer, *Ra Ma Da Sa, Sa Say So Hung*, which translates to: "Sun, Moon, Earth, Infinity. I am that Infinity that I belong to and contain."

While I worked on the beam, I was interrupted occasionally by my fellow Chanters who wanted to know what I was doing. When I would tell them, they would just shrug their shoulders and smile. Each of them knew that the task itself had no logical significance. The paint chips on the beam were hardly noticeable from the ground and had been there for years without bothering anyone. There was obviously a deeper purpose to this assignment, although I did not know what it was.

The longer I spent on that ladder, the more absorbed I became in the puffy white clouds that surrounded me. After a while, I began to melt into them, and the paint scraping work began to slow down as I got lost in the clouds. I was having such a beautiful experience up on the ladder that I was even reluctant to come down for lunch. I sat with the rest of the group mostly to be polite, had a few bites of food, and then excused myself so that I could return to my strange little project.

By mid-afternoon, I was having one of those now-familiar experiences of holiness. Dr. Singh summoned me down from the ladder and sat down with me on a nearby bench.

"Do you know why I sent you up on the ladder today?" he asked.

"I have no idea," was my reply. "But I'm glad you did."

"Yes, I can see you had a beautiful experience up there. And you did your assignment perfectly." Then he explained that a 10-year-old girl we knew named Betsy was flying in a small commercial plane that day, and that the plane had experienced engine trouble. Through our intervention, we were able to prevent the plane from crashing and to save the lives of every-one on board.

"That is wonderful," I said, "but I didn't do anything. I wasn't even aware that any of this was happening."

Dr. Singh smiled at me. "You did much more than you real-ize, my friend. We needed your fear of heights to make this particular miracle happen. By transforming your fear into holi-ness, you created the energy we needed so that we could keep that plane in the air."

The next time we saw Betsy, she confirmed everything that Dr. Singh had said. During the flight, there had been a sudden loss of altitude. As the plane began to plunge, the passengers panicked. At first, Betsy was terrified, but then she thought of Dr. Singh, and suddenly her fear dissipated. A feeling came over her that somehow she would be protected and that everything would be alright.

After that, the miracles kept coming. A woman named Matilda came to see us because she was concerned about her boyfriend, Stanley. A few weeks earlier, Stanley's mother had died after a lengthy illness. Having had a very close bond with his mother, Stanley became so despondent over his loss that he even considered suicide. As a hospital psychiatrist, he had access to a wide range of drugs that he could use to kill himself. He also had a loaded handgun that Matilda discovered in his briefcase one day.

Dr. Singh chose me to be the "point man" in the intervention we would be taking on Stanley's behalf. He instructed me to connect with Stanley's spirit and to make the case against suicide. But more importantly, he asked me to shield him from any harm he could do to himself.

"What I am asking you to do is an advanced technique," he said. "One day, maybe in ten or twenty years, you will be a Master and you will be very familiar with this approach. For now, I want you to travel forward in time, to become your future self, so that you can help save Stanley's life."

"And what should I do?" I asked.

"Just put yourself in the way of anything he tries to do to kill himself."

Looking back on that healing, I believe that Dr. Singh chose me to play this role because of the similarities between Stanley and myself. We were both from the same ethnic background, had training in psychology, and were passionate about the people in our lives. When my grandfather—with whom I had had a very strong connection since early childhood—had died several years earlier, I did not consider suicide but I felt that the best part of my life had ended. I could not imagine my life being happy or fulfilling without him in it.

We all gathered in the Song Chamber to perform a healing ceremony. As the ceremony began, I could feel Stanley's presence as if he were sitting in the room with us. I focused on being my future self, just as Dr. Singh had instructed. As I did, a Sufi chant came to mind. The words of the chant, which are *Bismillah E-Rachman E-Rahim*, are a plea: "In the name of God, most merciful and compassionate."

As soon as I began to chant these words, I had the following realization: Stanley's death would be his mother's greatest nightmare. No parent would want a child to die on his or her behalf. Through my chanting, I was pleading with him to realize the implications of his actions.

When I communicated with Stanley's spirit, I shared this realization with him. Then something very strange happened. I felt my body undergo a transformation of some kind. It was as if I were vaporizing. In a moment of clarity, I knew what I needed to do. I moved into Stanley's body and became his shield. If he tried to shoot himself, I would take the bullet. If he tried to poison himself, I would ingest the toxin and keep it from entering his body. I knew that there was nothing he could do to harm himself at that point, and I made sure that Stanley knew that, as well.

When the ceremony was over, I felt confident that our intervention would keep Stanley alive long enough to get him through his period of depression and to let the thoughts of suicide pass. The next time Matilda talked to Dr. Singh, she let him know that Stanley had gotten rid of the handgun and seemed in much better spirits.

More recently, one of the newer Band members informed Dr. Singh of a close friend of hers, Irwin, who was hospitalized with an aneurysm in his heart. Immediately, Dr. Singh sprang into action, rallying everyone together for a series of healing ceremonies. He knew that the aneurysm would be fatal if we did not intervene.

When Dr. Singh called me that morning, he asked me to take time throughout the day to perform the following visualization: I was to envision the plaque that had built up in Irwin's arteries softening and loosening as I transmitted unconditional love and a sense of serenity to him. Then at midnight, I would do an intense chanting and drumming to blast through the softened plaque deposits. Meanwhile, my fellow Chanters would be performing related ceremonies in their homes. None of us were aware of the roles the others were playing in the healing. We just focused on our part.

As I carried out Dr. Singh's instructions, I chanted the following prayer: "Fill my heart so I can know you in every moment and in everything." I knew that this chant was perfectly suited to the ceremony I was performing because it would allow unconditional love to fill my own heart. Then, I could just direct that flow into Irwin's heart, where it would dissolve the plaque.

The next day, Irwin underwent a series of tests, but there was no aneurysm to be found. His attending physicians wondered if their initial diagnosis had been incorrect because they could not understand how an aneurysm of that type could dissolve and vanish overnight.

In the past few months, we have performed an increasing number of healing ceremonies for Mother Earth. Dr. Singh has said that some of the radical Earth changes that have been anticipated by Chanter prophesy are currently unfolding and will produce, among other things, a worldwide shortage of potable water due to a combination of drought and chemical contamination.

In the past year, the desert areas surrounding Tucson have experienced a period of severe drought. Usually, winter months bring at least a few rainstorms, but not this year. By March, the desert was drier than I had ever seen it. Even the hardiest cacti looked burnt and wilted.

Dr. Singh asked me and a few other Chanters to go out into the desert to perform a healing ceremony for Mother Earth. When we set our intention in this ceremony, we did not request or demand rain. As Dr. Singh has emphasized to us on many occasions, it is not our place as Chanters to ask for anything. We are simply instruments through which healing and blessing can take place. Our personal desires do not come into play.

During the ceremony, we became a channel through which the Big Beautiful Spirit could give Mother Earth—and specifically the deserts of Southern Arizona—what she needs and take from her what she does not. We chanted these words: "Earth my body, water my blood, air my breath, and fire my spirit." While chanting, I envisioned a rain not of water but of unconditional love, compassion, and forgiveness, falling on those parts of the planet that are most depleted of those qualities. More than moisture, the Earth thirsts for peace during times of unprecedented turmoil.

At one point, Ricardo and I sat under a mesquite tree with another Chanter and just honored the desert surrounding us. We admired the subtle beauty and the diversity of desert life. For a few moments, I experienced a sense of complete emptiness in which I no longer existed as a separate entity. My consciousness merged with that of the desert landscape and I became the desert. I could feel the harsh effects of the drought on the plants, animals and even the soil because my spirit was intermingled with all of them.

Within two weeks of our ceremony, the Tucson area was hit by two rainstorms. Although both were short-lived, they provided enough moisture to ease the strain that the drought had placed on the desert flora and fauna. Since then, the drought has resumed. We know this is just part of a purification process that will continue to unfold throughout the planet over the next decade or more. As healers, we can help alleviate the suffering that this process may cause. At times, our efforts may even help to reshape the course of events in a way that minimizes their impact. But we cannot stop all of the Earth changes that are coming, and it would be foolish for us to even try.

Protecting the Planet

Dr. Singh likes to say, "Be thankful for what didn't happen." For every catastrophic event that occurs on this planet, such as the tsunami of 2004 or Hurricane Katrina, we manage to avert any number of disasters. Just consider all of the monumental environmental changes that are being created by human activity: global warming, the depletion of the ozone layer, the destruction of the rainforests, over-fishing of the world's oceans, chemical contamination of groundwater, and increases in atmospheric radiation levels. Any one of these developments alone could make the Earth uninhabitable. Yet somehow, we have avoided the most severe repercussions of our own carelessness.

Long before I met Dr. Singh, I had a feeling that someone or something was protecting the planet. As his apprentice, I have had the chance to discover how accurate this feeling really was. A few months ago, Dr. Singh announced to us that he was taking an unanticipated trip to Mexico City. This was very unusual for him; he hardly ever left the Band to go traveling on his own.

Before he left, he told me the purpose of his assignment. He had been summoned to an emergency meeting of Chanters. It seems that all the talk that had been circulating about bird flu was more than just unfounded rumors. According to Dr. Singh, a deadly virus was expected to enter the United States in the following weeks. The Masters had indicated that there was a small window of opportunity for averting this epidemic, but that it would require immediate and concerted action on the part of Chanters throughout the planet.

Dr. Singh informed me that during his trip to Mexico, he would be performing a full moon ceremony at the pyramids of Teotihuacan—specifically at the pyramid known as the Temple of the Moon. At midnight on the designated night, I was to stare at a photograph of this temple until the image was emblazoned in my mind. Then I was to close my eyes and fly to Teotihuacan to witness the ceremony that Dr. Singh was performing.

I found an image of the pyramid on the Internet. After downloading it, I gazed at the image for several minutes until my eyelids started to feel extremely heavy. I made every attempt to keep my eyes open and to keep staring at the image, but within seconds, my eyes just closed on their own. Once they were closed, I could see Dr. Singh in my mind's eye, standing halfway up the pyramid. He stepped into what looked like a solid rock wall and moved inside the Temple of the Moon. I could see through the temple walls as if they were made of glass. Inside the temple, there was a giant lens designed to focus the reflected light of the moon. Dr. Singh began chanting in a language that was foreign to me—perhaps Zapotec—while doing a ritualized set of movements that I could only describe as a sacred dance. In this dance, he was taking the focused moonlight and redirecting it towards those in need of healing. Somehow, Dr. Singh was using moonlight to help neutralize the bird-flu virus.

I was amazed and honored to witness this ceremony. Late at night and in the most invisible way possible, Dr. Singh was doing his part to avert a major public health crisis. A few weeks earlier, I had heard an interview with an infectious disease expert from the Centers for Disease Control who described the widespread problems that could arise in an epidemic. First of all, shipping would come to a halt because workers in the freight industry would not want to subject themselves to unnecessary risks and because their employers would not want to spread the disease through the goods they were shipping. Most supermarkets are stocked with no more than a three-day supply of food, which means that severe food shortages would occur almost immediately. Plus, air travel would grind to a halt, and most businesses would shut down. Hearing this interview, I realized that something as simple as the flu could bring an entire nation to its knees in a matter of days.

I thought that the healing process for this flu epidemic had ended with the ceremony at Teotihuacan, but I discovered how wrong I was the day after Dr. Singh returned from Mexico. That day, I began to feel ill. It was the middle of one of the hottest summers that Tucson had ever experienced. Almost from the start, I ran a fever so high that my body would alternate between sweats and chills. I had every flu symptom imaginable: muscle aches, coughing, sneezing, congestion, sore throat, nausea, loss of appetite, and general weakness. What I was experiencing felt like the worst cold or flu I had ever had in my life, multiplied by a factor of 10.

When I called Dr. Singh to get his medical advice, he described my symptoms to perfection and then told me that he was experiencing the same thing. Then he warned me not to seek treatment. "No doctor is going to be able to help you, my friend. This is not something that fits the traditional medical model."

"Then what is it?" I asked.

"This is your chance to be a true healer," Dr. Singh replied. "Sometimes you have to take on pain and illness to keep others from experiencing something much worse."

At that moment, I realized that my participation in the healing process for this flu epidemic was far from over. *Now comes the hard part*, I told myself. *I have to endure these intense flu symptoms in order to shift the energy and to keep the epidemic from taking hold.*

Then Dr. Singh told me something that let me know he was reading my thoughts. He said, "This experience does not need to be hard for you. Just surrender to it and then it will start feeling like heaven instead of hell. Remember that you are being a good servant by taking on these symptoms."

As soon as I heard his words, my attitude changed. I understood that it was an honor to be used as an instrument of healing in such a significant way. If having what felt like a bad case of the flu for a few days could help prevent an epidemic from spreading, then I was more than happy to take on the symptoms.

Over the next few days, the symptoms just intensified. I promised myself that I would not take my temperature because I knew that my fever was so high, it might frighten me and send me racing to the emergency room. I was confident that Dr. Singh would not expose me to something that I was unable to handle. So, I lived through nights of restless sleep and days of dragging my body as if I had a 100-pound weight strapped to my back.

The next time I spoke with Dr. Singh, he asked me how I was feeling, and I told him that the symptoms had gotten worse. Then he made me an offer: "If you like, I can just take your symptoms and they will go away by tomorrow."

Hearing his words filled me with a sense of determination. "I can't let you do that," I replied. "This is my assignment as well as yours, and I know it's an important one."

"Yes, it is," he said. "But maybe I can do something to make it a bit easier for you."

"I am supposed to go to Seattle to visit my family in 10 days. If possible, I would like the symptoms to go away by then."

"Yes, it's important that you be strong and healthy so that you can be a good servant to your family while you're there," Dr. Singh agreed. "I will take the symptoms from you slowly. Starting tomorrow, you will feel a little better each day, and by the time you get on the plane to Seattle, your symptoms will be gone."

Needless to say, things played out exactly as Dr. Singh had described. I woke up the next morning feeling slightly better, and the symptoms became less intense each day. Then a few days later, my fever broke and my energy level started returning to normal. By the time I arrived in Seattle, I felt fine.

As you know, there was no flu epidemic that summer. By the fall, all of the concern about the bird flu seemed a bit silly, and Americans wondered if the whole thing had just been media hype designed to play on people's fears. In my heart, though, I know that the epidemic was much closer to taking hold in the U.S. than most people realize. Of course, I have no way of proving that, and it really does not matter what others believe, anyway. All I know is that I am thankful for what did not happen.

Healing without Attachment

Dr. Singh has often said that Chanters cannot afford to get attached to the outcome of a healing ceremony. We are here to serve the Divine Will and not to impose our own. I learned this lesson the hard way when my friend Richard called me to say that his father, Henry, had been diagnosed with liver cancer. Although I had never met Henry before I visited him in the hospital, I knew a great deal about him through Richard.

By the time Henry was five, he had lost both his parents. He went to live with his maternal grandparents, who resented him because they felt that he was to blame somehow for his mother's death. Henry was not allowed to set foot in his grandparents' house; instead, he slept and ate in a nearby shed.

When Henry met his wife Rosalie, who had also come from a broken home, the two of them promised each other that if they ever had a family, they would raise their children in the kind of loving, supportive home that they never had. They did manage to have children—11 of them, in fact—as well as 54 grandchildren and 37 great-grandchildren. And every single member of this enormous clan looked up to Henry as the wise patriarch.

From the time I met Richard, I had heard all kinds of stories about his father. All of Henry's children looked up to him and consulted with him before making any major life decision. They respected his common sense, his adherence to basic moral values, his sense of fairness, his clear thinking, and his compassionate heart. And from what I knew about Richard and his siblings, all of them were successful in terms of having happy, stable family lives of their own.

Henry and Rosalie had created an amazingly close-knit and harmonious family out of thin air. They had taken the pain of their own childhood and transformed it into something beautiful, breaking the old patterns and replacing them with new ones grounded in the ideals of faith, integrity, decency, and unconditional love. In my mind, Henry and Rosalie were heroes. They literally changed the world by producing a family of over 100 happy, loving, well-adjusted people.

The day after Richard called me, I paid Henry a visit in his hospital room. I brought him a crystal that Dr. Singh had asked me to give to him and a Latin music CD that I thought he would enjoy. Although Henry was in good spirits, I knew the seriousness of his condition just by looking at him. Jaundice had caused his skin and eyes to turn a fluorescent orange-yellow color. I could see that Henry's liver was shutting down fast.

From the moment I met Henry, I felt an intense sense of kinship with him. We spoke openly and lovingly to each other, like two old friends. At one point he confided, "I'm not afraid to die, but I don't want to leave my family." I knew at that point that Henry's powerful attachment and commitment to his family were likely to prolong his suffering and his death, possibly for weeks or months.

The next time I saw Henry, three days after our first meeting, his health had worsened and he was moved into the hospice unit within the hospital. So much fluid had collected in his legs and feet that he was unable to walk or even to wear his pajama pants. Amazingly, though, Henry was relatively free of pain without morphine or other pain medication.

Dr. Singh had asked me to invite Henry and his family to come to the Conservatory in Sonora for a healing ceremony, but by then Henry's physical condition had declined so quickly that his doctors and his family were set against the idea of moving him. Instead, we agreed that the healing ceremony would come to him.

On a Friday evening, Harper and I performed the ceremony, along with two other Chanters. Dr. Singh had given us very specific instructions on what to do. In my case, he told me to focus on the powerful love and connection that I felt for Henry. He said that I needed to be willing to lay down my life for him.

When Dr. Singh had told me the same thing before, in the case of Doña Carmen, I was unprepared to follow his instructions. At that point, I had been too attached to my own life and health to sacrifice them for another person. This time was different, though. I felt that if I did not do everything in my power to help Henry, I would not be able to go on living. Somehow, this man had touched a very deep place in my heart, and I was determined to do whatever was needed to save his life.

Dr. Singh had given me two warnings, along with the instructions for the ceremony: One was that it was up to Sister Death—not me—to determine whether or not Henry would survive this illness. The second was that if we were able to save Henry, my life would be changed forever. People would begin to see me as a powerful healer and would come to me for miracles. Dr. Singh expressed his concern that I might not be ready to handle that kind of attention. And, of course, he was right. I was not ready because I still had too much attachment, especially to people like Henry that I wanted to help.

We arrived at the hospice on a Friday evening. Dr. Singh had advised me to gather the family elders, including Rosalie and her children, in one room. I asked them to pray and to send love to Henry while the healing ceremony was taking place. I also requested that no disruptions occur during the ceremony. One of Henry's daughters asked me if I thought a miracle was possible, and I replied that I would not have come otherwise. As it turned out, my words may have given the family false hope, but it was a hope that we all shared.

Henry's family let me know that he had been moving in and out of consciousness all day. When we arrived in his room, he had his eyes closed and was saying something unintelligible. It sounded to us as if he were speaking in tongues. We proceeded with the ceremony. Each of us stood on one side of the bed, with me at his feet. First, we recited the Lord's Prayer and then we chanted the Greek words, *Kyrié Eléison*, which translate to "God have mercy."

During the chanting, I suddenly had the feeling of all the energy being drained from my body. I knew that this was my opportunity to lay down my life for Henry, just as Dr. Singh had instructed. I had no choice but to lie down on the floor. As the others kept chanting, I surrendered my life. Everything went silent, and I lost track of what was happening in the room. I know that I experienced death that night, and I did so gladly. It was my honor to give my life for my beloved friend Henry.

I have no idea how long I was in that state, but when my eyes opened, I saw Harper staring down at me, making sure that I was alright. After indicating to her that everything was fine, I took a few moments to reorient myself. Here I was, returning from the dead, and at first it was a bit of an adjustment. Slowly, I stood up and tried to make sense of what had just happened. That is when I realized that we had made a miracle in that room. My death experience had been a vehicle through which we were able to give Henry something he needed.

The following afternoon, Henry died in his sleep. When I spoke to Rosalie at the memorial service, she said that the doctors had checked up on him that morning and had told her that he was well enough to live at least a few more days, and possibly even several more weeks. Hearing her say that, I realized what the miracle was that we had created. Through our ceremony, Henry was able to let go of his family, which was the one thing keeping him bound to this life. The day of the ceremony was the first time that Henry had taken any pain medication. Until the last 24 hours of his life, he had managed to be relatively free of pain. Had he held on much longer, the pain would have intensified and his dying process would have become much more of an ordeal, not just for him but for his entire family.

I attended Henry's memorial service with a sense of shame. In my mind, I had failed to deliver the miracle I had promised his family. Seeing the looks on some of the family members' faces, I knew that they felt the same way. And yet there was no way to convince anyone—including myself—of the significance of what had happened. I sacrificed myself for Henry out of pure love and compassion for him. In doing so, Sister Death let me serve as an instrument to facilitate his transition. Granted, this was not the outcome I had hoped to facilitate. I would love to have had more time with Henry, as would every single member of his family. Yet I will always value the time we spent together. I continue to be inspired by the things I learned from Henry during our short acquaintance.

Sister Death

One of the most powerful lessons I gained from that experience was about death. As Dr. Singh has pointed out to me on many occasions, every Chanter has to learn to face Sister Death with a sense of humility and detachment. In our healing work, we have very little say over matters of life-and-death. It is not our job to persuade or convince Sister Death of anything. We offer only our intention that events unfold in a way that best serves the spiritual needs of the individual.

At the beginning of my apprenticeship with Dr. Singh, he had me sit down one afternoon and watch the classic Mexican film, *Macario*. The film tells the story of a poor, hungry peasant named Macario who longs for just one good meal on the Day of the Dead. Wanting to fulfill his wish, his wife steals and cooks a turkey for him and then sends him out to the forest where he can have this feast to himself. There, he meets three apparitions: the Devil, God, and Death. Each asks him to share his turkey, but he refuses all except Death. In return, Death gives him a bottle full of water that has healing power.

Death informs Macario that the water can only be used under certain circumstances. When Death appears at the foot of the bed, Macario can administer the water in order to save a patient's life. But when Death appears at the head of the bed, the patient is destined to die. Death warns Macario to resist every temptation to intervene in such cases.

As I began to take part in healing ceremonies, I had to heed the same warning. Fighting against Sister Death is an exercise in futility. Every Chanter must learn to accept the fact that Sister Death is an ally and that some lives are not meant to be saved. Healing does not necessarily mean the extension of life. In some cases, the spiritual needs of the individual require that the person be allowed to make the transition to the next phase of his or her existence.

Knowing that death is not the end, Chanters have to accept the fact that the healing and enlightenment of the individual can be served by dying just as much as by living. Obviously, Sister Death makes the determination of who will live and who will die. But sometimes death is not the outcome that best serves the spiritual needs of the individual. It is in these cases that Chanters have the opportunity to intervene and to persuade Sister Death to extend a person's life.

When someone is destined to die—as was the case with my friend Henry—we Chanters have the sacred responsibility of making sure that the transition happens in a way that is most beneficial to that person. Without even realizing it, I did meet my responsibility to Henry's spirit. Through my willingness to surrender my life for him, I made it easier for Henry to let go of his attachment to his family so that he could move onto the next phase in his spiritual development.

The Chanting Circle

Because I am a Chanter, most of the healing ceremonies I have performed have taken the form of chanting circles. Although there are many types of healing ceremonies, the chanting circle is what I know best—and also what I love the most. I am attracted by its beauty, simplicity, and power. In the context of a chanting circle, a group of people can make miracles happen. I know this for a fact because I have experienced it firsthand.

The healing power contained within the chanting circle is extraordinary. But to access this power in a safe and effective manner is an art. If you are going to organize this type of healing ceremony, there are some important things you will need to keep in mind. The ceremony proceeds in stages, and each stage requires some degree of care and attention on the part of the facilitator.

Preparation. The effectiveness of a chanting circle depends to a large degree on the setting. Your intention in organizing this circle is to bring together a group of people who will generate healing energy and direct that energy to wherever it is needed. As the facilitator, you must take into account all of the factors that can affect the energy of the chanting circle. These factors include the qualities of both the space in which the circle is being held and of the individuals taking part in the circle.

There are two types of chanting circles in which I take part. The first is the weekly Global Chant circle, which is open to the public. We never know who is going to be attending this circle from week to week. The event is listed in the local newspaper. Our listing includes our name, the starting time and location, contact information, and the following: "Group chanting from all traditions. No musical experience necessary."

Attendance in the weekly chanting circle is in the hands of the Big Beautiful Spirit. The members of this circle trust that the right people will be attracted to the circle at the right time. We have little control over the composition of the group, except when we invite specific people to attend. Global Chant maintains an open-door policy: Individuals can come and go as they wish.

The second type of chanting circle is called together in

response to a specific healing crisis in the community. For instance, if a Chanter has a friend or family member in the hospital, he or she may request a special healing ceremony for that person. In that case, participation in the circle is by invitation only. The facilitator determines who will be invited based on consultation with the Masters. If you are assembling this type of chanting circle, use your guidance to identify the Chanters whose energy is specifically needed in the circle.

The facilitator is also responsible for creating a sacred space. Choosing a suitable location for the chanting circle is an important consideration. If possible, select a neutral site rather than someone's home. For instance, there are probably churches, synagogues, schools, or other meeting spaces in your community that may be available either free of charge or at a very low cost. Usually, all it takes is a few phone calls to locate the right space.

Once you have found a meeting space, you need to prepare it so that the energy is right. Arrive early and smudge the room with sage. Also, light candles and incense if you can. Some facilities have rules prohibiting any kind of flame in their meeting rooms. If you cannot light a fire in your meeting space, then use holy water instead of sage to smudge the room. You can prepare this water by pouring it into a bottle that you set on your altar. At the beginning of your daily meditation, you can open the bottle and smudge it with sage while directing healing energy and blessings to the water. After a week of doing this, your holy water should be ready. When smudging with this water, just sprinkle it lightly as you walk around the room.

When preparing the space, make sure to pay attention to lighting and to ambient temperature. I find it most effective to have a moderate amount of light in the room, making sure that it is neither too bright nor too dark. As for temperature, that is considerably trickier. Even if the meeting space has a thermostat, you are unlikely to find a temperature setting that makes everyone happy. I have noticed that there is a great deal of variation in terms of temperature preferences. No matter where you set the temperature, someone in the room is either too warm or too cold. My recommendation is that you keep the space slightly cool—especially if you are meeting in a small room—because the energy generated by the chanting circle is likely to warm things up considerably.

Ideally, the meeting space should have some flexibility in terms of seating. Global Chant is fortunate to have access to a space that includes folding chairs, benches, and cushions. I always make sure to arrange the seating in a circular configuration. The chanting circle is just that: a circle. Any other configuration flattens the energy of the space. I have visited chanting circles in which the musicians are sitting on one side of the room and everyone else is facing them. This configuration changes the healing ceremony from an interactive experience into a performance; it sacrifices the power of the circle in exchange for benefits that are unclear—at least to me. If you are fortunate enough to have musicians taking part in your ceremony, just integrate them into the circle. In fact, spreading the musicians around the circle can enhance both the sound quality and the dynamics of the space.

In the center of our circle, we keep the following items: songbooks containing the words to all of the chants we know, a set of small percussion instruments such as shaker eggs for those who wish to use them, and a "blessing basket." Here, we place the names of the individuals to whom we would like to direct love, healing energy, and blessings. We write these names on small pieces of paper that we burn every few weeks. The ritual of burning these papers signifies that we are surrendering to Divine Will. In other words, we are placing the fate of the individuals whose names we have written down in the hands of the Big Beautiful Spirit.

I usually try to arrive at the meeting space early enough so that I can have a few extra minutes to meditate after setting up the room. As a facilitator, one of my most important responsibilities is to set the tone for the healing ceremony. If I can align myself with each of the Seven Keys, then I can share these values with the other members of the chanting circle. In essence, I am imbuing the space with my own sense of serenity, detachment, forgiveness, humility, compassion, selfless service, and unconditional love. The only way that the circlc will generate healing of any kind is if each member enters into it with the purest intentions—beginning with the facilitator.

By arriving early, I also have time to welcome and greet every person who enters the space. Many of the people who are attracted to chanting circles have their own healing issues. My initial greeting is an opportunity to offer love and blessings to each of them as they come through the door. There are other such opportunities during the ceremony, but a good facilitator knows how important it is to seize every single one of them. By welcoming those who take part in the circle, you also get to make them feel at ease if they are first-timers, to learn their names, to find out how they are doing, and to get a sense of their needs, concerns and issues.

Opening the Circle. Once all the members of the circle have arrived and are situated comfortably, we select the chants that will be included in the ceremony. In 11 years, we have collected over 100 chants and have assembled them into a songbook that gets handed out to every member of the circle. At the start of each session, we take a few minutes to look through the song-book and to choose the chants that call to us. The reason we have room for such spontaneity is that I have learned every single chant in our collection well enough to lead it.

When you start out as the facilitator of a chanting circle, nobody is going to expect you to know 100 or more chants. But you need to learn at least 5-10 chants well enough to lead them. The task of leading chants can be shared by several members of your circle, but it is important that these duties are delegated in a clear and consistent manner so that the chant leaders know in advance when it is their turn to lead. Also, you need to know that these individuals are dependable enough to arrive early and to come prepared.

There is a crucial distinction between the role of facilitator and that of a chant leader. Someone who leads a chant simply needs to know the words and music well enough to get the chanting started. The facilitator, on the other hand, is responsi-ble for overseeing every aspect of the chanting circle, which includes setting the tone for the ceremony and keeping the members of the circle focused. For the facilitator, the most important objective is to align the chanting circle with Divine Will, which allows the group members to tap into the ultimate source of their healing power.

That is why the first order of business for any chanting circle is to set the intention. Simply by intending to serve as instruments of healing, we align ourselves individually and as a group with Divine Will. And by intending that the energy, love and blessings that the group generates be allowed to flow freely to the recipients, we initiate that flow. The word, *intend*, comes from the Latin *tendere*, which means "to stretch." When we set an intention, we stretch the inner and outer world so that they connect. This connection allows for the realization of our ideals, our dreams, and our visions because our intention stretches the universe a little bit—just enough to accommodate this intention.

I usually ask the members of the circle to get comfortable and to take a deep breath, using their exhalation to release any strain or tension that they may be carrying from their day. Then I say the following words: "This is the time when we set our intention for this circle. Each of us can dedicate the love, the energy, and the blessings that we create together to whomever or whatever we would like. As a group, we always direct healing energy to Mother Earth in this time of global environmental turmoil. But there also may be specific people, places, animals, plants or other entities to which you would like to dedicate this chanting. So, please take a few moments to set your healing intention."

We also have a chant that we use specifically for this purpose. While singing the following words, each of us focuses on our intention:

Send it up, send it out,
Blessings, love and joy.
Let us serve the world with purest intention.
Make us a vessel for your love.
May we bring healing to our sister and brothers,
And end this suffering for once and for all.

After the intention has been set, we invoke the forces that guide the chanting circle and that represent the source of it healing power. We use a number of different invocations to open the circle. One of the simplest is the sacred Sanskrit word, OM, which we chant three times. This connects us with the infinite creative power and consciousness of the Big Beautiful Spirit. Or we may chant OM, AH, and HUM, which serve to purify our actions, speech, and thought, respectively.

If we are guided to do so, we may open the Four Corners in the manner taught to us by Dr. Singh. This type of invocation includes the two prayers I described in the last chapter, which are part of my daily meditation ritual (pp. 163-164). One is a variant of a traditional Native American prayer to the Big Beautiful Spirit. It begins with the line, "Oh Big Beautiful Spirit, whose voice I hear in the wind, and whose breath gives life to all the world, hear me." At times, we have integrated this prayer into the following chant, which is based on a Navajo prayer:

As I walk, as I walk, as I walk in beauty,
The universe is walking with me.
In beauty it walks before me,
In beauty it walks behind me,
In beauty it walks below me,
In beauty it walks above me,
Beauty is all around me,
As I walk in beauty.

The second prayer is the Tibetan Buddhist "Eight Thoughts of a Great Being," which aligns us with the Seven Keys and with our true spiritual purpose as Chanters. This prayer helps to ascertain that the intentions of the chanting circle members are pure and selfless. It reminds each of us who take part in the circle that there is no room for personal agenda—not even the satisfaction of a job well done. To serve the healing needs of others effectively, we must give ourselves completely to the process from the outset.

In recent months, we have added another chant to the opening ritual. This chant invokes the power of the Four Directions, of Father Sky, and of Mother Earth. Its words are as follows:

Open up the circle of healing and light.
To the South, innocence and joy,
To the East, new beginnings,
To the North, cool winds of reason,
To the West, nighttime for dreaming,
Up above, the source of light, Father Sky,
Beneath our feet, the womb of life, Mother Earth,
Open up the circle of healing and light.

The Journey. Once our intention has been set and the invocation is complete, we are ready to undertake our journey of healing. This is the process by which we break free of our bubble, enter our inner temple, and transport our consciousness into other dimensions of reality. In these other dimensions, we are able to access the wisdom and the resources needed to bring healing to those we are serving.

This is the core of our experience and service as Chanters. Until now, I have described it as an individual journey, but it is much more powerful when done in the context of a chanting circle. The combined intention of a group of Chanters acting in unison has a synergistic effect on the capacity of each individual to penetrate into the flow of Divine Love from which all healing power emanates. I will discuss the dynamics of this synergy in much greater detail in the next chapter.

Chanting is our rocket ship. As Chanters, we know the power of this simple, ancient activity to free us from the limitations of our own minds and to propel us into the pure experience of holiness. From there, we can fly into other realms of existence and find the ultimate source of all healing through our connection with the Big Beautiful Spirit.

To get the journey started, everything you need to do can be summarized in two words: just melt. If your intention is to expe-

rience holiness and to travel into other dimensions to bring healing to those you serve, this is where you need to begin. You have
heard quite a bit already about the process of melting. In the last
chapter, I shared some of the techniques I use in my daily meditation practice to create this experience. But the most powerful
tools I know for facilitating the melting process are the chants
themselves.

Throughout this book, I have shared with you a number of
my favorite chants. But there are many others, some of which I
save specifically for healing ceremonies. For instance, I find
tremendous power in the Hebrew chant, *Baruch Kevod Adonai
Mimkomo*. These words translate to, "Blessed is the Glory of
God in Heaven and on Earth." More importantly than their
meaning, the words themselves carry a vibration that can draw
me out of my bubble.

Hebrew is one of several languages that have this power;
Sanskrit is another. One of the most powerful Sanskrit chants
that I know is: *Jai Ma*. This simple two-word chant is an
acknowledgement of the stream of pure love that emanates
from the Divine Mother and that flows through all things. It
serves as a reminder that this love will always prevail. Even
though the words themselves do not translate well into
English—the closest translation would be "Victory to the Divine
Mother"—the power of the chant extends far beyond our ability to comprehend its meaning.

Closely related to Sanskrit is the sacred Tibetan language.
One of the first chants I ever learned is based on the Tibetan
Buddhist mantra: *Om Ah Hung Benza Guru Pema Siddhi Hung*.
This mantra represents a purification of our thoughts, speech,
and actions. Moreover, its twelve syllables are said to carry all of
the blessings contained in Buddhist teachings. By chanting these
syllables, we invoke the wisdom through which our minds can be
liberated from ignorance and suffering.

From the Sufi tradition, there is the simple chant, *Hu Allah*,
which refers to the Divine Presence. When the word *Hu* is
chanted softly—almost in a whisper—it conveys our breath to

those around us. This serves as a reminder that the Divine Presence resides in us and is transmitted through our breath. In essence, *Hu Allah* connects us to the Big Beautiful Spirit. It serves as a powerful acknowledgement of our role as instruments of Divine Will.

Another chant, drawn from the Sikh tradition, is: *Tapo Hari Japo Hari*. The word *Hari* means "creation in action." It refers to the creative force of the Big Beautiful Spirit. The chant encourages us to meditate on this force (*Japo Hari*) and to become ablaze with it (*Tapo Hari*). We use this chant in our healing ceremonies because it aligns us with the ultimate source of our creative power. Only this source can determine whether and to what extent healing will take place.

The vibrations created by these chants are as powerful a vehicle for the healing journey as anything I have ever encountered. The trick is simply to immerse yourself in the experience of chanting, which allows your consciousness to be transported into hidden dimensions of reality. When you lose yourself in the chants, experiencing them as pure vibration, your spirit will begin to move freely through the universe. It will go wherever it is needed in order to facilitate healing. By setting your spirit free—even for just a few moments—you tap into a reservoir of healing power far beyond anything you can even imagine.

At first, you may not be aware of where the chanting is taking you; all you may feel is the perfect bliss that comes from breaking out of your bubble and stepping into the inner temple where holiness resides. But because of the pure intention with which you and the other members of your chanting circle have initiated this journey, you can rest assured that you will end up in exactly the right destination. Your spirit knows what to do, where to go, how to align itself with Divine Will, and what outcomes are possible. The main thing your mind needs to do is to get out of the way. Chanting is a perfect tool for quieting the mind and letting your spirit fly.

As the facilitator, part of your role is to create the right conditions for this journey. In order to do this, you will need to tune into the experiences of each member of your circle. This is one of the reasons why it is so important to develop and refine your intuitive abilities (see Chapter 2). The guidance you receive from the Masters will determine how long each chant lasts, the amount of silence between chants, and when the chanting ends.

At the end of the chanting, there should be a period of at least 10-15 minutes in which the members of the circle have the opportunity to sit in silent meditation. This is when the participants really take off on their healing journeys. While the other members of the circle are journeying, you have important work to do. As the facilitator, it is your responsibility to transmute any unproductive energy that may be carried by the members of the circle. Most of us are carrying something—perhaps physical pain, emotional distress, or distracting thoughts. You can use a breathing exercise such as the Tonglin practice I described in the last chapter (p. 167) to purify this energy. Through your efforts, you will make it easier for the other members of your chanting circle to be effective in fulfilling their healing intentions. In essence, you are acting as an amplifier that boosts their signal.

Another way you can do this is by directing healing energy and intention to each member of the circle individually. During the meditation period, I always go around the circle and transmit blessings to each participant while silently chanting:

DO YOU KNOW YOU ARE LOVE?
ONE THING—FLOWING THROUGH EVERTHING

Doing this has a profound ripple effect. The members of the circle will end up sharing whatever love and healing energy they receive through this simple blessing to many others in what can be considered a spiritual "chain reaction." This is ultimately the point of the ceremony: To expand our circle of healing outward so that it encompasses an ever-growing number of our beloved brothers and sisters—not just on the dimensions that are familiar to us but throughout the universe.

Closing the Circle. Once I have finished blessing each member of the circle, I know that it is time to end the period of silent meditation. As the facilitator, it is my responsibility to call the members of the chanting circle back from their journeys. In doing so, I want to remind each of them to bring back something that can benefit the recipients of the healing. That is the very reason each of us in the circle began our journeys in the first place. Motivated by compassion and unconditional love, we gave of ourselves and jumped into unknown realms in order to facilitate the healing and enlightenment of others.

But how do we know if our efforts were worthwhile? The answer is that the only outcome of our ceremony and of our personal journey that matters at all is healing, which occurs simply as a result of our intention. Remember that healing means wholeness, and that this wholeness arises from our connection with both the Big Beautiful Spirit and with each other. When we enter the chanting circle, we are acting from our own sense of interconnectedness.

In calling back the other Chanters from their journeys, I say, "In a few moments, we will be closing the circle by chanting OM three times. But before we do, I just want to remind you of the love, the energy, and the blessings that we are creating together. Each one of us has a responsibility to take these gifts with us and to share them with others—with the people we love, with those who are suffering or in need, with plants and animals, and with our brothers and sisters in other places and in other dimensions."

In uttering these words, my intention is to help reconnect the members of the chanting circle with their original healing intentions. It is not enough just to take the journey and to have an interesting experience. As Chanters, we are obliged to bring back whatever healing gifts we can from our journeys and to radiate these gifts outward in an expanding circle of light and joy.

In truth, the chanting circle does not close even when the healing ceremony ends. The energy that has been generated continues to circulate long after the members of the circle have left the room and gone home. In fact, we can contribute to these positive "aftershocks" by staying mindful of what we have created in our ceremony. That is why I also offer my fellow Chanters this reminder: "Although we close the circle in our bodies, we keep it open in our hearts, in our spirits, and also in our dreams. Tonight, I will be here chanting all night in my dreams, and I invite you to come and join me in your dreams."

After we have chanted OM three times, all of the members of the chanting circle stand up and hold hands. As we close our eyes one last time, remaining quiet and still for a few moments, each of us feels the power of what we have created as a group. I end this brief silence by saying, "We give thanks for this wonderful gathering, and we ask that the energy, love, and blessings we have created together radiate out into the universe in a way that benefits all beings."

At this point, the ceremony is complete, although our journey of healing is never over. By venturing outside of our bubble and into our inner temple, we initiate a journey from which we may never return—at least not without meaningful, lasting changes to our identity. This is the ultimate act of self-sacrifice; we lay down our lives—or, more accurately, the lives we have known up to now—for the benefit of others. By simply taking this course of action, we create healing: We bring about an awareness of wholeness in both ourselves and in those we serve.

In an interview with journalist Bill Moyers, Joseph Campbell told the story of a police officer who dove off a cliff in order to save a young man who was attempting suicide. The only reason that either of them survived is that a second police officer was able to grab them both and pull them to safety. When asked why he took such an enormous risk for the sake of a complete stranger, the first officer replied, "If I had let that young man go, I couldn't have lived another day of my life."

At the moment he grabbed hold of the other man, the officer had the experience of no longer being a separate entity in the universe. For an instant, he felt a deep connection with the man he was grabbing. Whether he was aware of it or not, the officer had brought about healing through his actions. He had given rise to a universe in which there is perfect unity and wholeness. Even if he did this only for an instant and only in his own mind, the fact of the matter is that a healing occurred.

As Chanters, we can create this sense of wholeness in ourselves. Beyond that, the outcome of our healing ceremonies is outside of our control. More importantly, our personal desires cannot come into play. Although we may want the recipient of the healing to live, to get better, and to be happy, we are in no position to impose our will on the process. In fact, for us to tell the Big Beautiful Spirit what we want to happen would be an act of arrogance.

That is why the only request we can justify making is to act as an instrument of healing for those we serve, transforming ourselves into a conduit through which the Big Beautiful Spirit gives them what they need and takes from them what they do not need. Who are we to say what is needed and what is not? That determination is in the hands of the Divine and not in ours. And we would not have it any other way. As one of our invocation prayers reminds us, we are "small and weak." How can we possibly know enough to say what is in someone else's best interests? As Chanters, we are not here to dictate the spiritual needs of others but simply to serve those needs in any way that we can.

The most important element of the healing ceremony happens at the beginning, when we are opening the chanting circle. Before we even start our healing journey, we set our intentions. In a sense, we have returned from the journey before we ever leave. Simply by intending to serve as an instrument of healing, we provide healing. And by intending that the energy, love, and blessings we generate flow directly to those we serve, we allow them to flow. When we make an intention, we stretch the universe in a way that can accommodate the reality. But we also stretch ourselves. Breaking free of the limitations imposed by our physical senses, by the linear mind, and by the bubble in which we have been imprisoned, we melt into the stream of pure love that flows through all of creation.

Although our intentions are essential to the healing process, they are not enough. As Dr. Singh has often reminded me, the spiritual path of a Chanter is one of action. Through our intentions, we may stretch the entire universe—starting with ourselves—but then comes the real challenge: We have to live and function in that new universe. The entire healing process is set in motion the moment we state our intentions, but we still have to carry out the actions that arise from those intentions. If for no other reason, we take action because we have to do something, and this is far and away the best thing we can do. By acting in service of others, we step into the very universe we have envisioned—the one in which healing and enlightenment are realities for all beings. That step is a miracle, and any one of us can make it happen.

CHAPTER 7

One Voice, One Skin, One Spirit

On a cold cloudy night in Sonora, Dr. Singh instructed me to lie down outside and meditate on the night sky. He told me that my destiny as a Chanter was literally "written in the stars," and that I would be able to see it if I just emptied my mind. Lying under a set of wool blankets, I looked up at the sky and saw only clouds. But the clouds were beautiful, and the more I watched them, the more tranquil I became. After a while, a tiny patch of sky opened up—just enough for me to spot the Pleiades.

Known as the Seven Sisters, this constellation occupies a relatively tiny place in the night sky, and yet it is prominent in world literature and mythology. I have always been drawn to this cluster of stars, and as I stared at it that night, it transported me into the future. I caught a glimpse of the radical planetary changes that will be taking place in our lifetimes.

Most of these changes will be related to the Earth's water cycle. As global warming melts the polar ice caps, the world's ocean levels will rise and many coastal areas will be flooded. This flooding will contaminate our oceans, waterways, and even groundwater. At the same time, weather patterns will shift so that inland areas will experience intense drought. Accompanying these changes will be an increase in seismic activity that will result in devastating earthquakes throughout the planet.

We have already had glimpses of these changes with

Hurricane Katrina and the 2004 tsunami. As the changes intensify over the next decade, much of the world will become uninhabitable, and millions of people will die. There is nothing we
can do to stop this process from happening; the changes have
already been set in motion. But as I saw into the future, I
became aware of the role that Chanters will play in alleviating
suffering throughout the planet, in reducing the severity of the
impact of these cataclysmic changes, and supporting the shift to
a more sustainable and balanced way of life.

Although the changes I foresaw will be harsh, they will usher
in a new era of peace and stability throughout the planet. From
a spiritual standpoint, these changes will serve as a cleansing.
They will mark an evolutionary shift in the way human societies
are organized, resulting in a rediscovery of basic spiritual values.
For half a century, many of the world's greatest minds have been
warning humanity that our existing way of life is out of balance
and non-sustainable. Now, these warnings are about to be vali-
dated by a series of dramatic natural events.

As Chanters, our role is to serve as protectors of the planet.
We can help create a spiritual atmosphere conducive to healing
and enlightenment. In this era, our role is intensifying and
becoming much more pronounced than ever before, primarily
because of the magnitude of the events that are about to unfold
at a global level. But even if such changes were not occurring,
Chanters would still have an important mission in this life.
World events have no influence on our decision to follow our
spiritual path, because the need for healing and enlightenment
is always present. Moreover, the wisdom of the Masters who
guide us in our spiritual lives is independent of space and time.

And yet, the trends we are seeing create a sense of urgency
in us. To be the most effective spiritual servants we can be in
these turbulent times, all of us who choose to embrace our roles
as Chanters must take advantage of the learning opportunities
we are being given. As I have discovered in the past year, these
opportunities are coming at us with increasing frequency and
intensity. It is clear that the Masters are speeding up our

progress at a time when the need for what we do as Chanters is becoming so great.

Time seems to be moving at an accelerated rate. Things that used to take me a year to do now take a month, and things that used to take a month now take less than a week. I know that the Masters are pushing me—and every Chanter on this planet—because our spiritual advancement has a huge ripple effect. As I have said before, the enlightenment of even a single individual can be felt throughout the universe.

Given the magnitude of the changes that will be unfolding on this planet and of the spiritual needs that will accompany these changes, the demand for enlightened beings is high. As a result, the Masters are creating a unique window for those of us devoted to our spiritual path. At this point in time, enlightenment is more in reach for a greater number of people than at any other time in human history.

The current generation of Chanters has unprecedented spiritual resources at its disposal. We have access to a number of living Masters who are here to serve us. Besides that, every Chanter is part of a fellowship through which we support each other on our spiritual path and catch one another when we fall—something that is bound to happen to every Chanter sooner or later.

If you have been reading this book from the beginning, you know that I have stumbled on more than one occasion. Those times would have been much harder had I not had the love and support of my fellow Chanters. When you jump into your spiritual life, you learn—sometimes the hard way—that there are some things you cannot do on your own.

Entering the Chanting Circle

Because of the way I was raised, I have mixed feelings about spiritual community. On the one hand, I am drawn to the possibilities of creating deep and lasting bonds with those who share the same passion and commitment to their spiritual path. On the other hand, the very idea of spiritual community can trigger my fears of losing my individual identity and of getting drawn into a cult. Some of these fears are based on legitimate concerns. Since the 1970s, Americans have become extremely familiar with disturbing real-life horror stories such as Jonestown, Heaven's Gate, and Waco, in which cult members followed their charismatic leaders down a path of self-deception and mass suicide. American culture has treated these stories as cautionary tales— reminders of the danger associated with blind faith and devotion.

But those of us who have grown up in Western countries, particularly the United States, also have to remind ourselves that ours is an individualistic society that treats all forms of community with an element of suspicion. Regardless of whether the suspicion is warranted, it is founded to some degree on the fear of "losing ourselves"— of sacrificing our individuality and becoming defined instead by our group affiliation. The decision to identify with a group is seen as a form of weakness in a society that values independence above all else.

This reaction to community is not universal. Many of the world's cultures are collectivist, meaning that they place more emphasis on the needs of the group than on the individual. If you travel to Africa, Asia, or Central and South America, you will find societies in which people define themselves in relation to their families and their communities. The members of these societies tend to think of themselves as interdependent rather than independent.

It took me a while to get accustomed to being part of a spiritual community. When Harper would tell me that our connection as Chanters is such that we share in one another's feelings and experiences, I was skeptical. But then when I began to experience painful transitions in my spiritual path, I could see by the reactions of Harper, Ricardo, and Carmina that they were taking on my pain. To be honest, that made things worse for me—at least in the short term—because the last thing I want is to pass along my pain to the people I love.

Then I realized that they were honored to take on my pain,

just as I would be to do the same for them. Because of our shared path as Chanters, there is a deep and powerful bond among us. We know that the mission we are undertaking, both individually and as a group, is not an easy one. If healing and enlightenment were easy, then all of us would have gotten there a long time ago. But it takes courage, passion, and devotion to walk this path because you have to let the old self die so that you can awaken into your spiritual life. You may have lapses— moments in which your inner strength is depleted. At such moments, you can draw upon the strength of others.

Nobody can understand the process of spiritual transformation unless they are undergoing it themselves. Even then, your process is unique, and even the people closest to you may not be able to fully grasp the nature of the challenges you face. The way that people respond to you during the hard times is the true test of their friendship. I have found, at those times, that the love and compassion that my fellow Chanters show me is unwavering. They may not be able to give me what I want, but they serve my spiritual needs, which is far more important. Sometimes, the things we think we want are not necessarily in our best interests—at least not from a spiritual standpoint. These things may actually indulge our minds and egos, shoring up the walls of our bubble rather than tearing them down.

Among other things, I can count on my fellow Chanters to tell me the truth, from their perspective, even if it hurts me to hear it. When we were in Oaxaca, I made a pact with Harper and Ricardo that we would let each other know when one of us seemed to be straying from our spiritual path. To have someone in your life to "call you on your BS" is an extremely valuable asset, whether you are able to appreciate it or not. That helps you make sure that you never lose sight of what is really important to you.

Anyone who jumps into this spiritual path becomes part of a powerful fellowship. Unlike a cult, the fellowship to which I am referring has no leader. Every Chanter is led only by the inner guidance that the Masters offer each of us individually. Dr. Singh has chosen to remain in the shadows so that he is never placed in a position of power by anyone. You will never find him, no matter how hard you search. He has made certain that there will never be a central authority for the network of Chanters that is now beginning to form around the world.

I am certainly not that authority. None of the wisdom in this book originates from me. I am just the host of a small chanting circle in Tucson, Arizona. The circle itself is important, but I am not. The significance of the chanting circle is that it is an outward manifestation of an inner connection. This connection, which exists within every Chanter, begins with our voices.

One Voice

In a very real sense, the entire universe is created from a single breath. For many cultures, spirit and breath are one and the same. In some languages, the same word is used to denote both: *ruach* in Hebrew, *prana* in Sanskrit, and *mana* in Hawaiian. The breath that gives rise to the universe also produces a vibration that is heard as sound. This is the music of the spheres—the sound from which all of creation emanates.

When we lift our voices in song, we resonate with this sound. Through the act of chanting, we reconnect with our origins and draw ourselves into alignment with the ultimate creative force of the universe. We chant in order to celebrate, to glorify the Big Beautiful Spirit, and to express our appreciation for the opportunity to take part in this magnificent, never-ending creative process. Our breath becomes the Divine Breath, and the sound we project with our voices becomes the music of the spheres. All of this happens simply through our intention to connect with the Divine from a spirit of joy, gratitude, and adoration.

The Sufi chant, *Ishk Allah Mahebood Lilla*, reminds us that "the Divine is love, lover, and beloved." As we chant, we draw closer to our ultimate lover and our true beloved—the Big Beautiful Spirit. Even if we chant by ourselves, we open a circle in which love flows freely between the Big Beautiful Spirit and ourselves. But of course, this love is the Big Beautiful Spirit. And so, through our chanting we merge our personal consciousness momentarily with the infinite consciousness that is our origin and our destiny. It is the drop of water finding its way back into the ocean from which it came, and then dissolving into it.

When the chanting circle is expanded, this effect intensifies. Each new member of the circle contributes to the overall intention and experience of the group. As Dr. Singh points out, a synergy is created that brings each individual closer to the Divine: "When Chanters come together, one plus one is never equal to just two." If even one member of the circle has a momentary experience of holiness, it triggers a chain reaction that everyone in the circle feels.

I have seen this reaction many times over the years. In fact, it has become an almost weekly occurrence in the Global Chant circle. The group will be in the middle of doing a chant that we have done a hundred times before, such as the Hindu mantra, *Om Namah Shivaya* (which is a recognition of the Supreme Consciousness that dwells in all things), when suddenly I will feel the unmistakable sensation of having my heart open, and the walls of my bubble begin to dissolve. As I look around the room, I can tell by the expressions on the faces of my fellow Chanters that they are experiencing something equally intense. After we have closed the circle, each one will come up to me and tell me about their experiences. Invariably, they will say something like, "The chanting was so powerful tonight."

The chanting circle is a dynamic body that grows and evolves constantly. We now see beautiful new people coming into Global Chant on a weekly, if not daily, basis. I feel so much compassion for each of these novice Chanters, because every one of them goes through similar highs and lows to the ones I have experienced. Mostly, I feel so much admiration for them, because I know that nobody gets to this point without overcoming some major hurdles.

When I began my apprenticeship with Dr. Singh, I noticed

that he ended many ceremonies with the following phrase: "one voice, one skin, one spirit." I did not realize until much later that he was describing the process by which each Chanter becomes integrated into the chanting circle. One day, when Cassady and I were still living together, Dr. Singh sat down with me in his office at the Conservatory and explained the process:

"First, you have the experience of being one voice. This happens to people when they come into the chanting circle for the first time. There is a moment when they can't tell the voices apart. It all merges into one sound.

"Next, you have the connection of being one skin. You have had this sensation with Cassady, where you don't know where you end and she begins. At times, you are able to feel in your body what she is feeling. If she has a pain in her leg, so do you. If her throat is scratchy, you cough.

"But the ultimate connection is with the Big Beautiful Spirit. I didn't really make that connection until I was 45, when I started to feel the Big Beautiful Spirit inside of me. I could sense it in my body, right here (he points to his throat chakra).

"Now that I am able to experience it, sometimes I feel like I'm going to explode. I am filled with happiness to the point of overflowing. And at the same time, I want to die, because this little body cannot handle all the love, all the energy, and all the happiness that I feel.

"When you become one with the Big Beautiful Spirit, you want to share everything you have—everything you are—with others. I want to shatter into a thousand pieces so that I can spread myself around. I want to be everywhere where beings are suffering so that I can take their suffering from them and replace it with my joy.

"I feel so responsible when I hear the 'Eight Thoughts' prayer. It demands action on my part. Just think of the line, 'May I take upon myself the great burdens, the difficult to endure sufferings, of beings in hell and the other realm.' That is a big task, a big responsibility, but also a great source of happiness. To be able to give yourself entirely to others is the best thing in the world when you are one with the Great Spirit. You will see.

"I have faith that you will get there one day, as I have. Part of the reason for my faith is that you have the chanting circle to support you and to make your path easier. The Masters call the United States the 'land of the dead.' That is because there are so many people walking around who are the walking, living dead. They may have life in their bodies but not in their spirits. The challenge of awakening spiritually in a place like that is especially great. Anyone from that culture who intends to pursue the spiritual path of a Chanter needs extra support. That is why the chanting circle is so important. Chanters must create a fellowship that makes it possible for them to support one another."

The spiritual life of a Chanter represents a radical departure from the everyday existence of modern people, especially in the United States. Everything I have described for you is a challenge: jumping onto your path, tuning into your guidance, stepping out of your bubble, aligning yourself with ideals such as selflessness and compassion, living those ideals 24/7, and helping create miracles for the healing and enlightenment of others. Nothing comes easily on this—or any other—spiritual path. But the path gets easier if you band together with other Chanters.

If you are like me, the idea of spiritual community may be appealing but the reality of it is much trickier. Before I started Global Chant, I was used to being completely autonomous and to following my heart wherever it would lead me, with little concern for the repercussions my decisions and actions would have on others. I did not want to give up my freedom to anyone, which is why I did not marry until I was 36. And when I married Catherine, she understood that she was not to "domesticate" me in any way. In fact, we lived in adjacent houses, seeing each other primarily at dinnertime and bedtime.

When I began taking part in the weekly chanting circle, this sense of autonomy began to change slowly. I underwent the exact process that Dr. Singh has described. First, I discovered my connection to fellow Chanters. Chanting in a circle is a powerful form of communication—in some ways, more powerful than any conversation or dialogue. Through your voice, you can express what is in your heart. If you are angry or prideful, those emotions show up in the way you chant just as much as joy or love can.

From the first time we chanted together, all of us who took part in the chanting circle knew that we were engaged in something extraordinary. Although none of us were particularly adept singers, our happiness and the purity of our intentions more than made up for our musical deficiencies. In these ceremonies, we often became "one voice." Our individual voices would blend into a single unified sound so that it would be impossible to distinguish one person's contribution from that of another. By the end of each ceremony, I felt that something powerful and important had been shared among us. I would leave with a genuine sense of appreciation and love for everyone in the room.

One Skin

The second stage in my integration into the chanting circle— the stage that Dr. Singh calls "one skin"—came much more slowly. From the beginning of my acquaintance with other Chanters, I was aware of our connection at a conceptual level, and I could feel that connection when we chanted together. But I did not feel the same level of connectedness to them outside of the circle. I did not really know the sensation that Dr. Singh describes as not knowing where you end and the other person begins until I met Cassady.

For reasons that I may never understand, Cassady opened up my sense of compassion in ways that nobody else ever had. I knew when she was experiencing physical or emotional pain, because I could feel it too. I could also feel her joy and excitement. It was exhilarating for me to be so connected to another human being.

When my relationship with Cassady ended, part of the reason I was so devastated is that I felt that I had lost this intense connection. My devastation was so profound that it killed me in every sense except the physical. I let go of my attachment to everything: my past, my identity, my possessions, my hopes and dreams. They all washed away in a seemingly endless stream of tears.

Being with Cassady had not just opened my heart—it had left it naked and exposed. For weeks after she moved out of the house, my tears would flow at the slightest provocation. At first, I thought that I was crying over my own pain. That was my misinterpretation of what I was experiencing. In truth, my sense of compassion was getting magnified. I was picking up on the emotional experiences of friends, neighbors, family members, and even strangers.

One day, I was describing these experiences to Dr. Singh when he asked me, "Do you know why Cassady left? Do you realize what caused her to jump so intently into her spiritual path that she had to move out of your house and into the temple?"

"No," I said. "I have not even had a chance to talk with her."

"Even if you asked her, she might not be able to tell you. But there is no question that everything changed for her when she read your book."

Dr. Singh's words stunned me but I also knew the truth of what he was saying. When Cassady had moved in with me, she asked if she could read this book. I was delighted to share drafts of the chapters that I had already written. Cassady read through the first three chapters in the time we were together. Although she never commented once about any of it, I could feel that she was absorbing everything she was reading.

At the beginning of this journey that you and I have shared, I relayed a disclaimer to you that Dr. Singh had urged me to include. He warns that this book is a manual for building the spiritual equivalent of an atomic bomb. The teachings that I have included here—ones that have come to me directly from Dr. Singh and the other Masters in my lineage—have the power to wipe out the life you have been leading up to now so that you can step fully into your spiritual life.

I know this is the case because that is exactly the effect this book has had on my life. The first atomic blast created by the book was in my own back yard. Through the book, I ended up opening a door for Cassady in her spiritual life. At the same time, I annihilated myself, because the loss of my relationship with her set off a chain of events that caused the remaining structure of my old life to simply collapse. As I write the last few pages of this book, I know that I am not the same person who began the writing process a year ago. That man no longer exists.

In his place is someone who has finally discovered his role—in the chanting circle, in the world, and in the universe. I now realize that I am here to open doors. That is my mission in this life. It is why I began the chanting circle over a decade ago. A number of people have found their spiritual direction through that circle, including me. It is also why I continue to teach college courses; although the course material has diminishing relevance for me, I know that I am there to serve the spiritual needs of my students. I met Cassady in a classroom, and although she was not my student for long—she had decided to drop out of school by the time we became lovers—it was through that interaction that she met Dr. Singh and found her spiritual path.

My need to open doors for you in your pursuit of healing and enlightenment is the only reason I am writing this book. You are my kin—my fellow Chanter—whether you know it or not. I know the pain and despair you have experienced because I have felt it, too. It would be my great honor to know that this book has served you in some way, perhaps giving you a glimpse of who you really are or making your path just a little smoother.

The day that Cassady walked out of the house for the last time, I spoke with Dr. Singh and he told me that another woman would be coming into my life soon. This woman would need my help to overcome some big hurdles in her life and to find her true spiritual calling. Dr. Singh warned me that I would need to love her with complete detachment, which would not be easy because of the intensity of our connection. "With this woman, it will be important for you to open the door and then get out of her way," he told me.

At the time, I was not ready to hear any of this. The idea of being with someone other than Cassady seemed repulsive to me. It also hurt me to realize that I had blocked Cassady's path to any degree. While I was opening a door into her spiritual life, I had also stood in front of that door, saying to her, "Take me with you." In doing so, I stopped being her servant and became another obstacle for her to overcome. I believe that part of the reason she cut off all contact with me is that she was afraid I would draw her back into her old life rather than encourage her to pursue her new one.

In retrospect, I am very proud of the fact that I was able to open a door for Cassady. She is undoubtedly a shooting star, progressing on her spiritual path as a Chanter with incredible speed. A shooting star is something beautiful to behold. You cannot help but be inspired by the focus and determination that propels someone into their spiritual life with that much intensity.

In the meantime, a second shooting star came into my life, just as Dr. Singh had predicted. The day after Cassady left, Chi showed up at the chanting circle for the first time. From the moment I saw her, I felt something unique—a sense of familiarity, perhaps, or a tingle of anticipation. Immediately, I was struck by her exuberance, her sweetness and her warmth.

Less than three weeks after we met, Chi let me know—with subtlety at first—that she was interested in me. When I told Dr. Singh about the attraction, he said, "This is the woman I told you about. She needs your help to let go of her fear and to heal herself. Give her unconditional love, with no attachment, and you will see her blossom like the beautiful flower that she is."

This time, I decided, I would try opening doors for someone without getting in her way. Chi and I became close friends but not lovers. For the first time in my life, I was able to separate spiritual intimacy from physical intimacy. Chi and I could tell each other anything; we established a level of trust and openness the likes of which I had rarely experienced before. By steering clear of the emotional traps that can occur in sexual and romantic relationships, we were able to create a very deep connection.

I gave her the nickname "Chi" because of the tattoo on her ankle depicting the Chinese symbol for energy, or chi. At the time she had gotten the tattoo, Chi had no idea what it signified. As it turned out, the symbol she chose was perfect for her. Most of the people who meet her are struck by the sweet, joyful energy she exudes.

I felt the same intense compassion for Chi that I had felt for Cassady, although this time the feelings were tempered by a sense of detachment. I knew that I had to be as free as possible of any emotional baggage of my own in order to serve her spiritual needs. I also knew that Chi had some big hurdles to overcome on her spiritual path, starting with her physical health. Five years earlier, she had been diagnosed with lupus, a condition that is characterized by joint pain and fatigue, among other symptoms.

Lupus is considered an autoimmune disorder, meaning that the immune system attacks the body's own cells and tissues because of an inability to distinguish them from foreign bodies. Dr. Singh has said that lupus, along with other similar disorders such as chronic fatigue syndrome and fibromyalgia, has a spiritual component that extends far beyond the mechanisms understood by modern medical science. From a spiritual standpoint, these disorders are messengers, signaling that there is a pressing spiritual drive or need that cannot be ignored any longer.

In Latin, *lupus* means "wolf." Just as a wolf will bite off its own foot to escape a trap, Chi's body was beginning to destroy itself in an attempt to free her spirit from the bubble in which she had been trapped. This bubble consisted of deep-seated fears that seemed incongruent with everything else about her. In her heart, Chi is a spiritual adventurer. She jumped into Global Chant without hesitation and embraced the chanting circle from the first time she attended—something that most people have a hard time doing. And she was able to establish an intimate friendship with me in spite of differences in gender, age, and ethnicity, all of which were dramatic, and in spite of the fact that we had a strong mutual attraction upon which we chose not to act. Chi let go of her reservations about our unorthodox friendship as soon as she realized that I had no agenda except to love her and to help her find her spiritual direction.

The turning point in our friendship happened on a Sunday morning, when Chi and I attended a Buddhist prayer ceremony, or puja, at the invitation of my dear friend and spiritual brother, Mr. Bone. The puja was an invocation of Chenrezig, whom Tibetans revere as the ultimate embodiment of compassion.

From the first time I had heard the story of Chenrezig, I had felt a tremendous connection to him. The story goes like this: When Chenrezig recognized the amount of suffering that exists in the universe, he vowed that he would devote himself to ending all suffering and that he would not give up until all sentient beings were liberated. He even asked his spiritual teacher, the Amitabha Buddha, to destroy him if his thoughts ever wavered from this intention for even a moment.

After eons of meditating and praying for the liberation of all beings, Chenrezig opened his eyes and looked around him, only to discover that there was still as much suffering in the universe as there had been at the start of his vigil. For an instant, he was filled with despair as he recognized the overwhelming magnitude of the task he had undertaken. At that moment, the Amitabha Buddha honored Chenrezig's request by shattering his body into a thousand pieces.

Out of compassion for Chenrezig, the Amitabha Buddha put him back together, giving him a thousand arms instead of two. With the additional arms, Chenrezig was able to multiply his efforts and to reach out to more beings than ever before. He was also given the mantra of compassion, *Om Mani Pemé Hung*, which has the power to end the suffering of those who use it.

On a beautiful Sunday morning, Chi and I arrived at the Buddhist temple where the Chenrezig puja was being held and sat down at the back of the room, leaving ourselves the option of sneaking out if either one of us felt bored or uncomfortable. A few minutes after we got there, the lama who was conducting the ceremony entered the room and began the puja.

Almost from the start, I slipped into an experience of holiness. I could feel a powerful, loving presence in the room with us, which I realized was Chenrezig himself. His boundless compassion began to fill my heart, and suddenly I could feel the suffering of other beings, just as I had during my first experience of holiness in Sonora nearly two years earlier.

This time, though, the sensation was different: Tears streamed down my face as I realized that this sense of compassion would be a permanent condition for me. In the past, my compassion would come in short, intense bursts. Now, my heart was really open, and I knew that all I had to do in order to experience the suffering of other beings was just to tune into it.

At that moment, I reached the level of connection that Dr. Singh calls "one skin." Only I realized that the circle to which I am connected extends far beyond anything I had ever imagined. It includes anybody or anything that comes into my field of awareness. Since that day, I have begun to learn more about how to take on the suffering of others. It is a beautiful sensation, filling my heart with so much tenderness and love that I feel it is going to explode. I never forget, even for a moment, that this suffering does not belong to me. I simply take it into my heart, transmute it into pure love, and send it back out.

After the puja, Chi and I sat down and talked about what we had experienced there. At one point in the conversation, Chi began to cry. Instinctively, I moved closer to her, opened my arms and drew her to me. As she rested her head on my shoulder, the emotions she was experiencing seemed to intensify until she began to sob. The sobbing continued for several minutes. Once it subsided, Chi began to tell me about what she was feeling.

"Every day, when I go walking in the park after work, I see at least one or two homeless people," she explained. "I always make an effort to greet them and to talk with them if they let me, but most of them are too ashamed even to make eye contact with me. It hurts me so much to see this. I want to reassure them, to let them know that everyone deserves to be loved and that nobody should be treated like an outcast."

When Chi shared these feelings with me, I was awestruck. I realized that her experience at the puja had been almost identical to my own. Both of us had made contact with the spirit of Chenrezig in a way that had heightened our sense of compassion. This realization came as a surprise to me. Here was this young woman who could not be more different than me in terms of age, race, or upbringing, and yet the two of us were connected by our shared compassion. We really were "one skin," and more than that, we were "one heart."

What happened next was even more amazing. For the first time in my life, I made love to a woman without touching her. Chi and I connected to each other through our eyes. As we looked intently at each other, we melted together in a way that I had not experienced with anybody else in my life, except perhaps Cassady. But this experience was different; we had done this without being sexual. Moreover, it was a very deliberate and intentional process for me. From the time Chi and I became drawn to each other, I had begun to prepare for this moment. Over the previous few weeks, Dr. Singh had encouraged me to move beyond my own needs and desires—and especially my sexuality.

"When you first came to me, you were concerned that your sexuality would interfere with your spiritual path, and now you know that it can be can be a gift and not a hindrance," he said. "The next step is to go even deeper. Try making love without a body. Find new ways to share with your beloved all the love, energy, and blessings that you have to offer."

This is exactly what I did with Chi. I focused my intention on melting into the flow of pure, divine love and then directing that flow completely to her. In doing so, I gave her everything beautiful that I was feeling in my heart, including the expanded sense of compassion that Chenrezig had inspired in me that morning. And I knew she was doing the same for me. When Chi and I made love in this new way, we became "one skin" to the point that we could draw upon one another's experiences and make them our own.

Dr. Singh later confirmed what I already knew, which is that Chi had experienced a spiritual awakening that day. She discovered her spiritual calling through the puja and through our connection afterwards. I believe that Chi's discovery that "everyone deserves to be loved and that nobody should be an outcast" will be the driving force in her life from this point forward. It will be the vehicle that takes her everywhere she needs to go spiritually, dictating the kind of service that she will offer as a Chanter and pointing her consistently in the direction of her own enlightenment.

In the week that followed, Chi continued to have powerful realizations. She was starting to experience holiness and for brief moments, she would even fly. As she read through the first five chapters of this book, Chi's experiences began to match the ones described in whichever chapter she was reading at the time. For instance, the same day that she read my account of the time I watched Dr. Singh transform himself into a powerful birdlike figure (p. 98), Chi had a moment in which she felt herself become a bird. For an instant, she had the sensation of being in a bird's body. As she looked down at herself, she could see her own wings and plumage.

Exactly one week into my unorthodox mentoring relationship with Chi, she told me, "I am ready to let go of my bubble." As soon as I heard this statement, I recognized the power of the intention behind it, and I knew that it would change everything for her. That evening, Chi asked me to guide her through the process that Dr. Singh had shared with me when he first taught me to fly. As she lay on a sofa with eyes closed, I instructed her to detach completely from the life she had been living. This meant adopting an attitude of passivity in which nothing in her life mattered anymore. Her only concern at that moment would be to melt into the flow of love and to experience holiness.

After a few minutes of trying this exercise, Chi announced, "It's not working." I found her comments ironic because I had begun to enter other dimensions just by guiding her through the process. At that point, it was getting pretty late, and I was tired from a full day of activities. I invited her to sleep over if she didn't mind spending the night on my sofa. Then I said goodnight to Chi, went into the bedroom, and fell asleep.

At 4 am, Chi came into the bedroom and awakened me excitedly. She wanted to describe the powerful things she had been experiencing throughout the night. A while after she had fallen asleep, she began to have the sensation of someone lying gently on top of her, caressing her body from head to toe. With each caress, she began to feel a flow of warmth and energy in her body. "It was not necessarily sexual pleasure," she said, "but just a heightened sense of bliss."

After that, an intense healing process began to take place that continued throughout the night. Here is how Chi described it: "There was a constant flow of peaceful, loving, cleansing energy. And by 'cleansing,' I mean a swap. The old junk was being replaced by new energy. It wasn't like I felt the old junk being pulled out of me, but I could feel a new sensation taking its place. There was no longer any fear, doubt, or sickness present in me."

As the night progressed, Chi felt someone blessing her and sharing spiritual secrets with her. She was given a specific breathing pattern to do, consisting of four short bursts. Each time she tried this breathing pattern, she would get "the most wonderful, intense sensations" moving through her body. Chi was also given a physical gesture to carry out that involved touching her shoulder and then circling her hand around her head. This gesture had the feel of a *mudra*—or sacred gesture—that can be used to facilitate the experience of holiness.

That morning, Chi noticed that she was free of physical pain for the first time in years. She had none of the familiar aching in her fingers, chest, or back. The symptoms of lupus that had become part of her everyday life were completely gone. In their place were feelings of peace and relaxation. The lupus symptoms did return eventually, but in a milder form than before. And with Dr. Singh's help, Chi learned to manage them.

One day, he told her, "The wolf is gone. Now all that is left is a little puppy dog that you will keep as your pet. The puppy is there as a gentle reminder of what you need to do on your spiritual path."

I was there to witness that conversation, and I watched the look on Chi's face as she grasped the meaning of Dr. Singh's words. Through his simple statement, Dr. Singh showed Chi how even a painful physical condition such as lupus will melt away if you resist the temptation to give it power over your life. He taught her not to take herself or her problems too seriously. By transforming the wolf into a puppy, she gained a new perspective on her illness that allowed her to make an important shift. This set off a chain reaction that led to other dramatic changes in Chi's life.

Over the next few months, Chi found a job and an apartment that she loved. The job gave her freedom to express her creativity, and the apartment brought light, beauty, and a sense of peace into her daily life. Chi also learned to cook healthy meals rather than eating out, and she began to exercise regularly for the first time in her adult life. More importantly, though, she found herself spiritually. She volunteered to mentor young girls who had been physically or sexually abused. At times, she would also work at local homeless shelters. And she never turned down the opportunity to take part in a healing ceremony.

Chi is a living example of a basic healing principle that Dr. Singh has always stressed: When you reach out to someone in need of healing, purely out of a sense of compassion and unconditional love, your own problems will dissipate. It is a great irony that the healer who acts selflessly will receive the greatest healing benefits. In putting someone else's suffering above your own, you break free of the thought patterns that gave rise to your suffering in the first place.

Because of Chi's openness and sweet disposition, people gravitated to her. They felt comfortable enough around her to confide in her and to share their problems. Many of them expressed concern about their loved ones: a younger brother who had developed a brain tumor, a friend who had been beaten and left for dead, a widowed mother who had fallen into a state of depression and despair. Through her compassionate heart, Chi expanded her circle to include all of these people. They became her brothers and sisters, and she took on their pain as her own.

As her circle grew, so did mine. When Chi would bring these people and their stories to my attention, I would feel an immediate sense of connectedness to them. As Chanters, we are responsible for the other members of our chanting circle—especially those who are suffering. It does not matter whether they even know that they are a part of our circle or that we are a part of theirs.

One Spirit

Through Chi, I came to realize how large my chanting circle really is. I began to have the experience of "one skin" even with people I had never met before. It was becoming effortless for me to offer my love and compassion to these people with no conditions and no limits. And as I did this, I could feel my circle reaching out to more and more individuals—not just people but animals, plants, spirits, and other entities.

During this period of transformation, I found one chant particularly compelling. This chant is based on a simple meditation technique in which you envision a circle of light and joy radiating outward from your heart and expanding to encompass the entire universe. The words of the chant are:

Circle of light, circle of joy,
Light and joy fill the universe.
I am the light, I am the joy,
Light and joy fill the universe.

When I do this chant, I have a clear sense of what the chanting circle really is. The circle is nothing more than a vehicle through which we share our light and our joy. As I expand my circle, I am transformed in such a way that I become the very light and joy that I am intending to share.

Through the chanting circle, we Chanters are able to tap into our essence so that we can share it freely. Once I made this discovery, I was ready to enter the third and final stage in my integration into the chanting circle. This is the stage that Dr. Singh calls "one spirit." It is when your consciousness merges with the Big Beautiful Spirit. At that point, your integration is complete—not just with the chanting circle but with all of creation. You experience the Divine in all things and at all times. This is the fulfillment of the prayer that I chant every day: "Fill my heart so that I can know you in every moment and in everything." It is also the experience of enlightenment.

After Cassady left, much of the pain I was feeling had to do with the fact that I had found a connection to the Big Beautiful Spirit through her. Somehow, being with her had given me little flashes of enlightenment. When the relationship ended, those flashes came to a sudden halt, leaving an enormous void in my life. I was desperate to re-establish that sense of communion with the Big Beautiful Spirit.

When I expressed this desire to Dr. Singh, he said, "So, you want to be enlightened. That is an important desire to have. But tell me: What is enlightenment?"

I shrugged my shoulders and replied, "I don't know. All I have had is an occasional glimpse or taste of it. I can't answer your question because I've never been enlightened."

Dr. Singh was quick to correct me. "Maybe not in this lifetime," he said, "but you have been there." Then he added, "Even if you don't remember, I want you to give me your best guess: Tell me what you consider enlightenment to be."

At that point, I thought of the Rumi poem I had been carrying in my pocket for the past several weeks. From the moment I had heard it, the poem had resonated so intensely for me that I had to write down the words and keep them close at hand at all times. The first stanza, in particular, felt like the only answer I had to offer Dr. Singh in reply to his question:

Soul of the world,
No life, no world remain,
No beautiful men and women longing,
Only this ancient love
Circling the holy black stone of nothing,
Where the lover is the love,
The horizon, and everything within.

When I showed Dr. Singh the poem, he read it silently and simply nodded his head. He never said a word about it. In fact, the conversation ended right there. Seemingly satisfied with my answer, he stood up and left the room.

The poem had touched my heart in such a powerful way that I would be moved to tears every time I heard or read it. But in truth, I did not yet understand its significance. Two days later, I lived through an experience that gave me direct insight into the meaning of this poem.

That day was my birthday, which came two weeks after Cassady had ended the relationship. When I first moved to Tucson, I had started an annual tradition of taking a long walk in nature on my birthday. On this particular birthday, I woke up very early with an overpowering sense of urgency. I had a feeling that his year, the nature walk was more important than ever, although I was not sure why. All I knew is that I had to get started as early as possible. By 6 am, I was at the Ventana Canyon trailhead, ready to start my walk.

The word *ventana* is Spanish for "window." At the top of this canyon is a rock formation known as Window Rock that has an opening through which one can see a panoramic vista of Tucson and the surrounding mountains. I had only heard about this rock but had never seen it for myself. When I began walking, I decided that this was the day I would climb the seven miles up to Window Rock.

The deeper I ventured into the canyon, the more I began to understand the significance of my walk. In my mind, this was no ordinary trail that I was following; it was the path of enlightenment. Every step I took brought me a little closer to my ultimate destination. And as I proceeded, I was faced with the challenge of letting go of everything I had ever known or cherished. I knew that I would not return from this walk, that I would be changed forever by it, to the point that the person I had been would cease to exist.

For the first hour, my heart was filled with turmoil. I passed a point on the trail where Cassady and I had stopped to have lunch just three weeks earlier. We ended up making love in that spot— an experience that had been profoundly beautiful for both of us. When I arrived there, all I could feel was a sense of loss and grief. I wondered why the relationship had to end so abruptly.

Then I had this awareness: The fact that nothing lasts forever makes everything that much more precious and beautiful. There is not a moment in this life to be taken for granted. Every instant is filled with blessings, and rather than dwell on the blessings that I had experienced in the past, I needed to take in the blessings of this particular moment. Otherwise, I would be showing the utmost ingratitude and disrespect for the Divine grace that was being bestowed upon me at this moment.

When I came to that realization, I began to experience a heightening of all my senses. Suddenly, I was hearing the majestic bird calls that surrounded me on all sides. I could smell the inspiring fragrance of spring blossoms and could see that I was surrounded by loved ones: trees, cacti, rocks, lizards, and insects. All along the trail, stink bugs were busy mating, not even slightly perturbed by my presence. I smiled as I watched them, making sure to send each of these little couples my love and blessings.

With every step, I could feel the walls of my bubble just dissolving. I was becoming immersed in the richness of the moment to the point that everything else stopped existing. There was nothing for me to be other than this flow of pure love connecting to everything around me. I could not even remember ever having been anything else. Nor could I aspire to be or to have anything that was not already here in front of me right now.

The closer I got to Window Rock, the more it grew in importance to me. I had convinced myself that when I reached that destination, I would attain enlightenment. There was something elusive and mysterious about Window Rock. For years, I had been told that it was visible from many parts of Tucson, but all of my attempts to see it had failed. I began to think of it as the "holy black stone of nothing" that Rumi had described in his poem. If I could just get to it, I would know what it is like to be enlightened.

About five miles into the trail, there is a small sign pointing to the turnoff for Window Rock. But I never saw the sign and ended up on a different trail. The trail I had inadvertently chosen was as beautiful as any I had ever encountered, but it was also overgrown and poorly marked. This seemed perfectly appropriate to me. It would make sense that the path of enlightenment would go through relatively uncharted territory. Only a small percentage of spiritual seekers ever get this far, I told myself. Most become tired or discouraged and eventually turn back.

What I failed to realize is that the path itself is enlightenment. I was looking for a particular destination, but enlightenment is an ongoing process. There is no single point in time, space or consciousness in which you need to be in order to experience enlightenment. The present moment is as good as any. I began to see that the path that I was following had all the elements of enlightenment right there. I never needed to get to Window Rock. In fact, when I would focus on that goal, it would pull me out of the moment and distract me from the profound experiences I was having along the way.

On occasion, I would encounter small cairns that let me know I was still on the trail. But these markers became more sporadic until they disappeared entirely. At one point, I lost sight of the trail and had no idea which way to go. After searching fruitlessly in almost every direction, I decided to sit on a rock and have my lunch. I knew that if I stayed perfectly detached, the trail would make itself known to me.

As I ate my lunch, I realized the significance of the Rumi

poem. The "holy black stone of nothing" is the condition of complete detachment, in which there is no more longing in your heart and life's struggles cease to matter. In this condition, you are enveloped in the pure "ancient love" that Rumi describes.

After lunch, I resumed my search for the trail. My attention was drawn to a spot occupied by a large fallen limb. It had not occurred to me to even look for the trail there, but as soon as I walked around the limb, there it was. I walked a few hundred yards farther until the trail ended at a large, impressive rock formation.

This was not Window Rock, but I did not care. The beauty of this rock formation, and of the spectacular views that surrounded it, took my breath away. I recognized the formation because I had seen it from my own doorstep. It sits squarely in the middle of Ventana Canyon, framed perfectly by the canyon walls. In a sense, it is a "window rock," because the canyon forms a window through which the rock can be seen.

As I stood next to the rock formation touching it with my right hand and looking out over Tucson and the surrounding mountains, I felt the exact sensation that Rumi had described, in which "the lover is the love, the horizon, and everything within." In this moment, I knew in my heart exactly what it means to be enlightened. I also knew that I would have to make my descent back into the world at some point, and that in doing so, I would have to face the remaining layers of my bubble. But now, the end of the bubble—and of all of the attachments that go with it—was clearly in sight.

The rock formation that I had reached that day would serve as a constant reminder of how close enlightenment really is. Not surprisingly, I named it Enlightenment Rock. That is not a particularly original name, I admit, and certainly not the first one ever assigned to this rock formation. Yet there is no better name for it. The rock is an important milestone on my spiritual journey. It is where I crossed the "point of no return" in my quest for enlightenment.

I know that I am not enlightened yet—at least not in any permanent way. But now I have a sense for the first time that there is nothing that can stop me from getting there. In fact, the only obstacle that has ever stood in my way is my self—namely, the dense little bubble I spent a lifetime creating. Dr. Singh is always reminding us of the line in the Four Corners prayer that says: "I seek strength—not to be superior to my brothers and sisters but to be able to fight my greatest enemy: my self." I am finally learning how not to be my own greatest enemy, which means not indulging my unproductive thoughts and emotions. One day, that stream of thoughts and emotions is just going to dry up because I will no longer be feeding it my time and energy.

Sharing Happiness

As I think about my experience at Enlightenment Rock, I am struck by two important realizations. The first is that this rock was not elusive or mysterious at all. I had seen it on many occasions and knew it was right there all the time. The point is that enlightenment is not as mysterious as we might think. It is simply a matter of knowing what to do and then doing it. To find Enlightenment Rock, all I had to do was to keep walking the path. I had to climb nearly seven miles to reach it, but every step of the journey was worthwhile.

The wisdom that Dr. Singh and the other Masters have shared with me and that I have relayed to you throughout this book represents a time-tested approach to spirituality. If you practice the Seven Keys and apply them with determination to every aspect of your life, you will attain enlightenment. I have no doubt about that because I am seeing the effects of this approach on a daily basis—in both myself and my fellow Chanters. Each of us has discovered the same thing in our spiritual life, which is that enlightenment is simply a matter of self-discipline and hard work. You cannot let up for even a moment, because as soon as you do, the old habits and unproductive thought patterns will take root once again. At the same time, I can tell you that this is not rocket science. Anyone reading this book can attain enlightenment in this lifetime. Of that, I am certain.

A second realization I had on my birthday walk is that enlightenment is fertile ground. When I looked up at Enlightenment Rock, I could see that the formation itself was largely black in a manner consistent with Rumi's "holy black stone of nothing." However, the rock was covered with lichens that created a wild multicolored mosaic, with patches of bright green, yellow, orange, and red.

It is easy to fool yourself into thinking that detachment and enlightenment are stark conditions devoid of any intense emotion, but in fact the opposite is true. That is why Dr. Singh made it a point of letting me know the intensity of the feelings associated with the experience of "one spirit." In describing it, he said that sometimes he has the sensation that "this little body cannot handle all the love, all the energy, and all the happiness that I feel."

When you feel that much happiness, you have no choice but to share it with others. This is what makes enlightenment especially fertile; it cannot be contained but has to proliferate. As I started my descent from Enlightenment Rock, I stopped at the place where I had gotten lost earlier. After removing the fallen limb, I marked the trail with a new set of cairns. This was my way of making sure that the next person walking the path would have a smoother journey than the one I had. One of the beautiful things about the path of enlightenment is that those who have gone before are more than happy to illuminate the path for those who follow in their footsteps. None of us has to walk this path alone; we have enlightened Masters at our disposal that are honored and delighted to guide us on our way.

A few days after my walk in Ventana Canyon, I decided to dedicate this new phase of my life to doing whatever the Masters needed from me. When I told Dr. Singh about this decision, he just smiled and said, "My friend, the Masters do not need anything at all from you. They just want you to be happy and to share your happiness with others."

This statement has simplified my life beyond belief. Now, when I wake up in the morning, I focus on one thing: Being happy. Most days, this means getting out of my own way, not letting my thoughts and emotions interfere with the condition of happiness that I am experiencing. I know that there is a large nuclear-powered generator in me from which all of my happiness emanates. Nothing I come across in the course of my day can affect this happiness generator in the least. Only I can interfere with my own happiness. I can pull the plug on the generator or just let the happiness dissipate.

But the thing I live for now is the experience of building up all that happiness within myself and then releasing it into the universe. This is not just the ultimate delight; it is my mission as a Chanter. Dr. Singh likes to tell us that "happiness is contagious." The best way to open a door for someone in search of their spiritual path is by sharing your own happiness with them. Everybody wants to be happy, and if they know that you have found the key to happiness, they are going to want to make a copy of that key for themselves.

And so, my friend, you and I have come to the end of this particular journey together. I have no doubt that we will share other journeys in the future. Until then, I will close with the words of my beloved friend and mentor, Dr. Pablo Singh:

"The spiritual path of a Chanter should be fun. That is why we are here: to fill our own hearts and the hearts of others with a sense of joy, love, and playfulness. Above all else, make sure to have fun."

Act On Wisdom Quick Order Form

To order copies of this book, either go to our website,
www.actonwisdom.com, or mail this form to::

Act On Wisdom
PO Box 12484
Tucson, AZ 85732-2484

Please mail my order to:

Name: _____

Address: _____

_____

Telephone: _____

Email: _____

_____ copies @ $14.95 each = _____

+ tax _____   (see below)

+ shipping _____   (see below)

TOTAL _____

❑ Please send me FREE information on chanting, spiritual
healing and other resources

Sales Tax:
Please add 7.12% for products being shipped to an Arizona address.

Shipping By Air:
US: $3 for the first book, $2 for each additional book.
International: $9 for the first book, $5 for each additional book.

Payment:
Please send check or money order only. For credit card orders,
please go to our website at: **www.actonwisdom.com**

Quick Order Form

To order copies of this book, either go to our website, **www.actonwisdom.com**, or mail this form to::

Act On Wisdom
PO Box 12484
Tucson, AZ 85732-2484

Please mail my order to:

Name: _____

Address: _____

_____

Telephone: _____

Email: _____

_____ copies @ $14.95 each = _____

+ tax _____ (see below)

+ shipping _____ (see below)

TOTAL _____

❑ Please send me FREE information on chanting, spiritual healing and other resources

----

Sales Tax:
Please add 7.12% for products being shipped to an Arizona address.

Shipping By Air:
US: $3 for the first book, $2 for each additional book.
International: $9 for the first book, $5 for each additional book.

Payment:
Please send check or money order only. For credit card orders, please go to our website at: **www.actonwisdom.com**